LETHBRIDGE
A CENTENNIAL HISTORY

William Lethbridge, after whom the City of Lethbridge was named, was an original shareholder of the North Western Coal and Navigation Company, Limited, which in 1882 began to exploit the coal resources of southern Alberta. He was born at Kilworthy, near Tavistock, Devon, England, on 10 February 1825. He was educated at Tavistock Grammar School and St. John's College, Cambridge (B.A. 1850), and was called to the bar from Lincoln's Inn, London, in 1861. He was managing partner with the news agency and book-selling firm of W. H. Smith and Son. In 1885, he retired to his country estates at Wood, in the parish of Southtawton, and at Courtlands, in the parish of Lympstone, Devon. He was a Justice of the Peace for Devon and High Sheriff in 1893. He never married. He left an estate of nearly 400,000 pounds sterling at his death on 31 March 1901. Wm. Lethbridge never saw the prairie city that bears his name.

LETHBRIDGE
A CENTENNIAL HISTORY

ALEX JOHNSTON and ANDY A. den OTTER

Advisory Editor

Hugh A. Dempsey

Published by
The City of Lethbridge
and
The Whoop-Up Country Chapter,
Historical Society of Alberta

Lethbridge 1985

ISBN 0-919224-42-3 cloth

Cartography: **Barry R. Peat**
Design: **Carlton R. Stewart**
Printed and bound in Canada
By **Ronalds Printing**, Lethbridge Division

Canadian Cataloguing in Publication Data

Johnston, Alex
Lethbridge

Includes Index.

I. Lethbridge (Alta.) — History.
I. Otter, A. A. den (Andy Albert), 1941-
II. Lethbridge (Alta.) III. Lethbridge
   Historical Society IV. Title

FC3699.L48J64 1985   971.23'4   C84-090194-1
F1079.5.L5J64 1985

43,907

4

Contents

Maps

Acknowledgements

Those who undertake to compile the history of a city soon find themselves in debt to many individuals and institutions.

We are indebted to the City of Lethbridge because the primary sources used herein were Council Minutes and other civic documents of the period 1891-1984. John Gerla, City Clerk, and M. Jean Potts, Assistant City Clerk, provided access to the Minutes, as well as to consultants' reports and other studies of the last 70 years.

Support was received from Mayor A. C. Anderson and City Council, which, on 17 January 1983, passed the following resolution: "That letter from Judge Ronald A. Jacobson, Chairman 100th Anniversary Committee, submitting a proposal from the Lethbridge Historical Society to prepare an illustrated history of the City of Lethbridge as a centennial project . . . be filed and further that the funding be included in the 1983, 1984, and 1985 operating budgets."

Others who contributed included Betty Balfour, James H. Carpenter, Drs. Robert and Jo-Anne Corbett, W. J. Elliott, L. Gregory Ellis, Ralph L. Erdman, Sharon E. Grismer, Helen Henderson, George Higa, Dennis Ito, Edward A. Keeling, John Kolpak, Patricia A. Marshall, Felix W. Michna, Cecil Murakami, David Obee, Linda Sears, Kenneth G. Sinclair, and Gwen L. Wilson.

Lethbridge oldtimers who shared memories with us over the years included Chris Gibson, George B. McKillop, Dr. Asael E. Palmer, Mrs. Annie Peat, Mrs. G. H. Starnes, Andrew J. Staysko, Dr. J. S. Stewart, George Watson, and many more.

Institutions that provided study materials and much other help included the Lethbridge Public Library, the Sir Alexander Galt Museum/Archives, the Lethbridge Herald, the Lethbridge Research Station, and the Glenbow-Alberta Institute.

Foreword
A Centennial Message From The Mayor:

We've come a long way! From our commercial beginnings as a whiskey-trading post, we have developed into a modern, progressive city — the envy of many of our sister cities.

Native people lived here for over 10,000 years before the arrival of fur and whiskey traders and, subsequently, of the North-West Mounted Police. Far-sighted men such as Nicholas Sheran and Sir Alexander and Elliott Galt were our first developers. Coal, railways, agriculture, and irrigation all played a role in the development of our city. Our history is rich with the stories of people who settled here. I am confident you will enjoy reading about our past in the pages of this book.

We are the third largest city in Alberta. We are proud of what we have accomplished. Our city is a showcase of educational facilities, retail facilities, industries, culture and recreational facilities, and parks and open spaces. We are fortunate that the University of Lethbridge and the Lethbridge Community College were established here. The appearance of our city is changing constantly; many new developments are underway or in the planning stages. Because of the relocation of the CP Rail marshalling yards, about 95 acres in the heart of our city are available for new development. And in conjunction with railway relocation, a major new roadway system is being built and will provide improved transportation through and around Lethbridge. The motto on the city crest reads, *"Ad Occasionis Januam,"* or *"Gateway to Opportunity."* I believe it to be true. Our future looks bright. I am confident that the years ahead will see us continue to grow and prosper.

Citizens of Lethbridge over the past 100 years deserve credit for the success of our community. Our citizens have contributed not only to their city, but to their province, their country, and the world in the areas of the arts, sciences, and humanities. And although we have grown, we have retained much of our former small town flavour. People here are friendly. We care about our neighbours. We warmly welcome visitors.

I would like to extend my thanks to the Whoop-Up Country Chapter of the Historical Society of Alberta, to Dr. Andy den Otter, and to Dr. Alex Johnston because, without the efforts of this organization and these people, this book would not have been written.

My personal thanks go to Alex Johnston for his unselfish service in recording the history of our city. He makes this material come alive. Through his writing, he encourages us to become aware of our past. I have often turned to him for material because I know that it will be meticulously researched. He has devoted uncounted hours to the production of this book. Thank you, Alex! And,

HAPPY BIRTHDAY, LETHBRIDGE!

A.C. Anderson

Mayor, City of Lethbridge
January 5, 1985

Exposures of Labuma till, called by the Blackfoot "Aksaysim" or "Steep Banks," in June 1883. The area is now known as Indian Battle Park.

Chapter One

Origins of Wealth

The origin and vitality of the City of Lethbridge are deeply rooted in its natural environment. The vast coal beds of southern Alberta attracted the entrepreneur and the miner, while the great expanse of fertile land lured the rancher and the farmer. When rainfall proved to be too scarce and too irregular for intensive agriculture, local rivers provided vital water supplies for irrigation. Coal, soil and water: these three resources gave Lethbridge its life and strength.

The creation of this natural wealth required an aeons-long process of geological and climatic changes, which slowly but relentlessly shaped and sculptured the landscape.

Lethbridge's coal was formed in the Cretaceous period some 70 million years ago when the natural environment was much different. Southern Alberta formed part of a low, broad western shoreline bordering a vast sea which covered the centre of the North American continent. Dinosaurs roamed the land, while the sea teemed with algae, diatoms, corals, bivalves, ammonites and marine reptiles. Luxuriant, subtropical plants flourished in the warm, humid climate. In the 12-month long growing season plants matured rapidly, died and fell into the stagnant swampy waters. The thick layers of dead vegetation were eventually covered by gravel and mud carried by water from the surrounding highlands. Heat, pressure and lack of air produced a chemical reaction which turned plant carbon into coal. At Lethbridge, this process produced a seam of medium-carbon, high-volatile "C" bituminous coal ranging in thickness from 4½ to 6 feet (1.2 to 1.8 m). This coal, mined with relative ease and ideally suited for domestic heating, became the foundation of Lethbridge's early economy.

Lethbridge's other natural resources took nearly as long to create. At the beginning of the Tertiary Period, an enormous geological event dramatically transformed the southern Alberta landscape and climate. About 60 million years ago in the vicinity of today's Selkirk Mountains, tremendous pressures in the earth's crust thrust up an entire mountain range, a predecessor of today's Rockies. Simultaneously, the plains also rose, the shallow sea receded, and, hence, the interior lost the moderating influence of a large body of water. When the new mountains blocked the warm, moisture-laden Pacific winds, Arctic air masses gained the upper hand and the climate became cool, dry and subject to seasonal fluctuations. New plants appeared in response to these profound climatic changes. They included species which produced seeds and thus suspended life during the cold season, trees which shed their leaves and thus endured the harsh winter months, and a few rudimentary grasses, which ceased to grow during the coldest and driest parts of the year.

As time passed, wind, water and ice wore down the mountains so that by about 30 million years ago all that remained were rounded hills. The warm, moist air masses from the Pacific once again circulated across the prairies and subtropical plants reappeared. Great rivers carried the debris of silts, sands and gravels from the mountains and deposited it in southern Alberta in a formation called Paskapoo. The Porcupine Hills and the upper parts of the Cypress Hills consist mostly of these sediments. (The Sweetgrass Hills, which also date from this period, are not sedimentary but rather intrusions of igneous rock called laccoliths.)

The sculpturing of the present day landscape of southern Alberta and the resulting climate began about 30 million years ago. The imperceptible movement of the earth's converging crustal plates slowly thrust up the modern Rocky Mountains. As before, the formation of the mountains drastically altered southern Alberta's climate. The region once again became cool, dry, and subject to seasonal variations. Three major air flows began to influence the climate and continue to do so today.

The most notable of these air flows are warm, dry winds from the west, called Chinooks. These begin when moisture-saturated air from the Pacific Ocean is deflected upward on reaching the coastal mountains. As the air mass expands and cools at higher altitudes, its moisture vapour is condensed and released as rain or snow. When the now cool-dry air mass reaches the eastern slopes of the Rocky Mountains, it loses altitude, thus compressing and heating the flow. Then the warm-dry air mass sweeps over the interior foothills and plains, often at great velocity, and well

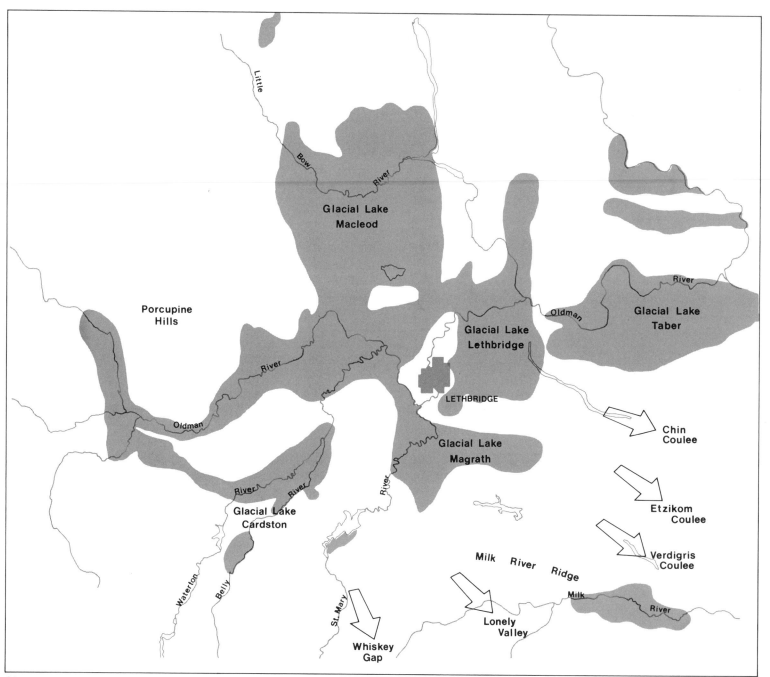

Glacial lakes of 12,000 to 15,000 years ago in southern Alberta and drainages.

deserves its winter nickname of "The Snoweater". An associated phenomenon often seen at Lethbridge is the Chinook Arch, which frequently appears in the western sky. It consists of a light band of sky below dark, altostratus clouds, the whole appearing as an arch because of the curvature of the earth.

The other two air masses which influence the region's climate are Arctic systems from the north and Gulf air from the south. Arctic air is dry because it is cold — sometimes, in winter, cruelly cold. The only significant carriers of moisture are air masses moving inland from the Gulf of Mexico. The long distances these winds have to travel to reach southern Alberta and the many obstacles they encounter en route make them unreliable sources of precipitation. In sum, the interaction of these three varied air masses has created a cool, semiarid climate at Lethbridge.

As always, the new climate produced new vegetation. Subtropical plants disappeared and a vigorous new family, the grasses, arose. Ideally suited to dry regions, the grasses originated in great variety only about 30 million years ago. They spread quickly over many parts of the world where the soil was fertile and the climate was too dry for forest but not dry enough to prevent the development of the kind of closed herbaceous cover that is lacking in steppe or desert. In these places the new plants created grasslands variously called prairie, pampas or veldt. One of the first, and eventually the most extensive, of these grasslands appeared in the lee of the newly risen Rocky Mountains. Subject to frequent fires, which tended to extend its boundaries, it stretched from Canada's Peace River country to Mexico's Central Plateau and eastward from the Rocky Mountains to the Mississippi River Valley. Thus the prairies of southern Alberta are the product of evolution and adaptation, of great geological events and sweeps of time. They have been described by Wallace Stegner as, "high plains country, chinook country, its air like a blade or a blowtorch, its sky fitting close and tight to the horizon, and the great bell of heaven alive with light, clouds, heat, stars, winds, incomparable weathers."

Although the general features of the landscape may have been similar to that of today, animal life was different. Many of the animals were very large — collectively called a megafauna — and included giant anteaters and armadillos, ten-foot (3.0-m) tall mammoths, and eight-foot (2.4-m) tall rhinoceroses. Even the birds were gigantic. Occasional visitors included the California condor with its six-foot (1.7-m) wingspan, and a similar-looking, carrion-feeding scavenger with wings spanning 12 feet (3.7 m). Many of the animals — elk, saiga, buffalo, mammoth, mastodon, wooly rhinoceros, even the black bear and the grizzly — had come to the southern prairies from Asia, moving across the Bering land bridge into North America. Others, notably the horse, travelled the other way. Hundreds of skeletons, many from Eocene deposits in the Cypress Hills, have shown how the horse evolved in North America from a small, four-toed mammal about the size of a fox terrier into a single-toed, pony-sized animal. Then it disappeared from the plains of North America, possibly because of an outbreak of some catastrophic disease, but evolved in Asia into the speedy beast of burden we know today. Many species displayed a herding instinct — camels, several kinds of buffalo and a variety of deer-like mammals. The latter included the modern pronghorn antelope, a true native of North America and the last survivor of a once extensive family of such animals. Other species exhibited a running or burrowing habit, similar to the jack rabbits or ground squirrels of today. Wide-ranging predators included the sabre-toothed tiger, dire wolves, and a kind of lion.

The geographical features and much of the animal life of this era eventually changed or disappeared in the face of several extreme climatic events.

About one million years ago, the winds from the north grew colder. More snow fell each winter than melted in the following summer. Over thousands of years, the snow accumulated and compressed into steadily-thickening icecaps. As pressure at the centre increased, the edges began to flow outward. The result was an enormous continental glacier, its front a towering wall of ice, 1,000 feet (300 m) high, which moved relentlessly southwesterly across today's Manitoba and Saskatchewan and into southern Alberta. Here it met a mountain glacier approaching from the west. Like a gigantic bulldozer, the continental glacier pushed everything before it. It ground rock into flour; it overwhelmed forests and prairies; it blocked drainages with debris. Wherever it approached, the flora changed to Arctic tundra and the fauna to caribou, muskox, polar bear, arctic fox, arctic hare and the elephant-like, wooly mammoth. But as before, the new conditions did not last, the climate moderated, the vast ice sheet melted, and eventually even its core disappeared.

At least four times in the last one million years vast glaciers

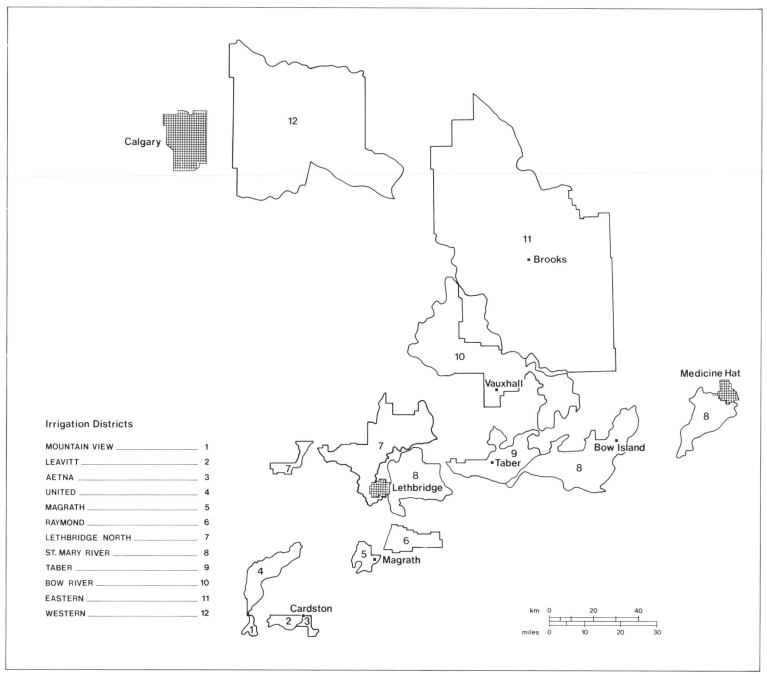

Calgary

12

11
• Brooks

10

Vauxhall
•

Medicine Hat

8

Irrigation Districts

MOUNTAIN VIEW _____ 1

LEAVITT _____ 2

AETNA _____ 3

UNITED _____ 4

MAGRATH _____ 5

RAYMOND _____ 6

LETHBRIDGE NORTH _____ 7

ST. MARY RIVER _____ 8

TABER _____ 9

BOW RIVER _____ 10

EASTERN _____ 11

WESTERN _____ 12

7

7

8
Lethbridge

9
• Taber

Bow Island
•

8

6

5
• Magrath

4

Cardston

2 3

1

km 0   20   40

miles 0   10   20   30

Southern Alberta's irrigation districts, which mostly occupy the beds of former glacial lakes.

crept across most of Canada, including the prairies. Although none of them covered as much territory as the first, all had a significant and lasting effect. The Wisconsin glacial advance, which was the last, melted and disappeared from the Lethbridge area only about 12,000 to 15,000 years ago and thus it sculptured most of the present landscape, especially north and east of the city. It and its predecessors scoured the Canadian shield free of earth and loose rock and dropped the material on the plains as till. ("Till" is unstratified glacial deposits consisting of rock fragments of various sizes, the most common of which is boulder clay). Wherever the ice front lingered, the till was thick and rocky; wherever it melted quickly, the till was thin. Occasionally, the advancing ice carried huge slabs of bedrock frozen to its underside. Some of these megablocks measured several miles in length and width and were a few tens of yards thick. One such slab, called the Laundry Hill Megablock, was carried at least 50 miles (80 km) and finally came to rest in the area immediately north of Whoop-Up Drive. About 1½ miles (2.0 km) long when it was released, it can be recognized as a grayish layer about 100 feet (30 m) above the flood plain on both sides of the river. Other features left by the glaciers are moraines, generally hilly areas that mark the farthest advance of the ice. Thus, at its maximum advance, the Wisconsin glacier deposited the Lethbridge Moraine, a gently-rolling area immediately south and west of the city. The Lethbridge Moraine has been traced from Calgary south to Lethbridge, then east to Etzikom and into Saskatchewan.

The glaciers did not create all of the landmarks in the vicinity of Lethbridge. The Milk River Ridge, at least in the Del Bonita area, was not glaciated because, beginning 30 million years ago, it somehow escaped the erosion that lowered the rest of the prairie in the region by from 1,300 to 1,600 feet (400 to 500 m). Thus, the ridge acted as a barrier to the advancing ice.

Just as climate and vegetation changed continuously over millennia, so too did the region's drainage system. During the formation of the Rockies, the ancestral Oldman River flowed eastward at a higher level than now and cut the spectacular S-shaped gap through the Livingstone Range by superposition. Leaving the mountains, the river flowed onto a five-mile (8.0-km) wide flood-plain, which was separated from adjoining watersheds by ranges of low-lying hills. Flowing eastward, the ancestral river roughly followed its modern course through Fort Macleod, Pearce,

and Lethbridge, and on to Medicine Hat. Approaching glaciers changed the river's flow. Some 12,000 to 15,000 years ago, the presence of glacial ice at Lethbridge forced the ancestral Oldman River to flow southward past modern Stirling and on to the Milk River by way of Etzikom Coulee. But, when the ice at Lethbridge melted downslope to the north, easterly-trending channels re-emerged and were utilized briefly as drainage-ways in their turn. Eventually, the Oldman River completed "The Bend," which now nearly encircles West Lethbridge, and once again joined the Hudson Bay drainage system.

The sides of the Oldman River valley provide a fascinating picture of the geological history of southern Alberta. At Lethbridge, the river has cut its channel into the bedrock of the coal-bearing Oldman River formation. Overlying bedrock there is a 20 to 30-foot (6.0 to 9.0-m) layer of sand, gravel and small boulders, which was carried by rivers over shallow ice from the eroding Rocky Mountains, called the Saskatchewan Sands and Gravels.

Above the Saskatchewan Sands and Gravels, which has been mined for aggregate at Lethbridge, there is a sequence of at least three glacial till sheets and at least two buried glacial lake horizons as well as a mantle of glacial lake sediments and loess on the surface. The till sheet immediately above the Saskatchewan Sands and Gravels is known as Labuma till. It is composed of very heavy clay, which was compressed when wet by 6,500 feet (2000 m) or more of ice, and now exhibits a dense, blocky, columnar structure. This till has been mined at Lethbridge and, because it is nearly impermeable to water when well tamped, has been widely used as fill. Another prominent layer at Lethbridge is the buff-coloured Lenzie silts, a thick sequence of glacial lake deposits.

Today the Oldman river is a collector of several streams fed by the melting snows of the Rocky Mountains. Every spring, as the warming sun melts the heavy mountain snows, the Oldman's water level rises, flushing and cleansing the ecosystem. By the time its swiftly flowing waters reach Lethbridge, its valley is one mile (1.6 km) wide and its banks, deeply scarred by coulees, are 300 feet (100 m) high. A rich profusion of shrubs and trees grow in the river valley microclimate, providing a migratory pathway and a wildlife habitat in the heart of the modern city. As the warm summer months approach and most of the winter snow has melted, the river's level drops quickly, its flow dwindles to a languid slowness, most of the rough gravel floor lies exposed and small islands appear.

Outcrop of main coal seam at Coal Banks, Belly River, 18 June 1881.

14

Exposure of Laundry Hill Megablock (the light-colored layer across the centre of the photograph) on the banks of the Oldman River valley at Lethbridge in 1984.

The Lenzie Silts

The Lenzie Silts are a prominent, buff-colored layer that has been exposed along the river valley at Lethbridge. They are fine sands and silts deposited by lakes and rivers. The downslope retreat of the continental ice sheets left large lakes at their fronts with rivers running through them to lower ground south of the ice. Sands and silts from these lake deposits produced very level terrain, for example, the land between Lethbridge and Taber. Silt exposures along the valley often show ripple marks left by waves or by stream currents. The Lenzie Silts date to the middle of the Wisconsin, about 59,000 to 25,000 years ago. West of the Lethbridge moraine, near Kipp, the glacier advanced several times into the lake formed in front of it, and there till and Lenzie lake deposits are intermingled. The Lenzie Silts were covered by till of a more recent ice advance with lake deposits laid down in turn over the till.

Unless a sudden rainstorm causes a flash flood, the river does not resume its vigorous pace until the following spring. Since the last ice age, the river has coursed through its natural cycles, its fluctuating tempo closely tied to the seasons; every year the meandering river flows relentlessly onward to the sea, constantly, even if imperceptibly, changing its immediate environment.

In contrast to the sheltered river valley, the gently undulating plains above it are exposed to heat and cold carried by strong, nearly incessant winds. The fertile soil that sustains the prairie grasses is the youngest and most fragile of Lethbridge's resources. Contrary to popular belief, soil profile development can take place in decades rather than in centuries or millennia. Soils are open, dynamic systems; in the last 12,000 years southern Alberta soils have been formed, buried, reformed, and destroyed several times. As late as 6,600 years ago a distant volcano, Mount Mazama in southwestern Oregon, added to southern Alberta's soil when it erupted and spread ash over an area extending from the Pacific slope to Saskatchewan, from Montana to north-central Alberta. Mazama ash covered Lethbridge with a two to four-inch (5.0 to 10.0-cm) readily-identifiable layer, which has been covered in turn by as much as six feet (2.0 m) of loess originating in the Fort Macleod-Pearce area. The soils of the Lethbridge region, therefore, are complex mixtures which have developed from both bedrock and till, or on lacustrine deposits, in response to vegetation and climate.

On a soils map, the western prairies look like three distorted triangles, set one within the other, with their base the border between Canada and the United States.

The innermost triangle, the semiarid Brown Soil zone, is the driest of the three. Annual precipitation averages about 14 inches (355 mm) but droughts lasting from several weeks to several months are common. It is in this region that the "rain shadow effect" of the Rocky Mountains is most apparent, so that areas 150 miles (240 km) east of the mountain front are almost deserts and receive only about 11 to 12 inches (280 to 300 m) of precipitation a year. The Brown Soil zone is a region of extremes. At Medicine Hat, records show a range of temperature from -50 F (-46 C) in January to 107 F (42 C) in July, and in annual precipitation from six inches (150 mm) in 1910 to 28 inches (710 mm) in 1927. The frost-free period ranges from 110 to 140 days. Because the whole region has been scoured by glacial ice, it has an immature drainage system; tens of thousands of temporary ponds or sloughs once collected water, which evaporated and often left the white alkali that is so characteristic of the dry plains. Thousands of these sloughs have been drained in the last 40 years, with disastrous consequences to prairie waterfowl and with unknown consequences in the recycling of spring runoff and summer rains. The original prairie vegetation, much of which is still used for grazing, is classed as Mixed Prairie and is a complex mixture of shortgrasses, midgrasses, forbs and shrubs. Except along the rivers and among sand dunes, trees do not grow naturally in the Brown Soil zone.

The second triangle contains the Dark Brown Soil zone. The climate is less extreme than in the Brown Soil zone, annual precipitation averages about 16 inches (405 mm), and the growing season ranges from 100 to 120 days. At Lethbridge, records show a range in temperature from -45 F (-43 C) in January to 102 F (39 C) in July, in annual precipitation from eight inches (194 mm) in 1918 to 28 inches (709 mm) in 1902, and a maximum wind gust on 19 November 1962 of 105 mph (171 km/hr). The original prairie vegetation of the Dark Brown Soil zone is classed as Mixed Prairie also, but it contains more midgrasses and tallgrasses than does the Brown Soil zone.

The third triangle is the Black Soil zone. Annual precipitation ranges from 18 to 20 inches (455 to 510 mm) and the growing

16

A 1950s flood in the river valley at Lethbridge. For the last 110 years and likely for millennia, the river has averaged a major flood about once every decade.

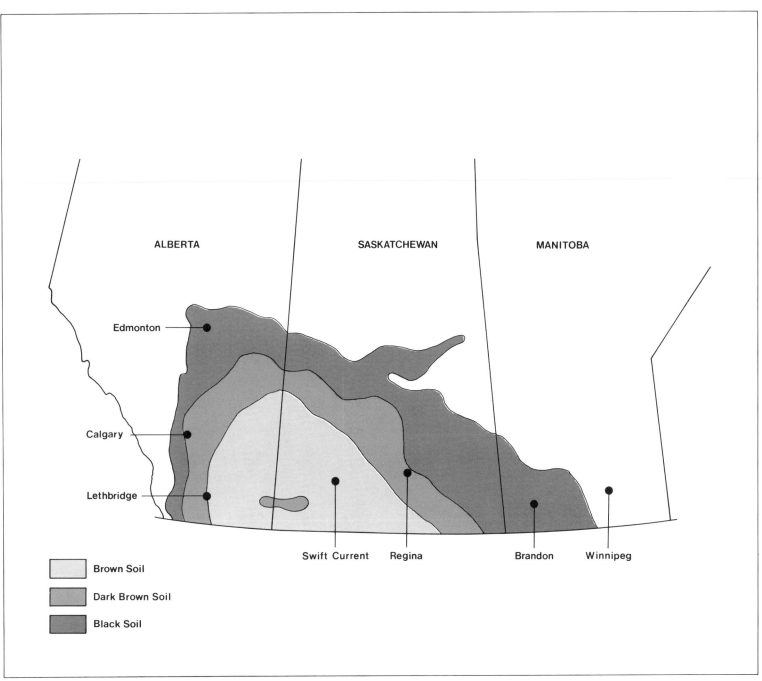

ALBERTA

SASKATCHEWAN

MANITOBA

Edmonton

Calgary

Lethbridge

Swift Current

Regina

Brandon

Winnipeg

Brown Soil

Dark Brown Soil

Black Soil

Soil zones of the prairie region of western Canada.

season from 90 to 110 days. The original prairie vegetation is classed as Fescue Grassland and is a complex mixture of tallgrasses, forbs, shrubs and trees. The area has been protected from prairie fires since settlement, hence, the cover of trees has increased, and there is a distinctive mosaic of prairie patches and aspen groves called the Parkland.

The wilderness territory, which encompassed the Lethbridge region, was a complex region of dynamic contrasts. In summer, the landscape presented an endless sea of waving yellow grasses, interrupted occasionally by a grey sage brush, a buff sand dune, or a white-rimmed alkali slough. Hot searing winds pushed temperatures into the high thirties causing an aridity rarely but spectacularly relieved by brief and heavy rainstorms often accompanied by violent thunder and lightning. In winter, a brilliant white snow sheet glistened under the hard blue sky, while cold, cutting winds drove temperatures far below freezing. Yet, suddenly, a warm Chinook wind might relieve the cold, melt the snow, and expose the vegetation. Only the hardiest of plants survived these harsh conditions. Precipitation, too infrequent to permit the growth of trees, fell too often to allow the creation of a desert. During prolonged dry spells, the short grasses flourished, while in wetter years, taller grasses and larger plants thrived. Thus ground cover changed with time, a delicate ecology transformed and shaped by climatic cycles.

Lethbridge was founded in the transition zone. It is situated in a region where the Brown soils of the semiarid plains meet the Black soils of the moister foothills. It lies between the Mixed Prairie of southeastern Alberta and the Fescue Grassland-Aspen Parkland to the west and north. It is located on the western edge of the eastward-sloping plains of Western Canada, at the foot of the Rocky Mountains.

The complex soil, the water and the coal, all of which gave Lethbridge its life, are the products of agonizingly slow yet relentless processes of nature. These majestic powers imperceptibly shaped and altered, moved and removed material. Millions of years of erosion and deposition subtly sculptured the landscape which greeted the founders of Lethbridge. In the 100 years since they came, the city builders have changed the environment more profoundly than had 100 centuries of wind, water and fire.

Fluted spearpoint, three inches (7.0 cm) long and about 11,000 years old. Found at bottom of a six-foot (2.0-m) ditch on 4th Street South in Lethbridge.

Chapter Two

The Prairie People

Long before the founding of the City of Lethbridge, native people roamed the yellow grasslands of southern Alberta. They were wanderers, who saw no economic value in the soil beneath their feet nor in the coal below the ground. Concerned mostly with food and shelter, they followed the buffalo and other herds across the prairies, abiding where game was abundant, departing when it became scarce. They seldom remained long in any one place, but came and went seasonally, leaving behind little to betray their sojourn. Their tools and weapons permitted little more than bare survival. Their numbers were small and their impact upon the environment minimal.

There are few traces of the earliest nomads. A controversial handful of bones of an infant, a crude stone chopper embedded in a buffalo skull, and a fluted spearpoint — these are the artifacts which suggest that early prehistoric people occupied the site of Lethbridge and its environs 11,000 years before the founding of the city. More positive proof of human occupancy is seen at the Fletcher archaeological site, near Lethbridge, which served as a buffalo killing site some 9,000 years ago. The scarcity of artifacts indicate that the bands of people were small, that they were wanderers, and that they lived in rock, brush, or skin shelters. Their weapons were simple, consisting of heavy spears which could be hurled a short distance or stabbed into a trapped or fallen animal. And yet these early hunters, between 11,000 and 8,000 years ago, were partly responsible for the disappearance of a megafauna of many species.

During the mid-prehistoric period from about 5,000 BC to AD 200, people came who left more evidence of their presence. The Head-Smashed-In Buffalo Jump, near Fort Macleod, dates from the earliest years of this era and represents a significant innovation: the communal kill and butchering site. Here and at other locations, medium-sized, notched or stemmed projectile points can be found. These were used with a spear thrower or atlatl, an important new hunting weapon which provided greater speed, range and impact than the simple spear. The various jumps and impoundments suggest that buffalo was the main source of food but lighter, more accurate weapons meant that smaller animals, such as antelope, deer or rabbit, were alternative quarries. Also novel to the time was the buffalo-skin tepee, a highly portable dwelling, easily moved as the band searched for food. More efficient hunting techniques left more time for cultural developments. Stone cairns and medicine wheels attest to the emergence of more complex societies. While their function is still not clearly understood, the structures were configurations of boulders arranged to serve as religious, artistic, navigational or astronomical markers.

Hunting techniques became even more efficient during the late prehistoric period, which lasted from about AD 200 to AD 1800. Material evidence is also more common. Arrowheads, which represent the most significant technological innovation of the era, are numerous, particularly at the popular buffalo jumps and occupation sites. The introduction of the bow and arrow had a dramatic impact upon the people. By significantly increasing the speed, range, rate of fire, and accuracy of the weapons of the hunt, food gathering took less time and survival rates improved markedly. Populations increased. More efficient hunting techniques left more leisure time which could be used for religious or artistic endeavours. Petroglyphs, pictographs, small stone effigies and even elaborate boulder carvings confirm a high level of artistic ability. Porcupine quill work emerged during the period. Pottery remnants are found in southern Alberta beginning about 1,500 years ago.

Transformations in human culture on the prairies accelerated dramatically with the arrival of Europeans during the eighteenth century. By then the eastern edge of America had been claimed and fur traders were travelling up-river into the heart of the continent. In 1690, Henry Kelsey, working for the Hudson's Bay Company, reached the prairies from the northeast. During the next 100 years, fur traders from London and Montreal became firmly rooted in the northern forests that rimmed the plains. They had little interest in the grasslands where the animals produced hides too large and too heavy to ship to European markets. Instead, they

Prairie covered with buffalo, 1853. John Mix Stanley sketch.

Blackfoot hunting buffalo near the Sweetgrass Hills in 1853. John Mix Stanley sketch.

22

saw the prairies as a resource for pemmican — buffalo meat, which, dried, beaten and mixed with fat and flavoured with dried berries, served as a nutritious, concentrated food staple for the northern trade. The fur companies built a chain of posts along the North Saskatchewan River where the Plains Indians could come to barter their produce for European goods.

Although the white newcomers seldom ventured onto the plains, their impact on human culture there was very great. The European trade dramatically altered the economies and customs of the prairie people. They became dependent upon such goods as pots and pans, knives and axes, clothing and tobacco. They began to hunt not only to satisfy their basic needs for food and shelter but to gratify a desire for material possessions they never needed before. The quest intensified for that most coveted of objects — the gun. First introduced by European traders on the Atlantic seaboard in the early 1600s, the gun made its way westward and a century later reached the prairies. At about the same time, the horse, brought to America by the Spanish in the 1500s, appeared on the northern plains. The horse and the gun formed a lethal combination which revolutionized life on the grasslands. The increasing emphasis on material possessions, for example, led to raiding and horse stealing. Intertribal hostilities occurred more frequently. Increased mobility and trade, and greater use of European goods, gradually eroded the differences in cultures on the prairies and blended them into a nearly homogeneous northern plains society.

The Blackfoot Indians, one of the oldest linguistic groups on the Plains, occupied the Lethbridge area just prior to white settlement. They were one of the prairie people dramaticaly affected by the European intrusion. The Blackfoot were a warlike nation, proud and fiercely independent. They embraced three tribes: *Sik-si-kah* or Blackfoot, so-named because of an incident whereby their moccasins became black from the soot of prairie fires; *Kai'nah* or Many Chiefs, now called Bloods, the latter from a Cree term *Mik-kwee-ye-ne-wuk* or Blood people, apparently from their use of red ochre; and *Api-ku-ni* or Scabby Robes (shortened to Peigan), so-named for a time when their hides were not properly tanned by the women. Collectively, they called themselves *Sow-ki-tapi* or Prairie People. European fur traders along the North Saskatchewan and Missouri Rivers first came into contact with the Blackfoot and, hence, this tribal name came to be applied to the entire nation.

Although the Blackfoot had only limited contact with the fur traders, the impact of the European presence was significant. They met Henry Kelsey in 1691 on their central Saskatchewan hunting

The Burial Tree of Seen From Afar

Three types of burial customs were practiced by the Blood Indians: underground burial, lodge or house burial, and tree or platform burial.

Underground burial is of recent origin, dating from the advent of Christian missionaries about 100 years ago.

Lodge burial was practiced when a notable chief or warrior died. A buffalo skin lodge was placed on a hill or in a secluded place, the deceased and his valued possessions were laid out within, and then the opening was sealed. After the beginning of the reservation period, small log or lumber buildings were erected over the remains of relatives.

The platform method of burial consisted of four posts, eight to twelve feet high, placed so as to make a suitable platform on top to hold the corpse. The body was properly prepared and laid on the platform, along with prized treasures of the deceased and gifts from friends.

In the tree mode of burial a large tree of suitable proportions and location was selected. The body was placed on a scaffold of branches in one of its crotches, safely away from the depredations of wild animals, while the coverings of the corpse protected it from the ravages of scavenger birds.

Tree burial was practiced, likely from the beginnings of Blood occupancy of the region, in the river valley at Lethbridge. Alma Isobella Forbes, later Mrs. Eli Hodder, on awakening in the William Stafford home after her first night in Coalbanks in 1883, looked out of her bedroom window and saw four tree burials nearby. The most famous local tree burial was that of the great Blood chief, *Peenaquim*, or Seen From Afar, who died in the smallpox epidemic of 1869 and whose burial tree was located a few hundred yards north of the present No. 3 highway traffic bridge on the east side of the Oldman River. It was undermined and washed away in the floods of 1902 and 1908.

Scout Joe Healy

grounds. In 1754, Anthony Henday visited a Blackfoot encampment of 200 lodges with many horses near modern Red Deer. By this time, the Blackfoot, armed with a few guns and mounted on horseback, had driven the Snake and Kootenay Indians from southern Alberta, taken possession of the territory, and extended their influence as far south as the Missouri River.

The Blackfoot were perfectly adapted to this vast, open landscape. Every niche in the complex ecosystem was exploited with great skill. They were nomads who roamed the plains in summer and sheltered in the river valleys in winter. They thrived on the enormous buffalo herds which ranged at will across the grasslands, sometimes forming an uninterrupted shaggy carpet of brown bodies or, at other times, a single plodding line.

Buffalo, supplemented by pronghorn, deer or elk and berries, provided the prairie people with all they needed: food, clothing, shelter. Thus, they attached no economic value to the agricultural potential of the prairies or to the coal exposed on the river banks. When guns and horses made hunting easier, they killed more than they required for their own needs and traded the surplus to the white newcomers for luxuries: tobacco, metal goods, weapons and utensils. Although trade changed their life-style, the prairie people remained nomads and in control of their own destinies.

Blackfoot culture prevailed because few traders or explorers ventured far into their territory. In the late 1700s, the Hudson's Bay Company sent David Thompson and, subsequently, Peter Fidler into the region. Fidler opened Chesterfield House at the junction of the South Saskatchewan and Red Deer rivers in 1800 and operated it until 1802. Donald Mackenzie and John Rowand reopened the post in 1822 but closed it again in 1823. Several Hudson's Bay Company parties explored the lower reaches of the Red Deer and Bow rivers and visited the Sweetgrass Hills.

For example, John E. Harriott reached the Sweetgrass Hills in 1822. His Indian guide claimed that one of the hills had a large hole in the top and when he looked into it he saw "a new country, herds of buffalo and Indian camps and everything like another world." Another Hudson's Bay Company man, Henry Fisher, crossed the Lethbridge area in 1824 on his way to the south. But the British-based company had only a halfhearted interest in the southern fringe of its empire, and thus relations with the Indians, although cool, remained peaceful.

Conditions were quite different to the south in the Missouri

Coal and the Indians

The native people of southern Alberta knew that coal would burn but had tribal taboos against its use, particularly in tepee fires. Indians of other regions, notably the Hopi of Colorado, mined and used coal from exposed seams for hundreds of years before the coming of whites, but the Blackfoot never did.

Taboos against the use of coal probably originated many years ago when whole families died mysteriously in their sleep from poisoning by carbon monoxide, the gas given off by a coal fire. Gradually the relationship of coal fires-mysterious deaths became convincing and tribal taboos evolved to provide the necessary protection.

Also, failure to use coal in any fires may have been due to apprehension and fear of the underground spirits by the Indians. Coal was almost always found underground, hence, fears of the underground beings may have become attached to coal.

The fuel used by the Blackfoot included the dried branches of willow and, particularly, poplar, which the women pulled down by means of a hooked stick on a long pole. Other trees and shrubs were burned, as was dried buffalo dung, later to be called *bois de vache,* the "wood of the cow" by the early explorers.

All of these fuels were widely and readily available, thus lessening dependence on a resource such as coal.

River region. In 1806, Merriwether Lewis, of the Lewis and Clark Expedition, met a small party of Peigans on Cutbank Creek. A fight ensued and two Indians were killed. This incident created such strong animosities that the Blackfoot fiercely guarded their territory against American trappers and mountain men for the next 30 years. Relations had improved somewhat by 1832 when a peace treaty was made and Kenneth Mackenzie built a fur post on the Marias River. However, bloody skirmishes remained the norm for the next few years. In sum, the risk of death for marginal returns kept the American fur traders and trappers out of Blackfoot country.

The Blackfoot also rebuffed Christian missionaries until the 1870s. In the 1840s and 1850s, Fathers Pierre-Jean DeSmet and Nicholas Point, working among neighbouring tribes in American territory, occasionally visited the Blackfoot. So did the Rev. Robert Rundle and Father Albert Lacombe, who ministered to the northern Cree, Assiniboine and Metis in British territory. None of them significantly influenced the Blackfoot. Nor did Rev. George and John McDougall, who in the 1870s spent most of their time with the Stoneys at Morley and only sporadically sought out the Blackfoot.

While the Blackfoot may have been able to control European penetration into their territory, they could not ward off the white man's diseases. Their bodies contained no immunity against these foreign illnesses nor did they have any cures. The results were tragic. In 1781, when the first recorded major smallpox epidemic broke out in the North-West, more than half of the native population perished. A healthy nomadic life-style quickly restored their numbers. But in 1837, smallpox struck again. It killed nearly two-thirds of the members of the Blackfoot and Blood tribes. When the disease struck, many of the Bloods were camped at the junction of the St. Mary and Belly (now Oldman) rivers near Lethbridge, at a site they subsequently called *Sow-kee Akai-nuskwi* (The Prairie Where Many Died). Scarlet fever claimed an unknown number of prairie people in 1865, while smallpox again killed nearly a third of the Bloods in 1869. Among the victims of the 1869 epidemic was the great Blood chief *Peenaquim* (Seen From Afar).

Disease was not the only effect of contact of the prairie people with the white newcomers. The trade in surplus buffalo meat brought a measure of material prosperity previously unknown on the plains. Greater wealth increased leisure time which in turn stimulated the growth of religious and social organizations. The prairie dwellers adopted such major ceremonies as the Sun Dance and the elaborate rituals of the opening and transfer of medicine bundles. These intricate pageantries served to redistribute wealth, prestige and power among the Blackfoot. At the same time, they established an elaborate system of age-graded societies based on common religious, military or social interests. These associations reflected fundamental changes in economic, religious and political life of the Blackfoot and a rapid increase in their numbers.

The transformation of the Blackfoot social organizations in the fur trade era reflected a desire to better exploit the new opportunities for wealth, power and prestige. In the earlier hunting and food gathering culture, for instance, women made an important

Blackfoot Sun Dance Camp in 1880s.

Life in the camps.

26

Fort Whoop-Up in the early 1880s.

contribution to basic subsistence. Once the Blackfoot began to barter with Europeans, however, this changed. The women picked and processed the berries, and prepared the meat, fat and hides for the trade. Consequently, the man who aspired to wealth and power required several wives. Polygamy increased and the average age at which women married decreased. (And women permitted the trend to polygamy because the increased warfare of the period created greater casualties and a relative shortage of husbands.) The quest for material possessions, virtually unknown before the fur trade, changed an important social relationship.

The most devastating change in Blackfoot culture, however, began shortly after the middle of the nineteenth century. America's industrial civilization was rapidly approaching the western plains. In 1853, Isaac I. Stevens surveyed northern Montana for a suitable transcontinental railway route and two years later signed a treaty with the Blackfoot on behalf of the United States government. Several American agents penetrated northward into British territory in an attempt to persuade the prairie people to sign the treaty and to bring peace to the region. One such messenger, Henry Kennerly by name, encountered Lame Bull's Peigan band at the junction of the modern Belly and Oldman Rivers. The American government, anxious to secure its authority in the west, wanted to impose peace and order among native tribes on both sides of the northern Rockies, to declare intertribal warfare illegal, to secure safe passage of whites through the region, and, in consequence,

to open the way for the rapid development of the territory's resources.

Meanwhile, the people of Canada also became interested in the rich prairie soils. As new farm lands became increasingly scarce in their eastern provinces, Canadians avidly absorbed the glowing reports of travellers to the North-West. The leader of a British scientific expedition, John Palliser, toured southern Alberta in 1858 and in the following year came within a few miles of the future site of Lethbridge. He proclaimed the black soils of the North-West — the Fertile Belt — fit for settlement. In the 1870s, the optimistic John Macoun, Dominion Botanist, called the whole western region an oasis. Once the concept of fertile lands and a suitable climate was firmly rooted in the Canadian mind, the government slowly but relentlessly pressed the Hudson's Bay Company to surrender its claim to the territory. Faced with adverse publicity against its old monopoly and the inevitability of western colonization, the company bowed to Canadian pressure. It relinquished its political and economic control over the prairies in 1870 and withdrew into the northern forests. The Canadian government, however, did not move into the North-West immediately, creating a dangerous void in political authority.

In December 1869, two American traders, John J. Healy and Alfred B. Hamilton, took advantage of the power vacuum in the Canadian North-West. By this time, it had become economical to ship buffalo hides from southern Alberta by wagon train to Fort

27

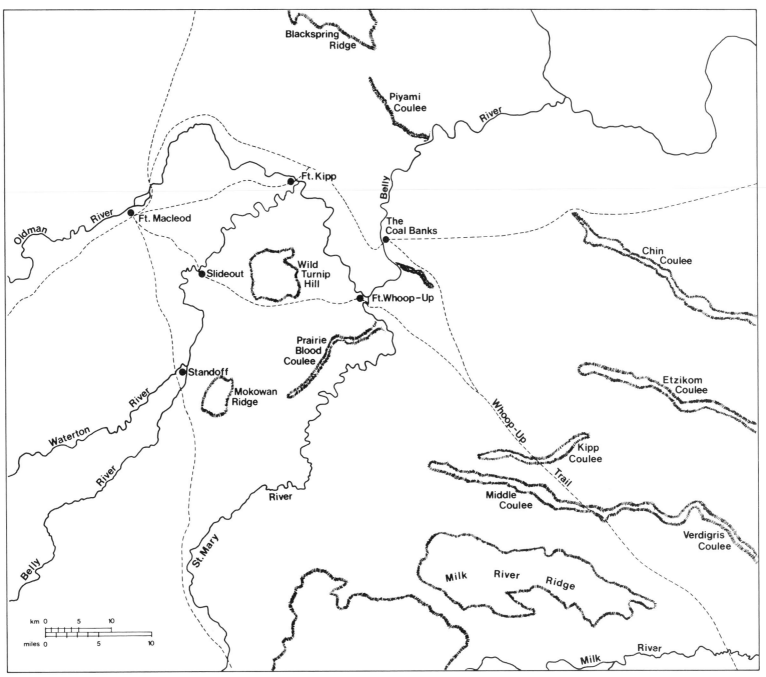

Part of Whoop-Up Country, about 1878.

28

Atso'Taoowayi, Chief Jim Shot Both Sides, whose forefathers for generations ruled over the Lethbridge region, was born on the Blood Reserve in 1914, the son of Shot Both Sides, Head Chief of the Blood tribe, and Drums In The Water. He was a member of a family that led the Blood tribe for at least 140 years: Seen From Afar (1840s-1869), Black Bear (1869-1870), Red Crow (1870-1900), Crop Eared Wolf (1900-1913), Shot Both Sides (1913-1956), and Jim Shot Both Sides (1956-1981, except 1965-1966). Jim Shot Both Sides presided over a Tribal Council which threw off the paternalism of the previous 70 years and assumed full responsibility for tribal affairs; developed industries on the reserve; created programs in road construction, housing and irrigation; and encouraged the development of Indian-run farms.

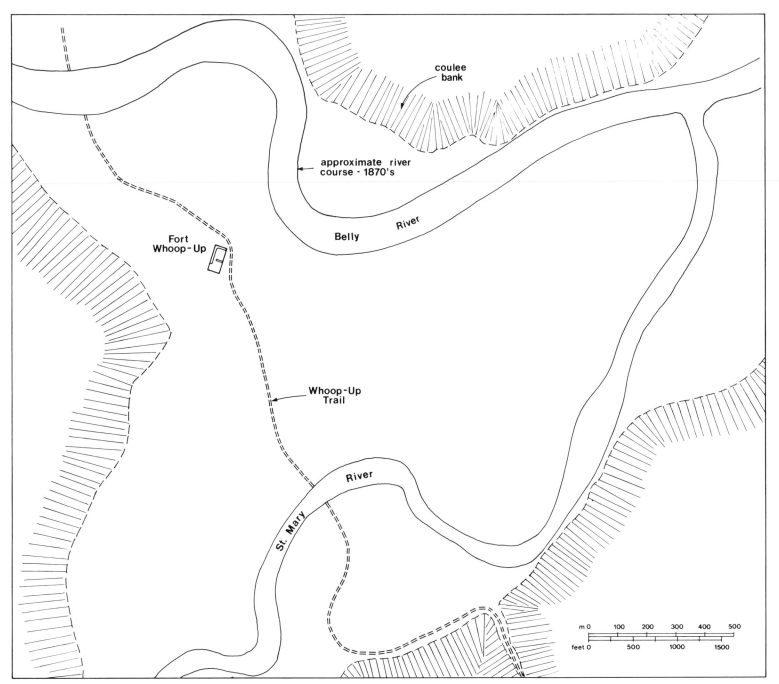

coulee
bank

approximate river
course - 1870's

Belly River

Fort
Whoop-Up

Whoop-Up
Trail

St. Mary River

m 0   100   200   300   400   500

feet 0   500   1000   1500

Fort Whoop-Up and vicinity, about 1872.

Alfred Baker (Alf) Hamilton was born on 2 September 1839 in New Haven, Connecticut. His mother was Grace Baker Hamilton, a sister of Isaac Baker of I. G. Baker and Company, merchants of Fort Benton, Montana.

John Jerome (Johnny) Healy was born in Cork County, Ireland, in 1840, emigrated to New York as a boy, and came west with the 2nd Dragoons in 1858.

31

Fort Whoop-Up

"One of the principal posts of the traders in that region was Fort Hamilton, commonly known as Whoop-Up, situated at the forks of the Belly and St. Mary Rivers. There were two walls, about a dozen feet apart, built of heavy squared logs, braced across by heavy log partitions about the same distance from one another, dividing it into rooms, which were used as dwellings, blacksmith shops, stores, etc., the doors and windows opening into the square. There were bastions at the corners, and the walls were loop-holed for musketry. Iron bars were placed across the chimneys to prevent the Indians from getting in that way. There were heavy log roofs across the partitions, and a strong gate of oak, with a small opening to trade through. All other posts merely had palisades, but they were strong enough for the purpose. The trader stood at the wicket, a tubful of whiskey beside him, and when an Indian pushed in a buffalo robe to him through the hole in the wall he handed out a tin cupful of the poisonous decoction. A quart of the stuff bought a fine pony. When spring came, wagonloads of the proceeds of the traffic were escorted back to Fort Benton, Montana, some 200 odd miles south of the border line."

--Col. S. B. Steele in "Forty Years in Canada."

"I skipped the Missoula country and went across the Line to Whoop-Up, supposed to be then a resort of the most desperate characters escaped from the United States. I saw some dead bodies there but the place was not so bad as represented. I was there partly in charge of the principal fort, when Col. Macleod and his Mounted Police arrived from Fort Garry to subdue the outlaws and drive out illicit traders. He came with siege guns to reduce our fort, which had been reported in Canada to be bristling with cannon and needle guns, and he came and found open gates, a cripple [Schafft had both legs amputated below the knees as a result of severe frostbite] as second in command, and six or seven peaceful-looking citizens. Our only Armament were two old steamboat cannons, and any amount of trade rifles, and our whiskey was cached at the bottom of the Belly River."

--Sketch of a Life: Charles Schafft.
Montana Magazine of History, January 1976.

Bull Teams

Bull teams were used in the 1870s and early 1880s to transport goods and supplies from Fort Benton, Montana, into southern Alberta. Travel was possible only for about eight months of the year, when pasture was available. The "bulls" (really oxen) were broken in as four-year-old steers, used for about four years, then sold for beef. In making up a team, the leaders were usually well-broken cattle. It was difficult to yoke up an unbroken team, hence, trains travelled in brigades so as to have plenty of help available if trouble occurred.

Teams, which consisted of six to eight span of oxen, were hitched to three wagons — lead, swing and trail — plus a cart to carry a cooking outfit, blankets, and a tent. The lead wagon carried 60 percent of the load, the swing wagon about 25 percent, and the trail wagon about 15 percent. About fifteen tons of freight were carried. Two men were detailed to each team. Brigades of six to eight teams also had a wagon boss, who rode alongside and directed all operations.

At river crossings, teams were taken to the far side, then wagons were hauled across one by one by means of a long chain. On very steep hills, two or more teams were coupled up. And on marshy or muddy ground, the wagons were separated and the team was used to haul each wagon across in its turn.

Wagons were strongly built, on a gauge of five feet. They were covered with heavy canvas, with bows on the wagon box, so that goods were kept perfectly dry, no matter what the weather.

The last bull train to pass through Lethbridge from Benton was in the spring of 1885, the outfit being in charge of F. Burel, wagon boss for I. G. Baker and Company, which owned the train. These teams were used for freighting in the Fort Macleod district until about 1889.

Benton on the Missouri River and then by steam boat to eastern factories. When U.S. industry expanded due to Civil War production, bison hides became popular for machine belting and the demand for them was insatiable. Healy and Hamilton built a cheap, crude post called Fort Hamilton at the confluence of the

St. Mary and Belly rivers, a favourite winter camp of the Bloods. Their primary purpose was to trade rotgut whiskey for robes and hides. The success of their venture owed much to Healy's personal relationship with the Bloods — he lived with a succession of Blood women — and their willingness to trade almost everything they owned for whiskey. After grossing $50,000 for their winter activities, Healy and Hamilton abandoned the fort but it was accidentally destroyed by fire when the bull trains were being loaded.

Stories of Healy and Hamilton's success spread like wildfire. Within two or three years at least 41 posts dotted the southwestern prairies. Most of the newcomers were blind to the beauty of the land, indifferent to the delicate balance of life, and contemptuous of the Indian's dignity. They saw the prairie people and its animals as items of exploitation and easy profit. Greedily, they encouraged the wanton killing of fur-bearing animals and, hiding in their strong forts, cheated and debauched the natives by trading them poisonous, adulterated whiskey. Of all these posts, the rebuilt Fort Hamilton, more popularly known as Fort Whoop-Up, was the most notorious. A solid, rectangular log structure, guarded by two bristling cannons, it protected the white plunderers from their alcohol crazed victims.

The chaotic violence, sown by the American traders, became the setting for the last great, intertribal Indian battle to be fought in North America. At dawn on 25 October 1870, a large Cree war party attacked a band of Bloods in camp on the banks of the Belly River, now within the city limits of Lethbridge. The Crees expected the Bloods to be gravely weakened by smallpox but unknown to them a large band of Peigans was camped on the other side of the river. These Peigans had fled their traditional Montana hunting grounds after United States Army troops under Major Eugene Baker massacred 173 of them in camp on the Marias River the previous January. Upon hearing of the Cree attack, the Peigans quickly crossed the river and routed the invaders, killing several hundred of them in the process. At a critical time in their history, the prairie people failed to bury their traditional hostilities. They fought and killed each other, while a common foe took over their land.

The lawlessness which reigned on the plains in the early 1870s sparked an uproar in central Canada. The Dominion government had to respond and in 1874 sent the hastily-assembled North-West

Old Buck

The first recruits for the hastily-organized "Mounted Police Force for the North-West Territories" signed on in eastern Canada in the autumn of 1873 and were sent west to Fort Garry. Lieutenant Colonel W. Osborne Smith, commander of the militia at Fort Garry, arranged accommodation for the men and erected stables for 50 horses, with harness rooms and storage space for hay and oats. Also, he purchased 33 horses for use by the recruits; among them was a seven-year-old gelding named "Buck."

On the great march westward in 1874, Buck was assigned to "the boy", 15-year-old trumpeter Frederick A. Bagley. On 21 September 1874, with the Force at the West Butte of the Sweetgrass Hills, Bagley was still mounted on Buck, as he had been since leaving Dufferin on 13 June.

Both Bagley and Buck accompanied Colonel James F. Macleod to the gates of Fort Whoop-Up on 9 October 1874 and to the site of the future Fort Macleod on 13 October.

Buck, by now referred to as "Old Buck" or "The Bagley Pony", is next heard of on 1 December 1894 when Superintendent R. Burton Deane, Commanding "K" Division, Lethbridge, reported: "The historic old horse 'Buck', which came into the country with the first expedition in 1874, and was then aged, is still to the fore. He has thus completed upwards of 28 winters, and nobody knows how many more."

"Old Buck" lived until 1898 in "K" Division's stables and paddocks, now Lethbridge's Civic Centre, until humanely put to death at age 32 on order of Superintendent Deane.

Mounted Police to the southwestern prairies to blot out the whiskey trade. The police quickly stamped out the most flagrant abuses but never fully eradicated the smugglers. Nor could they stop the reckless butchery of wild life. Greedy Metis and white commercial hunters continued to kill the animals and within less than a decade virtually destroyed the buffalo, pronghorn, elk and deer. The prairie people lost their basic food supply. Destitute and hungry, they turned to the white government for relief. The once proud native of the plains was reduced to a servile refugee, totally dependent upon the good will of the Canadian government.

Although the government was reluctant to spend much money to aid the natives, it had to act. Recognizing the value of the soil

David E. (Dave) Akers, from a sketch by lawyer C. C. McCaul.

George Houk and his wife, who was a Blood Indian woman.

Old Days at Fort Whoop-Up

This month's Canadian Life and Resources magazine has a cut of old Fort Whoop-Up, and the following article:

An interesting picture of old Fort Whoop-Up, near Lethbridge, Alberta, is here reproduced. This was the most important of all the whiskey trading posts in the Canadian West. The sale of liquor to the Indians was as lucrative as it was dangerous, in the lawless days of the 1860s. American traders came up over the border from Fort Benton with supplies, which they doled out to the Blackfeet, Crees and Assiniboines for their valuable buffalo skins. Fights were common and many an illicit trader left his bones to bleach alongside the buffalo's on the prairie. Forts Kipp and Whoop-Up were permanent camps erected by the most daring of these traders. Whoop-Up — so-called because one trader described himself as "whooping-it-up" at this particular spot, so rich was the harvest of trade — was a regular stockaded fort with a gun mounted at each corner. (One of these weapons can now be seen in the garden of Mr. Higinbotham at Lethbridge.) In the lawless days described by Captain Palliser and others, these camps were the centre of the worst kind of villainy and crime. It was to suppress them that the North-West Mounted Police were formed. When in the autumn of 1874, after their arduous march across the unknown prairie, the first body of this famous force reached the neighborhood of the fort, they lost their way and were only guided to their objective point by the famous half-breed, Jerry Potts, one of the most interesting characters of the early days in southern Alberta. When they found that the long-expected force had really come, the traders showed no resistance. All the illicit spirit had been got rid of and from the arrival of the NWMP lawlessness disappears from the annals of the Canadian West. The old fort building stood practically intact well into the 1880s and was at one time occupied by an amusing character, Dan Healy. [Likely this was Dave Akers, who remained in the fort for years after the whiskey trade was suppressed.] There was a great fireplace in the corner of the chief living-room and an acquaintance of the writer, who often went to Whoop-Up when Dan was there, had many a chat with him as the cup that cheers and also inebriates passed across the hearth. His squaw and half-breed child were the only occupants. On one occasion when he called, Dan would not smoke as usual. Enquiring the reason, Dan said he had given it up because it was making the child's face black! When it ceased to be inhabited, the building fell into decay, and the last of it was washed away by the swollen river some six or seven years ago in June [1902], after extraordinary rains which lasted seventeen days.

--The Lethbridge Daily Herald, October 19, 1909

for farm lands, Dominion administrators wanted the nomads settled on reservations. There the prairie people would be taught to farm and to become self-supporting. With the aid of the police and the missionaries, the government negotiated a number of treaties of which the seventh, signed in 1877 and amended in 1883, covered the southwestern natives. It was to be administered by Edgar Dewdney, the Indian commissioner, and his assistant, Elliott Galt, the son of a well-known Montreal financier and politician. Disease, alcohol and starvation had done the essential work and Dewdney's task was relatively easy. The prairie people had lost control over their own destiny. Bureaucrats from Canada imposed on them an administrative superstructure, designed to facilitate the rapid exploitation of the region's natural resources.

By 1880, government officials claimed that the Canadian North-West was peaceful and ready for agricultural settlement. Their claim implied that the prairies had a new economic function, a value which ranchers or farmers had to wrest from the soil through extensive pasturage or intensive cultivation. Raising livestock or tilling the soil, however, required structure, order and government. It demanded railways, roads and fences. The open, rolling plains had to be surveyed and subdivided into small parcels, each owned by an individual. The days of the nomads were over; the way was clear for the most rapid and dramatic transformation of the environment yet.

Sheran's Mine, the timbered entry to which was put in place in June 1881 after quarrying the outcrop with no protection since 1874. The miner is Nicholas Sheran.

Chapter Three

Coal Mines and Railways

The first settlers saw great value in the coal that, for millennia, had been ignored by the prairie people. By 1870, the industrial revolution had swept across settled North America and coal had become the predominant fuel. Visitors to the Canadian prairies noted the coal outcroppings on the river banks and recognized their utility as fuel for the projected transcontinental railway and the thousands of settlers expected to flood the plains.

As long as the transcontinental railway was only in the planning stages, coal mining in the North-West remained small scale. In October 1874, Nicholas Sheran, an Irish-American adventurer, opened the first commercial coal mine in the region at the Coal Banks (now Lethbridge). There he lived with *Awatoyakew*, a Peigan woman, who bore his two sons: Charles Sheran in 1880 and William Sheran in 1882. Sheran, an ex-sailor who had once spent three years with the Inuit after suffering shipwreck, had fought in the Civil War and pioneered in Montana. Involved in the whiskey trade, he turned respectable upon the arrival of the North-West Mounted Police (NWMP) in western Canada. Besides operating a ferry, Sheran mined coal from the river bank and sporadically prospected for gold in the mountains. He sold most of the coal to the NWMP at Fort Macleod and some of it to merchants operating from Fort Benton. The high cost of transportation, however, kept sales small.

One visitor who used Sheran's ferry was Elliott T. Galt, the assistant Indian commissioner. Galt, a tall, quiet man, then about 30 years old, visited Coal Banks in 1879 on one of several inspection trips. He noted the five-foot (1.6-m) thick seam of coal outcropping on the river bank and had a few samples analyzed. But, without an economical means of transportation to a sizeable market, the coal was worthless and Galt did nothing to exploit it.

In the spring of 1881, however, the Canadian Pacific Railway (CPR) decided to cross the southern plains rather than to follow the North Saskatchewan River. The decision solved Galt's transportation problem and the coal deposits he had noted on the southwestern fringe of the plains took on great value.

With transportation and a market assured, organizing a mining company was an easy task. Elliott's father, Sir Alexander T. Galt, the prominent Montreal promoter and then High Commissioner in London, marshalled the investors. Late in the summer of 1881, Sir Alexander hired Captain Nicholas Bryant, a Nova Scotia mining engineer, to prospect for coal in the southwestern plains. In a quick, preliminary survey, Bryant uncovered several large deposits of useable coal. His findings substantiated those by George M. Dawson of the Geological Survey of Canada, who had explored the region earlier that summer. Consequently, late in the fall of 1881, Sir Alexander had sufficient evidence to support an approach to British financiers. No doubt he bolstered his plea with stories of the fabulous real estate boom then raging in Winnipeg, a frenzy sparked by the start of railway construction. In any case, by April 1882, he had gathered a group of prominent investors incorporated as the North Western Coal and Navigation Company, Limited (NWC&NCo).

The initial group of backers was small but powerful. It included the wealthy William H. Smith, owner of the well-known news agency and bookselling firm, W. H. Smith & Son. Another member was William Ashmead Bartlett Burdett-Coutts, a wealthy American residing in England and recently married to the elderly Baroness Angela Burdett-Coutts, the richest heiress in England, admired for her devotion to charities. The most enthusiastic founder of the NWC&NCo was William Lethbridge, a close friend and associate of William Smith. These three men, and Galt, formed an influential core quickly joined by prominent investors from Canada and Great Britain.

With incorporation completed and financing arranged, Galt next sought government permission to mine coal. This was relatively easy to obtain because the Dominion government, which controlled the natural resources of the North-West Territories, was anxious to encourage the rapid development of the western coal reserves. Believing these resources to be inexhaustible, the administration felt that regulations could only hinder development. In December 1881, it provided for 24-year leases and minimal royalties, but a year later eased the rules and allowed free-hold purchases of limited acreages.

First Births:
Charles and William Sheran

Nicholas Sheran began to mine coal here in 1874, his first customers the North-West Mounted Police in their new post at Fort Macleod. His sister, Marcella Sheran, kept house for him in 1877-78 but left in July 1878 to get married.

On a trip to Fort Macleod in fall 1878, Sheran met a Peigan Indian woman, 20-year-old Mary Brown. Her Indian name was *A-wa-toy-akew*, or White-Tailed Deer Woman. By October, Sheran and Mary Brown were living together in a cabin at the Coal Banks, as Lethbridge was then called. A baby boy called Charles was born to the couple on February 24, 1880, the first child to be born in what is now the City of Lethbridge. In November 1882, another son was born and was named William. Unfortunately, Nicholas Sheran drowned in May 1882 and never saw the second boy.

Marcella Sheran, by now married to Joseph McFarland of Fort Macleod, was appointed administrator of the Sheran Estate. Also, Mary Brown turned over to her custody of the two children, reasoning that this might give them a better chance in life. Marcella McFarland arranged first for the two youngsters to be baptized in the Roman Catholic Church and, on 18 May 1884, brought Father Leonard Van Tighem from Fort Macleod to Lethbridge to perform the ceremony. These were the first recorded baptisms on the Lethbridge townsite. Afterwards, the two boys were enrolled in the Mission School at St. Albert, where they were taught by the Sisters of Charity, better known as the Gray Nuns of Alberta. The boys attended school until at least 1898 and must have been very well educated for the time. In 1900, both were living in Fort Macleod and both applied for, and received, halfbreed scrip, which entitled each of them to a 160-acre homestead of their choice. Neither seems to have homesteaded in Alberta and likely the scrip was sold to white speculators. We know nothing about the lives of these two young men, the first persons to be born in Lethbridge, after October 1900.

The NWC&NCo initially applied for five leases at various locations in southern Alberta and ordered Captain Bryant to choose the best of these. On 2 May 1882, Bryant and William Stafford, of the Acadia Coal Company in Nova Scotia, and several others went on a five-week western journey by train, Missouri River steamer, and horse to the far reaches of the prairies. Throughout the summer, the Nova Scotians explored the Bow, Belly and South Saskatchewan rivers as far east as Medicine Hat. They quickly eliminated three locations because of poor coal quality and narrowed their choice to two sites, one at Coal Banks on the Belly and the other at Blackfoot Crossing on the Bow River. Later that summer, Sir Alexander and Elliott Galt visited both places and after lengthy discussions chose Coal Banks. Although Blackfoot Crossing was located on the CPR main line, its coal was inferior to that of Coal Banks and its surrounding lands were unsuitable for the large colonization scheme the Galts, even then, associated with the mining venture. It was a momentous decision: it determined the location of the City of Lethbridge.

The Coal Banks site had a serious drawback. It was situated 109 miles (175 km) from the proposed CPR main line, a disadvantage which dictated a substantial investment in some efficient means of transportation. From October 1882, when the Nova Scotians opened a drift mine at Coal Banks, they produced only 22,000 tons (20 000 tonnes) of coal because the only accessible consumers were at Fort Macleod. To reach a substantially larger market, the Galts chose a relatively inexpensive transportation technique. In the summer of 1883 they built a 173-foot (53-m) sternwheel river steamer, the *Baroness,* and a small fleet of barges. Owing to the lateness of the season, the boat made only one trip that summer and delivered a paltry 200 tons (180 tonnes) of coal to Medicine Hat. During the winter, Sir Alexander tried but failed to gather financial and government support for a private railway to the CPR line. Because they wanted to demonstrate the value of their coal, the Galts constructed one more steamer, the 120-foot (37-m) *Alberta,* and shipped the much smaller tugboat *Minnow* in from Winnipeg. Low water foiled their plans again and the entire fleet delivered only a negligible quantity of coal during the summer of 1884.

With the inefficiency of the steamers clearly proven, Sir Alexander redoubled his efforts to win a government subsidy for a narrow gauge railway to Dunmore on the CPR main line near Medicine Hat. He found federal administrators anxious to secure

Sheran
Cabin

Indian
Battle
Coulee

Drift Mine
Entrance
(1881)

Five foot thick
coal seam

Ferry (now Sixth
Avenue Bridge)

This 1883 photograph by surveyor George M. Dawson shows the ferry started by Nicholas Sheran in 1874, the cabin built by him, and the mine entry opened by him in 1881.

a stable fuel supply for prairie settlers and western railways; they granted the NWC&NCo a precedent-setting subsidy of 3,840 acres per mile of railway (965 ha/km) free except for a ten cents per acre (25 cents per ha) survey charge. The government also sold the company 10,000 acres (4050 ha) of coal lands for $10 per acre ($25 per ha). Armed with this generous government subsidy, Galt concluded the difficult negotiations with his London backers. The gloomy economic climate of the mid-1880s had created a general mood of timidity among investors, particularly in railway shares, but Galt's comprehensive package of railway, coal and land development eventually won over his friends. Construction on the narrow gauge, begun in the fall of 1884, was completed the following summer. On 25 August 1885, the first train rolled into Coalbanks, officially named Lethbridge on 15 October of that year.

With the means of transportation assured, the NWC&NCo could commence full production, and it began to recruit miners from across the continent. Suddenly the mining camp throbbed with new life; town lots sold briskly and buildings shot up everywhere. By the end of October 1885, Lethbridge boasted over 60 buildings including six stores, five saloons, four billiard rooms, two barbershops, one hotel and a livery stable. Despite the hasty construction, overall development was orderly because the company, as the original landowner, had surveyed the site and laid out wide and straight streets in accordance with prairie custom. The scarcity of building materials severely limited the erection of private dwellings and for some time many of the miners lived in tents. Lethbridge had, according to the *Macleod Gazette,* appeared instantly "like a newborn infant city dropped from the clouds."

Created so quickly, Lethbridge was initially a rough town, plagued by numerous saloons, gambling dens and flagrant prostitution. John D. Higinbotham, a 21-year-old druggist from Ontario who arrived in Lethbridge in October 1885, found the mining town crude and teeming with noisy bars. Pay nights especially were filled with boisterous drinking and brawling. Yet, violent crimes such as murder and armed robbery were rare. The NWMP watched the town carefully and in 1886 established its K division (called "Cowboy K" because of the nature of its patrols) just to the south of the settlement. Through good humour and tact, particularly of commanding officers like Captain R. Burton Deane, the police were able to moderate the exuberance of an immature society. They also fulfilled a social function. Beginning in 1887,

the NWMP sponsored annual balls at the barracks and its band regularly performed at community affairs. Captain Deane, a former British military officer, clearly placed his stamp on the town. He was active in the Anglican church, visibly involved in local politics, and founder of a number of clubs, including a troupe of amateur actors.

Under the protective umbrella of the mounted police, the new town quickly achieved the basic stability needed to foster the growth of social institutions. These establishments were organized mainly by a small group of young and ambitious businessmen, professionals, and executives who saw in Lethbridge an opportunity for social and economic advancement. One such individual was Harry Bentley, an employee of an Ontario retail firm, sent West to start a store at Medicine Hat. Personal fortune beckoned, however, and Bentley borrowed enough money to set up his own store in Lethbridge. Within a year he was one of the wealthiest men in town, owner of a retail store, wholesale outlet, stage coach operation, and a partnership in a hotel. His interest was not limited to commercial dealings, however, as Bentley was a founding member of most of the town's social organizations, including the town council.

Some company officials, too, played a prominent role during Lethbridge's formative years. The most notable was Charles A. Magrath, the NWC&NCo's land commissioner. Like Bentley, Magrath was Ontario-born, young and aggressive. He established a close friendship with Elliott Galt, the company's resident manager. He also became a leader of the town's social elite, actively involved in virtually all its clubs and associations, elected as the town's first mayor in 1891 and later the same year as member of the North-West Territorial Council. Men like Magrath, Bentley, Higinbotham, Frank H. Mewburn, the town's physician, and Charles F. P. Conybeare, a lawyer, were members of a close and lasting circle of friends which provided a measure of social cohesiveness in a young and volatile community.

The voice of this small group was the *Lethbridge News,* a gossipy, lively weekly founded by E. T. (Si) Saunders in 1885, only months after the completion of the railway. Its editor, a former mounted policeman, was a westerner in the sense that he embraced the spirit of the frontier — the desire to create in western Canada the idealized features of the Ontario most of his readers had left behind.

Elliott Torrance Galt 1850-1928.

Sir Alexander Tilloch Galt 1817-1893.

41

Town of Lethbridge on 20 November 1886, taken from about 10th Street and 4th Avenue South.

This utopian vision, however, was based on the general belief, increasingly common in the western world, that economic progress was not only highly desirable but absolutely essential to a community's survival. Accordingly, the *News* faithfully recorded every step in the town's growth, constantly pleaded for more capital investments, and enthusiastically promoted any scheme which promised further expansion. Since economic progress was the weekly's prime concern, it focused all its attention on the people most actively engaged in the advancement of community institutions, the leading businessmen, company officials,

42

churchmen and professionals. The paper wanted to project for the benefit of prospective investors and citizens an image of Lethbridge as a progressive town with unlimited potential for future expansion. Consequently, its editor ignored the less tangible contributions of the miners, the railwaymen, and their wives and children; he glossed over labor difficulties or social problems; and he avoided discussing the dearth of recreational facilities for the workers, the physical hardships of mining, and the tedium of living in a small, isolated, one-company town. Instead, Saunders emphasized the positive features of life in Lethbridge, its picnics, sports days, quadrille clubs, and debating societies — in sum, the bright and pleasant aspects of sophisticated urban life.

Two institutions central to the cultivation of Lethbridge society were the church and school. Before the founding of Lethbridge, itinerant priests and pastors occasionally conducted worship services in the Sheran cabin or in William Stafford's large home. Subsequently, they moved to the townsite and used one of the larger saloons. The various denominations readily accepted free building lots from the NWC&NCo and by the summer of 1886 both the Presbyterians and Methodists had their own churches. The Anglicans and Roman Catholics built their churches the following year.

Like the churches, the school quickly abandoned informality. In the summer of 1885, the Howard F. Greenwood family hired a governess from Prince Edward Island, Miss Louise Nelson, who married Dr. F. H. Mewburn in 1887. Later in the year, Miss Edith Coe opened a private school. By April 1886, a properly constituted board had rented a one-room school house and hired its first teacher, Bruce L. Latimer. A year later, when the school population reached nearly 50 pupils, the board built a two-room school house and hired a second teacher, Miss Margaret Duff. Thus, well within two years, Lethbridgians had built a school house and four churches. The small structures, unadorned by beautifying shrubs or trees, stood starkly alone on their large, open lots, a forlorn isolation that aptly symbolized the role of the church and school in a young and male-dominated mining community.

Two individuals dominated the religious life of Lethbridge. Charles McKillop, the Presbyterian minister, was a tall, burly Scot, who had grown up in various Ottawa lumber camps. Always donned in proper eastern garb, replete with black top hat, he dominated the gritty streets of Lethbridge. He was an agile fighter who more than once thrashed an unsuspecting mocker. His physical strength and clear, loud voice commanded respect and his powerful sermons, while not learned, directly confronted the evils of alcohol, gambling and prostitution. Father Leonard Van Tighem, the Catholic priest, was a gentler man. A Belgian cabinet maker, he had only recently been ordained to the priesthood. An occasional visitor to Coal Banks in the early 1880s, he settled there permanently in 1888. Van Tighem did not attack vice as vigorously and as openly as McKillop nor did he appeal to the town's leaders but, instead, worked quietly among the European coal miners, most of whom were Roman Catholics. He founded a Catholic school in 1889 and a year later brought a small convent — the Faithful Companions of Jesus — to Lethbridge to staff the new school. Thus the clergy, each is his own way, tried to civilize an isolated, rough society with familiar and tried institutions.

The community, which Lethbridgians were building, was very much affected by the fortunes of the NWC&NCo, the mainstay of the town's economy. But the company's fortunes were not as bright as Lethbridge's boosters wished. The NWC&NCo depended almost entirely upon sales to the CPR, a company built on the premise of a rapidly expanding prairie population. But the flood of settlers did not materialize and the NWC&NCo's coal production was too small to repay the large investment in its highly mechanized operations. Owing to the nature of its product, the NWC&NCo could not significantly increase consumer demand through advertising. The only solution was expansion. The colliery could survive only if it broke out of the confines of the small western Canadian market.

To meet this objective, Galt persuaded several powerful Montana investors to help him build a railway from Lethbridge to the smelting industries of western Montana. The project was delayed several years because the CPR had a monopoly on all railway construction within 30 miles (48 km) of the international boundary. By the spring of 1889, however, Parliament had repealed the CPR's monopoly and approved a charter for a narrow gauge railway from Lethbridge to the international boundary to meet an American line coming from Great Falls. It also granted Galt's company a 6,400-acre per mile (1610-ha/km) subsidy. With his hand strengthened by the government's concessions, Galt transferred all the assets and liabilities of the NWC&NCo to a newly capitalized, London-based company, the Alberta Railway and Coal Company

Sir Alexander Tilloch Galt

Alexander Tilloch Galt was born in London in 1817, the son of John Galt, developer of the Huron Tract in Ontario. He grew up in an atmosphere calculated to give him a forward outlook and a broad vision of Canadian possibilities, both economic and political. His political career took him to high office in Sir John A. Macdonald's administrations where he became one of the Fathers of Confederation. His business career led him in 1882 to southern Alberta and to the complex of companies he and his son, Elliott, set up to exploit coal discoveries, to build railways, to irrigate semi-arid acres, and to build towns and cities. He died in Montreal on September 19, 1893, "as all good men might wish to die; at an honourable age . . . and mourned by an entire Dominion."

(AR&CCo), which built the Montana railway during the summer of 1890.

Although the company had widened its operations, the prosperity of Lethbridge remained entirely dependent upon the fortunes of the AR&CCo. Local businessmen were very conscious of their town's economic vulnerability.

The *Lethbridge News* often urged its readers to diversify the local economy in order to escape the domination of the coal company and its unstable market. This warning, however, never dampened its cocky, optimistic confidence that the great wealth of coal was the guarantee of nearly unlimited prosperity and progress. Lethbridge, according to the *News*, would grow unremittingly because it lay near an abundant resource being vigorously exploited by foreign capitalists. Tottering dangerously on the fine line which separates gross exaggeration from outright lie, the weekly boasted, "Built upon a coal mine of practically limitless extent, whose output is and always must be in great demand as being the best steam coal in the North-West, we have a sure foundation that ensures a steady growth and prosperity for our town." Although several seasons had proved otherwise, the *News* crowed that neither season nor climate affected production, and it unrealistically asserted that the CPR would always continue to buy Galt coal. "So long as the boundless prairies of the North-West are traversed by railways," the editor gloated, "there shall always be a sure market for Lethbridge coal and our town will

Elliott Torrance Galt

"The Father of Lethbridge" — that was the tribute paid by John D. Higinbotham, pioneer druggist and postmaster, to Elliott Torrance Galt upon the latter's death in 1928 in New York City at age 78.

Higinbotham went on to say, "It was due to his foresight, when travelling through this district as assistant Indian Commissioner in 1879, that the outcroppings of coal on the Belly River suggested to him the possibility of their development in order to supply the needs of the pioneer settlers, the Mounted Police, and the Canadian Pacific Railway. He reported to his father, Sir Alexander T. Galt, then Canadian Commissioner in London, and the latter organized the North Western Coal and Navigation Company, Limited, which opened up the coal measures and built a fleet of stern-wheel steamboats to convey the product to Medicine Hat. Those boats were later replaced by the railway from Dunmore to Lethbridge."

It fell to Elliott Galt, particularly after the death of his father in 1893, to manage the various companies set up by the Galts to exploit the coal discoveries, to build railways, and to construct irrigation systems. The companies were amalgamated in 1904 as the Alberta Railway and Irrigation Company. All of this took great financial and business skills and perseverance because, if the truth be told, most were poor investments. Investors received little in the way of dividends until Elliott Galt, in his last major business deal, in 1912 sold the AR&I Company to the Canadian Pacific Railway at a good price. All shareholders got their investments back.

Elliott Galt made his home in Lethbridge from 1883 until forced by ill-health to give up active management of the Galt companies in 1905.

His last official act in Lethbridge was to donate Galt Gardens to the city, to be used in perpetuity as a park.

steadily prosper." As far as he was concerned, Lethbridge was bound to become an important industrial, agricultural, and commercial centre and certainly the first or second largest city in the North-West. People would be attracted by its excellent facilities, its schools and churches, its reputation for law and order.

Drift Mines Nos. 1 (right) and 2 (left) in 1888.

For the first four years after its inception Lethbridge drifted along without any formal means of local government. The announcement in 1889 of the plans for the Lethbridge-Montana railway finally stirred the business community into action. They wanted an efficient organization to plan and stimulate Lethbridge's growth. On 16 September 1889, a group of men met in one of the smoky backrooms of the Lethbridge Hotel and formed the Lethbridge Board of Trade. Although the Board did lobby the federal government for such public works as a court house and land office, its primary aim was to seek the incorporation of Lethbridge

The Galt Mines

Having heard and read much concerning the opening up of the coal field in this district, we resolved to avail ourselves of the first favourable opportunity to witness the development of the mineral industry here. Arriving at Dunmore about midnight, we are informed that the cars for Lethbridge may leave about 6, maybe 8, and perhaps not until 10. Having purchased a document certifying that we and none other though in possession of said passport, were entitled to travel to Lethbridge, we find ourselves considerably after 10 o'clock, prepared to resume our journey. We are gratified to find the caboose fully occupied, thus bearing testimony to the popularity already enjoyed by the city to which we are hastening. Our fellow passengers are very friendly and we are priveleged to form pleasant acquaintanceships, thus tending to relieve the monotony of the journey. The railway, which is the property of the North Western Coal and Navigation Co., is a single one with three stations, where trains may pass. At one of these stations there is a telegraph office, and we understand it is contemplated to have offices at the other stations also. Lethbridge is reached about eight o'clock. Upon inquiry at the hotel, which is under the management of Messrs. Henderson and Hogg, we are informed that there is no room for us at the inn. Relying upon the hospitality of an acquaintance of former days, we proceed to his abode and find, greatly to our relief, that our confidence has not been misplaced. At personal inconvenience, our friend provides sleeping accommodation, where, though our sleep is light, our dreams are pleasant. Having been rested and refreshed we resume the pursuit of knowledge. In quest of this object we have to acknowledge the civility of all with whom we came in contact while we were placed under lasting obligation to Mr. Galt, the general manager, and Mr. Stafford, the mines superintendent, for their courtesy and attention on this occasion. The residence of Mr. Galt is pleasantly situated on an eminence in the valley where it is surrounded by brushwood in which are numerous tee-pees all tending to heighten the picturesque beauty of the scene. When passing the abodes of the noble red man the sounds proceeding from them impress us with the idea that the inmates are engaged in worship, and as we have no desire either to disturb the worshippers or join in their devotions, we visit them not. The saw mill at the edge of the river is fully employed. Proceeding down the banks of the river we reach the engine house [pump house], where is located the machinery for forcing the water from the river to the round house on the top of the hill. The keeper, an intelligent youth, proudly narrates the capability of his engine for the performance of its work. There is a boarding house in the valley. Several of the workmen have erected abodes for themselves on the brae face, while some with aspiring ambition have gone nearly to the top of the ridges. We climb to one of them and find its occupants busily preparing their mid-day meal. If we, in declining to accept their hospitality, have unwittingly broken any of the rules of Lethbridge etiquette, we trust the good-natured workers will overlook the mistake. The mines, which are three in number, for purposes of ventilation, have communication with an upcast shaft. Under the care of our cicerone, we examine the workings of one of the mines and are well pleased to observe the systematic manner in which the operations of stoop and room are being conducted for the purpose of getting the coal out. The coal, which runs in an almost horizontal position, is about four and a half feet thick and lies in two sections, the pavement section is about two and two-third feet thick and is separated from the upper section by a rib of foreign subtance varying in thickness from simply the position to four inches. It is pleasant to notice the intelligent interest taken by the miners in their work. In one of the working faces where the process of removing the stoop was taking place, grateful reference was made to a crown tree which had prevented the roof making a burst too near the face. When the workmen get their mine cars filled the same are taken by mule power to the opening of the mine, from whence they are taken by a pony to the foot of the incline. There is a photographer here today taking views of the surroundings, and if he favors us with a copy of them we shall be pleased to give them places in our sanctum, thus affording our visitors an opportunity of viewing the scenery of this place, through the work of the artist. Ascending the incline, which is about 750 yards long, we reach the scaffolding, a very substantial affair, where the coals are screened. On this screen there is a dross weighing machine, the collier being paid for the round coal at the present rate of $1.10 per ton. Great activity in prosecuting the work at hand is very observable. Work shops and other buildings are nearing completion, while whatever is finished reflects creditably on the design and workmanship. The locomotives, three in number, are from the Baldwin Locomotive Works, Philadelphia, and seem thoroughly capable of performing good duty. We had the pleasure of meeting the Rev. Messrs. Robertson and MacKenne who are exerting themselves to get church accommodation for the citizens and it was very gratifying to learn that their labours are being attended with a fair measure of success. We leave Lethbridge shortly before 6 p.m. fully impressed with the idea that at a no distant date it will become an important industrial centre, and thus add considerably to the importance of the North-West Territories.

--The Regina Leader, November 19, 1885

as a town. The charter members elected C. A. Magrath as their first president, a choice which he felt "turned out an excellent move, as it brought about a contact that grew into a harmonious and active co-operation between the citizens of Lethbridge and the Company for the development of the district which was of great moment to both." By June 1890 Magrath and a small committee had worked out the details of incorporation and set the initial taxation rates.

The major disadvantage of incorporation was the matter of taxes, and its advocates had to convince the public that municipal government would bring marvelous improvements to the town and personal prosperity to its citizens. In other words, the ultimate goal was worth the small tax levy. The editor of the *News*, himself a member of the Board of Trade, noted that incorporation was a necessary step in the settlement's evolution because only a town council could introduce stability and organization to the amorphous collection of houses and people. A municipal government could build the sidewalks, sorely needed when rains transformed the dusty streets into impossible quagmires; it could rid the town of the putrid garbage, rotting carcasses and stale ashes strewn about the streets. Only a town council could offer bonuses to attract the manufacturers and industrialists needed for the town's growth. It

could provide a water distribution system which would not only reduce the cost of water but provide fire protection and drastically reduce high insurance premiums. In sum, the taxes, which were to be set low, were justified, the paper argued, because local government would make Lethbridge a more attractive place for businessmen to come to and live in; incorporation was the essential step to ensure expansion to metropolitan status.

Despite the paper's impassioned arguments, the average Lethbridgian responded with a decided lack of enthusiasm. A referendum, held on 19 July 1890, attracted only a small crowd of supporters. Charles Magrath, however, was undeterred by the public's apathy and late in August he secured the territorial government's permission to incorporate Lethbridge. On 29 December another small number of voters approved the plan of incorporation. As the *News* explained, the workmen, "feeling sure there would be no opposition did not take the trouble to go to the poll." Coupled with the fact that incorporation made little

William Stafford Senior

William Stafford was born at Patna, Ayrshire, Scotland, in 1842. His father was an English mining engineer and, after a Scottish education, young Stafford followed his father's calling. In 1863, he married Jane Gibb of Auchinlech, Ayrshire. He emigrated to Westville, Nova Scotia, in 1867, and became manager of coal mines operated by the Acadia Coal Company of Pictou. In 1882, he was hired by Sir Alexander Galt to accompany Captain Nicholas Byrant west and to become the first manager and superintendent of mines of the North Western Coal and Navigation Company. It was William Stafford who made the final decision as to the location of Drift Mine No. 1 and, hence, decided the location of the City of Lethbridge.

Stafford became Inspector of Mines in 1894 and was succeeded as mines superintendent by W. D. L. Hardie. About this time, he became interested in ranching and resigned from the company to follow that pursuit. He maintained his interest in coal mining and, at the time of his death on May 12, 1907, had an interest in a mine at Carmangay.

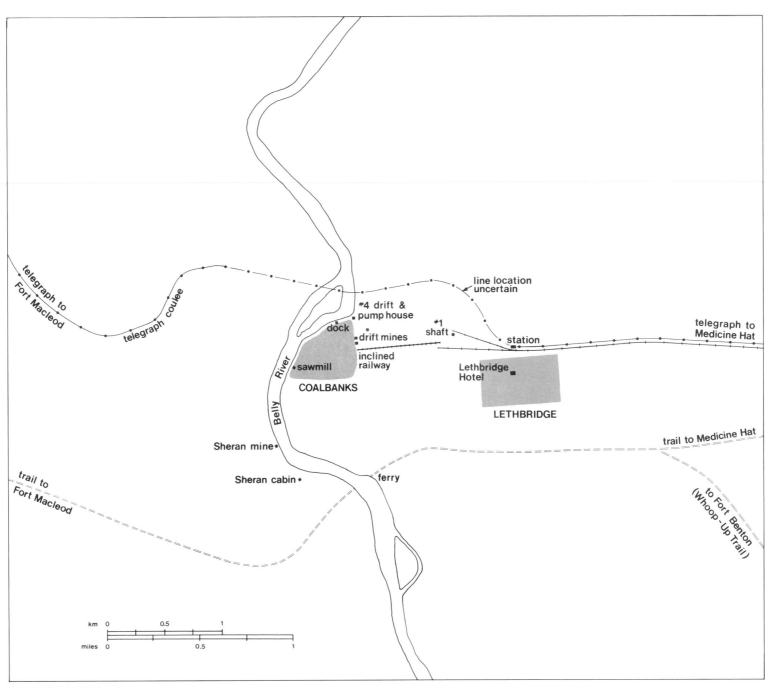

telegraph to Fort Macleod

telegraph coulee

line location uncertain

#4 drift & pump house

dock

drift mines

#1 shaft

station

telegraph to Medicine Hat

Belly River

sawmill

inclined railway

COALBANKS

Lethbridge Hotel

LETHBRIDGE

Sheran mine

Sheran cabin

ferry

trail to Medicine Hat

trail to Fort Macleod

to Fort Benton (Whoop-Up Trail)

km 0   0.5   1

miles 0   0.5   1

Lethbridge in 1885.

Notman Photographic Archives No. 1376

1376—MEDICINE HAT BRIDGE SASKATCHEWAN RIVER

The river steamers, Baroness and Minnow, and coal barges at Medicine Hat in 1884.

difference to the economic welfare of most miners or railwaymen, the newspaper's explanation was reasonable. The indifference of labour contrasted sharply with the activity shown by the town's middle-class and revealed the growing gap between these two groups. The aspirations of both segments of the community differed greatly as the workers did not share the merchant's dream of major metropolitan status for the town.

At the time of incorporation of the Town of Lethbridge, the population was 1,478 and the male: female ratio was about 3:1. It did not approach 1:1, indicative of a stable population, until about 1912.

On 2 February 1891, the newly incorporated town held its first municipal elections and chose Charles Magrath as mayor. Magrath, who was "closely identified with all the movements which wanted to advance and develop the town," firmly believed that the good of southern Alberta, the town, and company were inseparable. In his inaugural address the mayor stressed the friendly relations between town and company. Although Magrath did not mention that, at Elliott Galt's insistence, the Board of Trade had granted the AR&CCo a 20-year tax exemption, he did laud his employer's contribution to Lethbridge's economy. He fearlessly predicted that the abundant supply of energy, combined with a future railway to the minerals of the Crow's Nest Pass, would attract smelting and reduction industries to Lethbridge, while nearby sandstone, clay and water would lure other factories as well. In short, the newly-elected mayor was confident that because a progressive firm was developing the region's great coal reserves, Lethbridge would soon outstrip Winnipeg in size and become a leading industrial city.

But Magrath's industrial vision was based on an illusion because the economic future of Lethbridge was by no means certain. In fact, faced with increased competition in a limited market, the AR&CCo within the year was forced to curtail its operation and reorganize its financial structure. In 1892, as a first step, the Dunmore-Lethbridge rail line was leased to the CPR with an agreement to purchase it in 1897. The AR&CCo broadened its narrow rail gauge to accept the CPR's standard gauge rolling stock and on 25 November 1893 the first CPR train rolled into Lethbridge. Only months later, the coal company nearly lost the railway lease to its mortgage holders but a complete reorganization of its capitalization, brilliantly engineered by Elliott Galt, saved the day. These were desperate measures, made to avoid bankruptcy.

Charles A. Magrath and his first wife, Margaret (Maggie) Mair Magrath. Ca. 1880s.

To survive, the AR&CCo needed a major revival of the Canadian economy.

Through the depression of the early 1890s, then, Lethbridge remained dependent upon the collieries. It displayed all the characteristics of an isolated, single resource town, with a migratory population which grew and shrank with the fluctuating demand for coal. It was a male-dominated town, its lusty manliness accentuated by the miners' craft. One of the most conspicuous manifestations of the town's masculinity was a prominently displayed red light district sporting several gaudily painted brothels perched on one of the promontories, called The Point, jutting out

1—Shaft No. 1, with Coal Trestle in distance, from Bank Head, Alberta Railway & Coal Co., Lethbridge, 1890.

No. 1 shaft, opened in 1885, as it appeared in 1890.

C. A. MAGRATH,
PRESIDENT.

THOS. CURRY,
VICE-PRESIDENT.

W. A. GALLIHER,
SECRETARY.

THE LETHBRIDGE

BOARD OF TRADE AND CIVIC COMMITTEE.

Lethbridge, N.W.T., 16th Nov, 1889

The Board of Trade and Civic Committee was organized in September 1889 primarily to incorporate the town.

on the steep river bank just south of the mine shafts. Gambling was commonplace, conducted in a relatively professional manner in the saloons or hotel backrooms, more informally at prize fights or horse races, and most commonly in the miners' shanties. The police kept a casual eye on these activities and occasionally ran a particularly obnoxious individual out of town. The town council, ignoring its own morals by-law, tacitly approved the mounted police's policy of supervision rather than strict enforcement. The police also overlooked violations of the territorial liquor ordinance because government inspectors were supposed to enforce it. The inspectorate was lax, however, and in Lethbridge virtually non-existent. Consequently, its retail stores openly sold alcohol while its hotels contained noisy saloons with no regard for closing hours. The mounted police were loath to close the bars, obviously a highly unpopular task, especially when it fell outside their jurisdiction. As a result alcohol flowed freely in Lethbridge, notably on weekends when many miners seemed bent on spending their entire pay in one boozy whirl of revelling.

Not everyone approved of this lax law enforcement policy. In 1894, the Methodist and Presbyterian pastors called for a public meeting to discuss the "flagrant violations of the law relating to liquor-selling, gambling and public morals." Since public entertainment was never abundant in Lethbridge, a large crowd turned out and with great amusement heard the ministers angrily instruct the town council to rid the community of these evils, particularly the "soiled doves." The "soiled doves," however, had

sent a lawyer to the meeting and he rather forcefully argued that only the federal government was the rightful guardian of public morality and that therefore complaints had to be sworn before a justice of the peace who could prosecute under dominion statutes. Everyone, except the clergy, accepted this as sound advice. The town council, always eager to save money whenever it could, decided to leave the matter with the police. This was precisely what the police commander wanted. "If they (the parsons) would turn their attention to the juvenile depravity and promiscuous fornication that is going on under their own eyes and in their own congregations," he fumed, "they would be kept so busy that they would have no time to think of the professional ladies, who at all events are orderly, clean, and on the whole not bad looking."

The local newspaper tended to blame the town's rowdy behaviour on the central and southern Europeans living north of the railway tracks. In one editorial the *News* expressed the apathy and fear with which the Anglo-Saxons viewed the immigrants. "Many of them," the *News* warned, "bring hatred of Government, hatred of liberty, and hatred of humanity." The remark, written at the opening of a new school in Lethbridge, laid bare the basic fear that the strange Europeans threatened the establishment of British cultural values of western Canada.

The *News* and its readers, fearing the erosion of cultural institutions, evinced a strong concern for the education of children. They shared the belief of other English-speaking westerners that

52

Father Leonard Van Tighem

Rev. Charles McKillop

The Mushroom Town, 1885

On arriving at Lethbridge, the mushroom town, I was surprised to see a place of such a size, as the town is only about four months old. The buildings, as a whole, are more substantial than is usually found in a new town. There are now three good general stores, and I. G. Baker & Co. will soon have the fourth opened. The stocks carried by the merchants are first-class, being well assorted. Business is very brisk.

Beside the general stores mentioned there are several other places of business, and the Galt Coal Company are building, as speedily as possible, a large number of houses for their employees and renting at a very reasonable rental. Buildings are also being erected by private people in all directions, and I think there is every prospect of Lethbridge being the best town between Brandon and Calgary. Hotel accommodation is very deficient at the present time, but there are plenty of saloons. In fact, I was informed by a party that he seen more persons under the influence of liquor in one night than he has ever seen in Winnipeg, this being in a town where liquor is strictly prohibited. There is a small detachment of North-West Mounted Police stationed here. Sometimes in travelling through the western country I try to think what is really their duty.

Three of the boys hired an outfit and started immediately for Fort Macleod and Pincher Creek, a distance of sixty miles; but a traveller in the grocery line and the writer did not go any farther than Lethbridge, so we started to see the mysteries of the coal mine. On arriving at the brow of the hill overlooking the Belly River a very pretty scene meets the eye. The flats lie about two hundred and fifty feet below the plain, and the rugged banks across the river with the coal protruding out along the sides of the cliffs, and the Belly River winding so pretty through the valley.

After going down over the incline we reached the flats below, and we immediately started into one of the drifts, of which there are three, and, being our first visit to a coal mine, we enjoyed very much the novelty of being underground. The entrance to the mine is on a level with the flats. The seam of good coal is from 5 to 6½ feet in thickness. The drift is about 8 feet wide. Here and there as we passed in, I noticed drifts branched off on both sides. They are not so wide. At present the miners are at work as far in as 900 feet. Along this leading drift there is a tramway laid, on which the loaded trucks are drawn out to the entrance by horses. Each horse generally draws five trucks at a load, that being five tons. One driver informed me that he has drawn ten tons out at one time which shows that the tramways are in very good order.

Two miners work together, in which is called a room and on having a truck filled they run the truck the short distance to the leading drift and drivers come along and pick up one truck after another until they have the load. Then they start out for the entrance. Two miners average five and six tons of coal a day. They are paid $1.00 a ton for the mining of the coal and filling the trucks.

The top of the mine is well braced with heavy timber. The miner that was showing us through the mine took us to where the mine was caving in and I was very glad when he was finished with that part as a very strange feeling came over me about that time. Every one connected with the working of the mine carried a safety lamp hooked onto his cap, and in passing along the dark drift a person can see the glimmer of the lamp in all directions.

After the coal is drawn out it is taken to the foot of the incline preparatory to being drawn up. When the man in charge of that part has a load ready and the wire cable coupled on he gives the signal to the engineer by means of an electric bell. Then the five trucks which comprises a load begins the ascent of the incline the length of which is 2,100 feet. I rode up on one of the trucks and enjoyed very much the novelty of riding at such a speed up the hill. About half way, five empty trucks passed going down, so that when the five full ones arrive at the top the empty ones have reached the bottom. The full trucks are pulled up onto a high trestle, and there are men ready to run them forward to the dump and by means of a spring the truck is dumped onto a screen. Thus the dust is separated from the good coal, then the coal passes into a hopper and is weighed. From that the coal is dumped into the car ready for shipment to Dunmore. Each car holds ten tons, and each train consists of fifteen cars, thus each train pulls out with 150 tons.

Bull teams and the Macleod stage on The Square, now Galt Gardens, 1890.

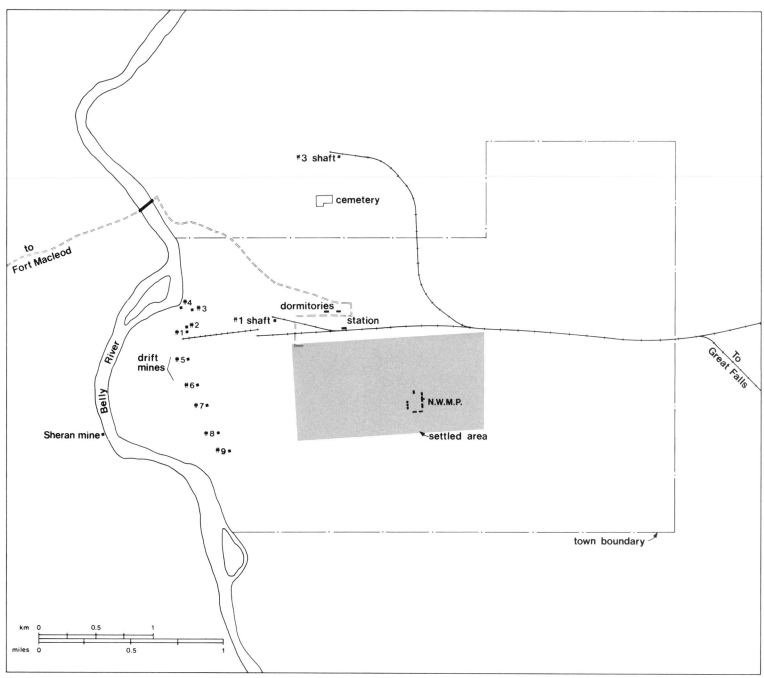

Lethbridge in 1891.

#3 shaft

cemetery

to
Fort Macleod

#4 #3

dormitories

#1 #2

#1 shaft

station

drift
mines

#5

Belly River

#6

#7

N.W.M.P.

Sheran mine

#8

settled area

#9

To
Great Falls

town boundary

km 0   0.5   1

miles 0   0.5   1

The output of the mine at present is about 300 tons a day, and the coal must be giving the public satisfaction as the coal company at present are not able to supply the demand. But in a short time that will be remedied as their other locomotive has arrived and a large number of coal cars. Before that they only had three locomotives and the trainmen were on duty as long as it was possible for them to be so.

The coal company have built a very good roundhouse. Close by is the engine house, in which there is a splendid boiler, and two engines are on each side of an immense drum; and, receiving the signal, the engineer quickly puts the engines in motion, and thus the wire cable is rapidly wound round the drum, and in a very short time the loaded trucks are up on the trestle (that I mentioned before). So that is the means employed to draw the loaded trucks up the incline.

The head offices at present in use are only temporary, as it is the intention of the company to put up a fine building shortly, to be used for the purposes. I was informed that the passenger and freight traffic was paying the running expenses at present. The fare is six dollars and a half from Dunmore to Littlebridge [sic]. The company at the present time have nearly 300 men employed, and the employees being paid regularly puts a good many dollars in circulation — and that is what makes the merchants happy. I may safely say that there is more money in circulation here than at any other point between Brandon and Calgary. The miners appear to be very happy. I noticed some of them on emerging from the mine after finishing their day work went home with a light heart. It appears to a novice on going through a coal mine and seeing the miners at work that it can not be very pleasant work to be engaged at, as they generally take their dinner with them, thus all day they are at their work in their small room, having to pick and shovel in all positions and for so many hours, never seeing daylight. Most of the miners are from Nova Scotia, men who have been brought up to mining all their life.

I left Lethbridge about six in the evening, had supper at Grass Lake at nine, arrived at Dunmore at 1:30 a.m., and boarded the CPR express going east at 5:30 a.m.

--*The Manitoba Daily Free Press, November 24, 1885.*

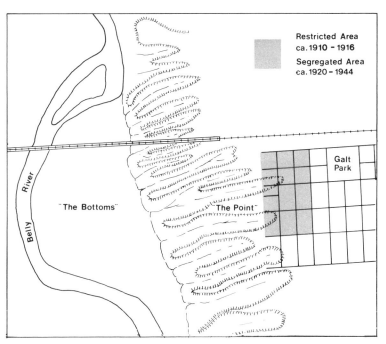

The Point, centre of prostitution in Lethbridge from 1890-1920; the Restricted Area, to which Chinese laundries were confined, 1910-1916; and the Segregated Area, which was the centre of prostitution from 1920-1944. Broken-down and aged prostitutes until ca. 1910 tended to gravitate to The Bottoms.

the public schools could eradicate the undesirable characteristics of hundreds of Europeans coming to the North-West annually, and could teach their children the basic moral and civic standards of Canada. The school, then, became the essential social institution in the North-West, the tool to set the future temperament of Canada. In its usual purple prose, the *News* concluded that "the public schools are the incandescent light that will illuminate the houses of the land."

Since Lethbridgians considered the school to be of prime importance, they were willing to spend money on it. Early in 1891 the town's school board closed its five-year-old wooden structure and opened the first Central School, a two-storey brick edifice with six classrooms. The Gothic structure, centred on four town lots, was typically ornate with its stone facings and window sills, its imposing double-door entrance, and its tower complete with belfry. In addition to this major project the board also built a small

The Post Office

Throughout 1883, mail delivery to the hamlet of Coalbanks was haphazard and mail was sorted in and picked up from the coal company's office. On May 8, 1884, Elliott Galt submitted a petition signed by 181 "employees of the North Western Coal and Navigation Company, Limited, doing business at Lethbridge, in the District of Alberta, North-West Territories," the petition "praying for the establishment of postal facilities at the Lethbridge Colliery." All that came out of this action was an order from the Postmaster General instructing Postal Inspector W. W. McLeod of Winnipeg "to establish a mail service from Medicine Hat to Fort Macleod via Lethbridge."

By June 1, 1884, a tri-weekly stage and mail service was in operation.

The narrow gauge railway line to Dunmore was built in 1885. McLeod determined that the line would be completed in August and proposed that mail for Fort Macleod, Pincher Creek and New Oxley [Claresholm] be sent by it to Lethbridge, then west by stagecoach. A mail contract was advertised calling for "the conveyance of Her Majesty's Mails three times per week between the Fort Macleod Post Office and the Lethbridge Railway Station or Coalhurst Post Office on and from the 1st October next." On October 14, 1885, Postal Inspector McLeod wrote to the Postmaster General: "Referring to your letter No. 286 of the 8th May last authorizing the establishment of a Post Office under name Coalhurst at Lethbridge, Alberta, with Mr. H. F. Greenwood as Postmaster, I beg to report that the said office went into operation on the 1st inst, and that it is supplied with mails three times per week by The North West Coal & Navigation Company's Narrow Gauge Railway from Dunmore Junction, 109 miles, at four cents per train mile, the mails being conveyed in charge of baggagemen . . . As instructed by you, the name of this office will be changed to Lethbridge from the 15 inst."

schoolhouse, the North Ward School, forerunner of the 1906 Westminster School, where most of the immigrants lived, so that no children needed to be deprived of an education because of the long walk and danger of crossing a busy railway yard. Obviously, the community believed that the cost of instilling the many newcomers with Canadian values was a worthy investment.

The townsmen were less willing to spend money on other amenities. Caught in the prevailing economic depression, the town council prided itself on keeping taxes to a minimum; it endeavoured to spend as little as possible and to pay its debts promptly. Improvements (sidewalks, for example) were built gradually. In 1891, private citizens, not the town, erected street lights and a telephone network. Even such a basic service as a hospital was built by Sir Alexander and donated to the town. In fact, the economic symbiosis between town and company, coupled with the veneration of the patriarchal Galt, became a crucial factor in the attitude of Lethbridge's citizenry. The majority of its inhabitants were content to let the AR&CCo provide basic services and stimulate regional development. While a few leaders cheered the efforts of the Galts and supported, for example, their bid for government irrigation subsidies, they were unwilling to spend much money on this enterprise themselves. Everyone heartily agreed that Lethbridge must diversify its economic base in order to escape the dominance of the Galt company, but few were willing to levy upon themselves the requisite taxes. When the prevailing economic depression discouraged major outside investment in Lethbridge, local businessmen were unable to translate their ambitious vision for the town into concrete action.

Consequently, in 1896, Lethbridge was little more than a coal mine and railway town where people threw their garbage behind their houses and their ashes on the street. Even though its leaders continually prophesied that within a few years Lethbridge would be the largest city on the prairies, in reality cows, chickens and even pigs roamed its roads at will. The dream of major metropolitan status was still alive, but while Lethbridgians waited for wealthy capitalists to recognize their town's industrial potential, the realization of the vision grew more remote with every passing year.

Lethbridge Public School in 1888; principal Bruce L. Latimer and teacher Margaret Duff are in the doorways.

Town of Lethbridge flume, about 1900, looking west-northwest from 7th Avenue and 13th Street South.

Chapter Four

The Rainmakers

By 1896, the collieries at Lethbridge were still the largest producers of coal in the North-West Territories. In that year, its miners extracted 120,000 tons (109 000 tonnes) of coal, twice as much as their nearest rivals. But the market for coal, either in Alberta or in Montana, was too small to support the large, heavily capitalized mines. More than 1,900 miles (3000 km) removed from the industrial heartland of North America, the Galt mines barely survived the economic depression of the early 1890s. That they endured at all was due largely to the extensive land grants the company had earned building its railways. It was the land and its soil, rather than the coal, which ultimately determined the character of Lethbridge.

Although the land on which Lethbridge was founded is fertile, the scarcity of rain and the presence of desiccating winds permitted only the growth of hardy grasses. These nutritious grey-yellow grasses flourished and fed large numbers of animals. The Galts realized that 19th century farming techniques could not cope with the semiarid conditions and they planned to sell the lands to large ranching companies. Consequently, they took their grants in alternate townships rather than the usual sections. They soon discovered, however, that they could not compete with the generous grazing leases offered by the dominion government nor the free grasslands in Montana. They had to find different buyers.

It was the Mormon Church which eventually solved the Galt's problem. One of its members was Charles Ora Card, a very talented and ambitious leader. Card had escaped to Canada in 1886 while under arrest on polygamy charges. In the spring of 1887 he bought from the NWC&NCo a large tract of land near the St. Mary and Waterton rivers on which he settled a number of Utah families. Card recognized that the rivers of southern Alberta could be used to overcome its rainfall deficiency and make the company's land suitable for agriculture. He convinced Elliott Galt to sponsor a large-scale irrigation project. By 1893, Galt had concluded an agreement with the Mormon Church but he failed to interest his London friends in the venture. For ten years, these investors had

backed Galt's southern Alberta enterprises with little return for their money. In the general economic depression of the 1890s they refused to risk even more. The irrigation project was premature.

Galt and Magrath considered the Londoners' rebuff but a temporary setback. Elliott Galt founded a new firm, the Alberta Irrigation Company, for the purpose of buying from the AR&CCo lands for irrigation purposes. C. A. Magrath, meanwhile, lobbied the dominion government for financial assistance. His work was aided by the *Lethbridge News* which published editorial after editorial arguing that irrigation should receive the same liberal subsidies as railways. For the moment, it was a futile effort. With immigration to the North-West slowed down to a trickle, the government wanted to dispel any notion that the plains needed irrigation. They dismissed Magrath's campaign but did allow him to consolidate most of the company's lands into a solid block south of Lethbridge.

In the 1890s, a complex of factors dramatically improved the prospects of irrigation. Perhaps it began with the spectacular gold discoveries in South Africa and the Klondike which helped to arrest the general decline of world wheat prices. Certainly, the end of the free lands in the United States focussed attention on the vast Canadian plains. The refinements of dry-farming techniques opened the semiarid regions to settlers, while the development of grain elevators, railways and large grain ships made bulk wheat shipments cheap and speedy. Grain became one of Canada's great export potentials and her western prairies began to attract farmers. When the Canadian government revamped its immigration program and increased its advertising, thousands of American, British, and European colonists responded. And, as the trickle of settlers swelled into a flood, western Canadian developments once again lured foreign financiers and made irrigation an appealing investment.

The southern Alberta irrigation scheme was also helped by the Canadian government and the Canadian Pacific Railway. The new

Liberal administration, elected in 1896, forgave the AR&CCo the survey dues owing on its land grant. The government also subsidized the CPR's Crowsnest Pass extension and the company began to build that line in 1897. The Crowsnest railway opened the vast coal reserves of the Pass, leading to the founding of several towns and the creation of a market for agricultural products. Lastly, the CPR contributed $100,000 to the Galt project.

With the favourable turn in circumstances, Galt and Magrath renegotiated the old contract with the Mormons. The church agreed to provide labourers for the construction with wages paid half in cash and half in land. On 26 August 1898, Charles Ora Card plowed the first furrow for the ditch and for the next two years sometimes as many as 300 teams worked on the excavations. By the summer of 1900, the workers had completed 95 miles (153 km) of canals, including the main canal (which tapped the St. Mary near the international border), and branches to Stirling and Lethbridge.

Once construction was completed, Elliott Galt redoubled his efforts to develop the countryside. A brochure stressed the certainty of good crops with irrigation, saying "The farmer is his own rainmaker." He launched an advertising campaign to lure settlers to the company's lands. He built the St. Mary's River Railway to link Cardston to the Montana line at Stirling. He encouraged the construction of a sugar plant at Raymond and he donated land to start a model farm under William H. Fairfield near Lethbridge. Meanwhile, he improved and enlarged the canal system. Although the wet years at the time retarded the sale of water rights, the overwhelming optimism of the first decade of the century spread to southern Alberta and the company's land sold well. By 1905, Galt's efforts were bearing fruit and Lethbridge was fast becoming an agriculture centre.

For the time being, however, Lethbridge was still a coal and rail town and its population ebbed and flowed with the production cycle of the mines. Prosperous times often sparked an influx of migrants most of whom were men. Many of them moved into company or private boarding houses located near the mine entrances or just south of the railyards. Others preferred to stay in shacks and shanties scattered along the river valley and tablelands. Most of the married coal workers lived in small, often company-owned houses near the mine shafts. In these homes the men were the breadwinners and masters. They expected their wives to remain quietly in the background, serving them and their children. Recreation and social activities, in their closely knit neighbourhoods, catered to the men and stressed the manly virtues of strength and virility.

Norman Photographic Archives No. 8491

Constructing an irrigation canal with an elevating grader near Lethbridge in 1904.

The irony of irrigation: the first of two major floods in 1902, which washed out much of the new irrigation system and made farmers think of drainage, not irrigation. The former William Stafford home is in the left foreground.

One of the results of the town's masculinity was occasional bouts of rowdyism, considerable drunkenness, gambling and prostitution. Captain R. Burton Deane, commander of the NWMP, developed a relatively lenient policy of permitting the segregated red-light district, which he could watch and control. It was a difficult position to maintain because church officials constantly pestered the police to enforce the law rigidly and stamp out prostitution. At the same time, the town council expected the mounted police to patrol the community and collect its license fees for free, even though they had no jurisdiction in Lethbridge. The

uneasy relationship came to an end in 1895 when a small group of men revenged the suicide of a cuckolded husband. They hauled Joseph Donaldson out of bed, sprinkled some tar and feathers on his head and escorted him out of town. Captain Deane discovered, to his dismay, that one of the vigilantes was the town constable who had also fled with the town's license receipts. When Deane learned that the town council held the mounted police responsible for the stolen money, he told council to look after their own law enforcement. For the next two years council engaged their own inspector to maintain law and order and collect taxes and fees. In

1897, the NWMP took on the task again but only after council repealed a recently-approved morality bylaw. Although council's action enraged the clergy, Deane won the day and a specially appointed NWMP constable patrolled Lethbridge for the next few years.

Meanwhile, the forces of morality redoubled their efforts to rid the town of the red-light district. In the summer of 1898, their efforts seemed to have borne fruit. Lethbridge passed another morality by-law that ordered fines for the keeping of bawdy-houses, houses of ill-fame, and disorderly houses, and threatened to arrest anyone not a bona fide resident found in such a place. The police were unhappy with the legislation because they believed the prostitutes would move their operations outside the town boundaries making control much more difficult. At a hastily called meeting, the NWMP commander convinced the councillors to change their minds and leave the matter to police discretion. The zealous guardians of morality, led by Charles McKillop, did not accept defeat, however, and a year later, the Presbyterian pastor publicly accused the police of overlooking flagrant violations of territorial liquor laws. Captain Deane, who never retreated from a fight, countered with a lengthy letter to the town council in which he explained that because the territorial council refused to contest the appeals of those convicted of liquor offences, he had ordered the town constable to leave liquor-law enforcement to territorial officials. Ironically, the incident created so much publicity that police headquarters ordered Deane to remove the constable from town duty as of 1 January 1900. Lethbridge tried to hire its own man but was unsuccessful. At the end of the year, when the hubbub had died down, it re-engaged the NWMP.

Deane's policy of loose supervision rather than rigid repression triumphed again. From his cosy town office, a NWMP corporal looked placidly down the street to several brightly-lit, noisy saloons and brothels. Two of the more notorious brothels were run by "Swede Alice," last name unknown, and Carrie "Cowboy Jack" McLean, a working prostitute during the cattle drives before she acquired her own house in Lethbridge. The corporal's hands were never very far from the telephone so that should affairs get unmanageable he could call the barracks for reinforcements. Lethbridge's reputation for illicit entertainment and loose law enforcement endured. The saloons stayed open after regulation time, the gambling and prostitution continued. Single settlers, farm

Flood irrigation at the Dominion Experimental Station (now Research Station), Lethbridge.

Ott's Barbershop, ca. 1905.

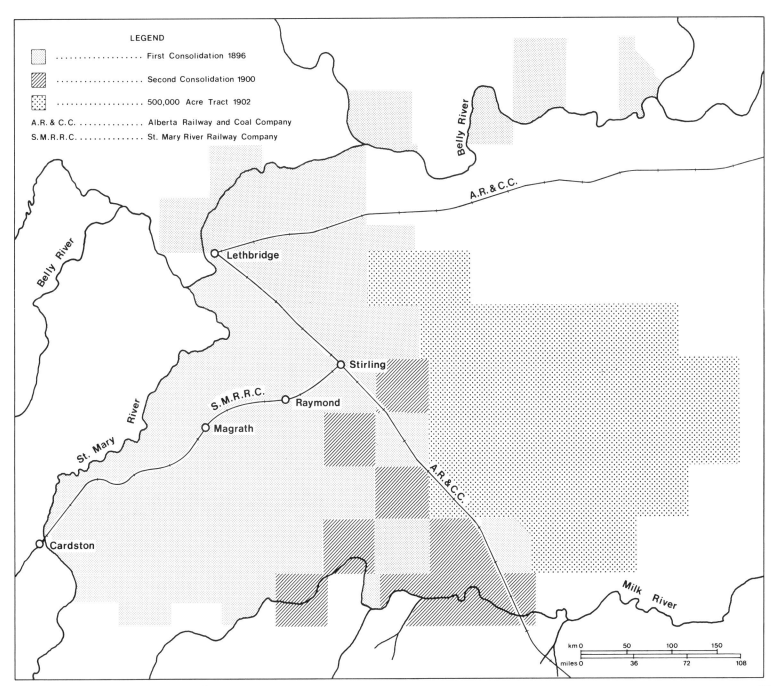

LEGEND

▨ .... First Consolidation 1896

▨ .... Second Consolidation 1900

⬚ .... 500,000 Acre Tract 1902

A.R. & C.C. .... Alberta Railway and Coal Company

S.M.R.R.C. .... St. Mary River Railway Company

Southern Alberta land holdings of the Galt companies.

James "Coyote" Henry

A local character in turn-of-the-century Lethbridge was James "Coyote" Henry, an old hunter of the district. He worked occasionally, usually as a sheepherder or a farmhand. He lived in a combination dugout-shanty on the north side of the railway tracks near the slack piles from the abandoned Galt No. 1 mineshaft. He kept several dogs and a mare, which from time to time had a colt. He had a gaily-painted wagon for his forays about town and for his odd out-of-town trip.

He was obsessed with, and frightened of, mountain lions. At first his comments were taken seriously — ("Mr. J. Henry, better known as Coyote Henry, recently came across several mountain lions in the vicinity of Chin Coulee and is looking for someone to co-operate in their extermination") — but soon everyone realized that the animals were figments of his imagination.

Once he got a haying job on the Hyssop Ranch, north of Lethbridge. While there, he stayed in a tent under a tree near the ranchhouse. One night the wind got up and broke off a branch, which fell on Coyote Henry's tent and bounced to the ground. Convinced that the mountain lions finally had him, he grabbed his ever-present shotgun and fired a barrage into the roof and sides of the tent, meanwhile wailing, "Save me! Save me! The mountain lions are after me!" Bill Hyssop heard the firing and realized that Coyote Henry was having another of his spells. He ordered his family into the basement where they would escape stray buckshot and, in the morning, gave Coyote Henry his time.

By 1911, his condition had worsened to the point where he took a shot at a neighbor and threatened the man's family. He was jailed by Pat Egan of the Lethbridge Police Force and examined by Dr. P. M. Campbell, a local physician. As a result, on August 18th, 1911, Coyote Henry was committed to the insane asylum at Ponoka, where he died a few years later.

was money to be spent and Lethbridge businessmen eagerly welcomed the weekly influx of farm and ranch hands. They overlooked the decrepit shacks of older, broken-down prostitutes in the river valley, the recurring brawls of drunken revellers, and the cruel robberies of besotted workers by crooked gamblers and thieves. Although McKillop's attempt to cure the ills of an urbanized society was perhaps impolitic and certainly outdated, Deane's approach, however expedient and wise, showed an inability to deal with the festering side-effects of an immature, isolated, and partially industrialized society.

The parsimonious town council finally hired its own constable in 1902 but staffing problems and a lack of citizen support prevented efficient law enforcement. While the moralists pressed the council to abide by its ordinances, the majority of Lethbridgians were still willing to tolerate a certain amount of illegal entertainment. The councillors approved yet another morality by-law in 1904, but it was not popular and thus could not be effectively enforced. The council did reorganize its two-man force in 1905 and hired a third officer a year later. Finally, twenty years after its founding, Lethbridge had laid the basis of a systematic approach to law enforcement but had not solved all its problems.

The red-light district and the excessive violation of liquor and gambling ordinances were not the only problems facing the mining town. The techniques of coal-mining required a large, cheap, and mobile labor force. Newly arrived immigrants, anxious to find employment, fulfilled this need. Lethbridge welcomed large numbers of central and south Europeans, including Hungarians, Slovaks, and Italians, as well as a few Croats and Poles, all popularly labelled as Slavs. Many of the Europeans were transients who chose mining as a temporary expedient to earn enough capital to buy a farm in Canada or back home. They were a hard working group, obsessed with accumulating this money as quickly as possible. But, they were also cliquish and their strange customs and impenetrable language isolated them from their Anglo-Saxon co-workers. The latter increasingly viewed the continental European with suspicion and distrust because they believed the "foreigners" drove down earnings by willingly accepting minimal wages. Many Lethbridgians even blamed the town's rowdiness on the immigrants, a belief based upon tales of disorderly weekend parties and noisy weddings, and an assumption made more believable because police and newspaper reports always singled out

labourers, and cowboys from miles around flocked to the town on weekends to join the miners and railroaders in unrestrained escape from monotonous loneliness and strenuous or dangerous jobs. There

Galt Hospital operating room staff in 1897: Nurse Millar, Nurse Chapman, Nurse Andrews, Nurse Vandervoort, and Dr. Mewburn.

ethnic troublemakers. They seldom labelled Anglo-Saxons who got into trouble nor those who owned the brothels and saloons.

The railway track, which divided Lethbridge, also exaggerated the town's ethnic division. Most of the continental Europeans settled north of the railway yards so that by 1901 they made up nearly half of the Village of Stafford and North Ward populations. In that same year, the British constituted 80 percent of the people living south of the tracks. This physical division of the town, clearly recognized by all, merely served to accentuate the ethnic tensions. The townsfolk continued to dislike the immigrants. Their newspaper often railed against the foreign labourers, accusing them of undercutting local wages, of causing labour unrest and violence. It also complained that many of the immigrants spent their wages only on the bare essentials and mailed the rest home to Europe. Beneath all this rhetoric there stirred the fear of the unknown and the unfamiliar; for a long time yet, the railway yards continued to symbolize the cultural division in the community.

The tracks also marked a religious split. In 1901, nearly one-third of all Lethbridgians called themselves Presbyterian. Fewer in numbers were the Anglicans (21 percent), the Roman Catholics (19 percent), and the Methodists (12 percent). In North Lethbridge, the Roman Catholics made up well over a third of church-goers, while the Presbyterians and Anglicans comprised only 16 percent and 12 percent of the population. The established churches also served a sprinkling of Salvation Army.

The churches founded at the birth of Lethbridge remained small, that is, they failed to keep pace with the town's rapid growth. Both Knox Presbyterian and St. Augustine's Anglican churches built extensions and became self-supporting in 1891, but their existence remained precarious. Although these mainline churches enjoyed the membership of the town's leading businessmen, company officials, and professionals, they both experienced financial difficulties. In 1893, for example, Knox could not afford a summer replacement for its vacationing minister, while a year later St. Augustine's abolished offertories for outside causes. At various times the Anglicans considered closing their church but they managed to survive with their bishop's help and budget restraint. But, even as late as 1901, when their pastor resigned, they talked of selling the rectory and seeking an unmarried replacement.

70

Southern Alberta has the finest land lying out of doors.	
RETAIL MARKET PRICES	
OF STAPLE COMMODITIES	
Rough boards	$16.00 per 1000 ft.
Dimension lumber up to 20 feet	16.50 " " "
Boards, dressed one side	16.50 " " "
Shiplap	18 to 20 " "
Siding, Flooring and Ceiling	27 to 29 " "
Cedar Shingles, No 1	3 per 1000
Barb Wire	4.40 per 100 lbs.
Nails	4.75 to 5.00 "
Wheat and Oats	1.00 to 1.50 "
Potatoes	1.00 to 2.00 "
Granulated Sugar	6.50 "
Best patent flour	2.65 per sack.
Rolled Oats	2.75 " "
Bran and Shorts	1.25 " "
Ham—best	16c. per lb.
Butter—creamery	30 to 35c. " "
" dairy	20 to 30c. " "
Eggs—fresh	20 to 50c. " "
Beef	7 to 15c.
Mutton	8 to 15c.
Pork—fresh	15c.
" —green salt	12½c.
Prices of Butter and Eggs are for Winter and Summer.	
The altitude of Lethbridge is 2,800 feet, and for chest complaints the climate is not surpassed.	

Retail market prices in March 1901; coal, not listed, cost $2.50 per ton.

In their annual reports the congregations often blamed their precarious position on the unsettled conditions of a migratory population. To be sure, fully 19 percent of North Lethbridgians specified no religious affiliation at all, the highest total anywhere in Alberta. The figure, undoubtedly reflected the presence of a large transitory population which wandered from place to place, people who had lost all contact with established institutions. Judging by the size of the churches, the figure could have been higher. Undoubtedly, convention, custom, or simply subconscious social

1885 – PAST and PRESENT – 1904

– OF THE –
HOTEL
LETHBRIDGE
N.W.T.

– 1885 –

– 1897 –

– 1904 –
HOW
ABOUT
PROGRESS?

– 1900 –

– 1902 –

The various stages of the Lethbridge Hotel from 1885-1904. Since 1904, the inset balconies have been filled in.

pressure compelled many to claim religious affiliation although they never attended church. The establishment churches made little effort to reach these lapsed attenders. McKillop's ministry was largely devoted to eradicating the most blatant and obvious sins, the visible symptoms of deep-seated ills of an industrialized society. His faithful ally, J. D. Higinbotham, took a more incisive approach by establishing a Sunday school for the town children. It was the only evangelistic outreach of the main line churches. They did not concentrate their energies on bringing the Gospel to the mine or rail workers, particularly those living north of the tracks. Nor did they help to solve the bewildering problems of the new, highly mobile, technologized society.

The only churchman active among the workers was Father Van Tighem. Ever since his first visit to Coal Banks in 1884, he had been deeply concerned with the spiritual welfare of the miners. He was able to converse with them in English, French, German, or even Flemish and he could hear confessions in Hungarian and Italian. His was a lonely task, however, for unlike McKillop, whose sermons were published sometimes verbatim in the *News,* Van Tighem did not enjoy the friendship and admiration of Lethbridge's social leaders, who belittled his work among the "foreign element." Nevertheless, Van Tighem continued his endeavours, particularly to establish a distinctly Roman Catholic education for the children of his parish. He fought hard to secure for his school a fair share of the district's taxes.

Father Van Tighem's school was disliked by Lethbridge's non-Catholic majority. They believed that uniform public schools were the essential instruments in setting the basic moral and civic standards in the community. In other words, the future character of western Canada depended upon the children's education; and, in a society made up of a myriad of ethnic groups, a single school system was the best instrument to instill common values into the nation's youth. Van Tighem's school, by catering to the children of the Roman Catholic, Slavonic coal workers, would, they believed, retard the homogenization of Canada's population.

In the next few years the student body grew slowly so that by 1898 the average attendance at both public and separate schools was less than 170 pupils. With the rapid influx of immigrants during the next decade, the school population more than doubled and in January 1906 Lethbridge opened Westminster School, another two-storey brick building. Obviously, the community felt

that the cost of instilling the many newcomers with Canadian values was money well spent.

Lethbridgians were more reluctant to spend money on physical improvements or economic stimulators. The optimistic boosterism, which marked the early years of Lethbridge, did not translate into concrete action. The depression of the early 1890s certainly contributed to the lack of results. So did absentee landownership. In 1891, nearly half of the town's assessed properties were owned by company shareholders, the largest proprietor being Sir Alexander Galt. Such extensive outside interests, coupled to a migrant population, meant that only a few people were involved in civic affairs.

Throughout the early 1890s, it became increasingly difficult to fill public offices or reach a quorum at council meetings.

The marked improvement in the world economy in the mid-1890s boosted Lethbridge's spirits. By the end of 1897 all the empty structures that had plagued the town for years were filled to capacity. Building activities increased so rapidly that the *News* proudly complained of a shortage of skilled workers. The Bank of Montreal expressed its confidence in Lethbridge's future by opening a branch in the town. And, as the surrounding countryside filled with eager settlers, Lethbridge grew steadily, a phenomenon heartily applauded by the town's second weekly, founded in 1905. Matching its competitor's preoccupation with economic expansion, the newly established *Herald* reflected the exhilarating optimism which grabbed hold of Lethbridge's business community and town council. Lethbridge joined the wild scramble for a share of the West's booming prosperity. Like their counterparts throughout the West, they abandoned their cautious fiscal policies and recklessly borrowed funds for lavish public works and bonuses to attract industries.

In the late 1890s irrigation and railways were still the prime objectives of Lethbridge's expansionary urge because both endeavours promised to lessen the town's dependence upon the coal mines. Harry Bentley, the town's mayor, spent several months in Ottawa during the summer of 1897 lobbying the government to induce the CPR to construct the Crowsnest Pass line from Lethbridge. A year later, the town council reacted quickly to a board of trade petition for a substantial bonus to the AR&CCo to extend the canal into Lethbridge itself. While it was by far the largest

Interior of Jim Rose's store, ca. 1900.

The First Automobile

The first report of an automobile in Lethbridge appeared in the *News* on 23 July 1903 and read: "Mr. E. T. Galt has imported a Wilton automobile from Cleveland, Ohio, which was taken out for a trial spin on Saturday [18 July]. The vehicle is of the latest improved construction, the propelling power being furnished by a 20 horsepower gasoline engine, the working parts being located in the centre under the seats. The wheels are rubber-tired and render travelling very easy and comfortable. It is reported that, on Sunday, the fiery steed was headed for Raymond but something went wrong with the machinery and it got stuck in a slough, a team being requisitioned to pull it from its damp location. The ride is said to have been quite exciting, the driver — Mr. Braderick [manager, E. H. Dyer & Company, then building a sugar factory at Raymond] — being designated a veritable steeplechaser. Needless to state, members of the equine race are greatly excited when they meet the new arrival."

The second automobile in Lethbridge was purchased by Manfred Freeman. By 1906, there were six automobiles in the city and Messrs. Bowman, Colpman and Vrooman were said to be getting machines. Howard Case, who set up the Lethbridge Motor Car Company in 1907, was building a garage for storage and care of the new machines and was installing machinery to handle repairs. And in 1907, also, a group of enthusiasts organized the Lethbridge Automobile Club.

Bobby McBeth at Redpath and Coutts (3rd Avenue and 9th Street South) in 1902 with fish from the irrigation ditch.

single expenditure for the community to date, a plebiscite in the summer of 1899 overwhelmingly approved the council's $30,000 debenture to be held by the AR&CCo for a promise to extend the main canal from Stirling and to deliver water to 20,000 acres (8100 ha) in and around Lethbridge.

As the pace of western development accelerated, so did Lethbridge's frantic rush to participate in the general affluence. Not only did it publish thousands of copies of promotional pamphlets and give out bonuses to attract industries, but it greatly increased its physical services to the community in order to maintain a progressive town image. With boundless optimism

Lethbridge expanded its civic administration, planted hundreds of trees, replaced wooden sidewalks with concrete, improved street lighting, and in 1904 completed the first stage of a $130,000 water and sewage system. At the same time, to entice the CPR and Alberta Railway and Irrigation Company (AR&ICo) into making Lethbridge a divisional point complete with a Union station, it granted them a 20-year tax exemption on all railway properties as well as free water. With all this activity the town's budget doubled within the eight-year period from 1897 to 1904. Municipal debt soared from a cautious, manageable $10,000 in 1899 to a costly $165,000 only four years later. The reckless spending, encouraged by the boom mentality of the business establishment, made the community a more attractive place in which to live, but it also led to financial difficulties which were not resolved until the establishment of a managerial system of civic government in 1928.

Most of the council's expenditures were for material items: miles of sidewalks, sewers, road maintenance, and fire-fighting equipment. The same attitude that contributed to the lack of control over the red-light district and the emphasis on the practical benefits

Temperature was 53°F, there was no wind, and Lethbridge won the baseball game, which was played on The Square (now Galt Gardens), by a score of 13 to 1.

of education set municipal priorities. The town spent nothing on recreational facilities. It made but a minimal annual grant to the town hospital, avoided responsibility for epidemics, and cautiously approached a bid to acquire a Carnegie-funded library. Like many of its western counterparts, Lethbridge bid furiously against other towns to attract a brewery or a flour mill but turned a deaf ear whenever a destitute family appealed for help. Railway tickets to Montana were the favorite form of welfare. Spending guidelines were entirely commercial and designed to yield a maximum amount of economic growth.

The provision of recreation rested entirely with the private citizen. For the sports-minded member of the English establishment, this was no problem. Opportunities were plentiful. With almost clocklike precision, Lethbridge witnessed the rise and fall of baseball, soccer, rugby, lawn tennis, and cricket clubs. The town square, which after a succession of abortive beautification schemes was still only a grassfield, served as a convenient playing ground. Bicycle enthusiasts formed the Chinook Cycle Club, which for years promoted casual riding, races, and rallies. In 1891, a turf association began a program of horse races. Few workers

75

Baseball Match in Midwinter

On 31 January 1906, headlines in the new weekly, *The Lethbridge Herald,* read: "Lethbridge Savages Win From Calgary. Baseball Match In Midwinter. Big Advertisement For The Banana Belt."

The news report told how, on 27 January, 800 people, most without overcoats, saw a seven-inning baseball game between Lethbridge and Calgary. The final score was Lethbridge 13, Calgary 1. It was a perfect day with no wind and a temperature of 53°F.

The local baseball team was called "Houk's Savages" as it was sponsored by George Houk, an old whiskey trader from the Whoop-Up era then in the wholesale liquor business in Lethbridge. Houk's halfbreed son, "Press" Houk, was catcher.

Here are several short items from the news reports:
"Last Saturday was as balmy as a May day. The baseball and lacrosse boys, in summer costume, practiced in the Town Square [Galt Gardens], and gamboled about never imagining it was the 27th of January. Hammond Bros. took a photograph of the scene, which will be reproduced in eastern papers to establish the claim that has always been made that Lethbridge has the finest climate of any place in Canada."
"Verily, Lethbridge is the banana belt. Where else in Canada could we find baseball and lacrosse being played in the latter part of January? Why do people travel to California to avoid the winter when they can enjoy good summer weather in the good Canadian town of Lethbridge."
"The news that a baseball match was played here last Saturday was sent all over North America by Associated Press: 'Lethbridge, January 26. The Calgary baseball team will play here tomorrow. The weather is magnificent and the diamond is in fine form'."

George Houk

George Houk was born in Newcastle, Pennsylvania, in 1840. He visited what is now southern Alberta with a prospecting party in 1864 and stood on the site of the City of Lethbridge years before the whiskey trade or coal mining began.

He had a varied career as prospector, sheriff, freighter, and Indian trader. He always identified with the west of stampeding buffalo, warring Indian tribes, pious missionaries, wolfers and traders. Throughout his life he was very proud of a .44 handgun presented to him by the "boys" during his tenure as sheriff of Choteau County at Fort Benton. Another prized possession was a Winchester rifle, with which he had shot many a buffalo.

He had lived with the Blood Indians, spoke their language, and married a Blood Indian woman. He could be counted on, in the early days of the Lethbridge Exhibition, to organize and lead a colorful contingent of braves in warpaint in the annual parade. A baseball enthusiast, for years he sponsored a team known as "Houk's Savages," which once won an Alberta championship in their class.

Houk became involved with the wholesale liquor and fine cigar trade when Lethbridge started to grow. There seemed to be a deliberate campaign on the part of assorted stool pigeons and police informants to entice Houk into committing minor infractions of the liquor laws. This, in turn, allowed the police to pounce and permitted some righteous, petty-minded judge to suspend his liquor license, or to lecture and fine him. News reports of the early 1900s remind one of a bunch of coyotes yapping at the heels of the old bull of the herd.

Houk died in Lethbridge in 1928, predeceased by his wife of many years and by his son, Press, an employee of the Great Northern Railway, who was murdered in Great Falls in 1924 in a fracas over a poker game.

Lacrosse team, coached by Dr. F. H. Mewburn, winner of Lavasseur Championship Cup in 1902.

Members and meeting hall of the Hungarian Sick-Benefit Society of Lethbridge in 1901.

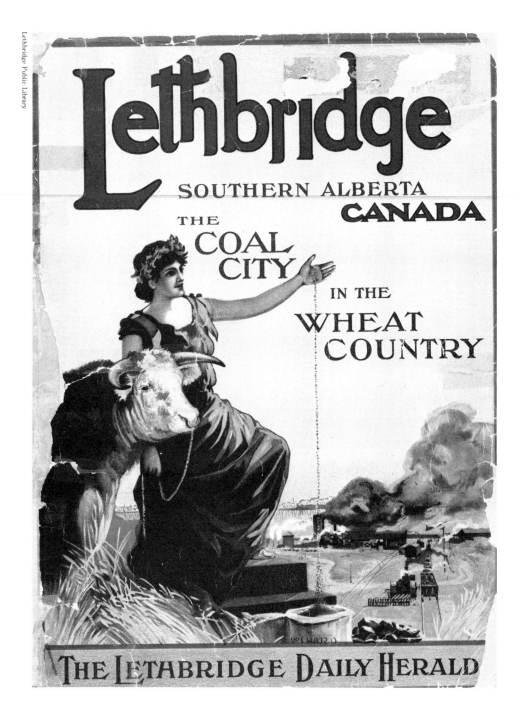

Cover of a special issue of the Lethbridge Daily
Herald, which used the slogan, "The Coal City in the
Wheat Country."

participated in these activities. While they had their colliery band, most of them preferred to relax at home after a hard days work, or sit in a nearby saloon, shoot a game of pool, or merely lean against a favourite wall and tease girls. As late as 1906, the *Herald* scolded the young men for loafing downtown on Saturday nights, crowding the sidewalks so that ladies could not pass without being jostled about and ruining their skirts in the streams of tobacco juice. With the onset of winter, activities went indoors. The churches had social groups for men, women, and children. Several lodges, debating societies, and music clubs provided another form of diversion. So did public dances and card games. Political meetings, too, were a popular pastime. Touring theatrical groups and musicians were rare and second-rate, and so the townsfolk organized their own variety programs with local talent. As the town grew larger, the inhabitants older, and society less intimate, all these forms of public amusement became less frequent and were replaced by private house parties and invited gatherings.

By 1906, when Lethbridge was legally incorporated as a city, it was taking on more and more of the trappings of a modern urban centre. A few large, brick buildings, like the functional three-storey Bentley block or the new Hudson's Bay store with its modern showcase windows were replacing the motley collection of wooden structures. The streets were still gravel but many of the downtown sidewalks were cement. Spindly trees, placed in unimaginative straight lines, bordered the city square. The stately homes of druggist Higinbotham, lawyer Conybeare, and merchant Bentley proved that these successful men had confidence in the community's future. Most of the houses sprawled across the prairies behind the business districts were linked into the water and sewer system, the telephone network, and the electrical plant. The municipal council was even discussing the purchase of electric streetcars to whisk people about the city. With the flow or immigrants still unabated, Lethbridge's takeoff to metropolitan status seemed to be just around the corner.

Lethbridge, however, never became the industrial metropolis its promoters envisioned. The cows and calves, which tramped through the streets every morning as the town herder took them to pasture, symbolized the agricultural base of the city's economy. By 1906, Lethbridge was experiencing the effects of the settlement of its hinterland. A casual stroll through the business district would reveal this change in the community's economic orientation. Among the most prominent establishments was Bentley Company Ltd., a prosperous retail and wholesale firm, which had expanded its small 1885 shop into one large store and two warehouses in the city as well as branches in the Crowsnest Pass, and dealt in all manner of dry goods, groceries, and hardwares. Another firm thriving on the flourishing agricultural hinterland was that of George Rogers, a large wholesale lumber business with outlets in Raymond, Magrath, Stirling and Taber. An obvious sign of the agricultural revolution sweeping through southern Alberta was seen when Rogers was named agent for the Massey Harris farm implement company. Yet a third company was the Winnipeg-based firm of A. Macdonald & Co., with two general stores specializing in the ranching trade serving the city and its hinterland. In sum, a variety of stores, banks, dealers, artisans, and teamsters made Lethbridge the service station for its growing agricultural hinterland.

By 1906, Lethbridge was becoming a strange two-headed creature. One promotional pamphlet aptly called it a coal city in a wheat country. The wealth of coal beneath its streets was still vital to its economic wealth. But of increasing importance were the many farms being built in the surrounding countryside. The fertile soil, made more attractive through irrigation, gave Lethbridge its most enduring economic foundation.

Line-up at Dominion Land Office to file on homesteads at Del Bonita, 1912. On Sunday afternoons the Salvation Army held a service for the landseekers, who did not dare go to church because they would lose their place in the line.

Chapter Five

Boundless Optimism

The first decade of the twentieth century throbbed with optimism. As thousands of immigrants flooded onto the Canadian plains, a sense of euphoria gripped the nation. With the prairie population trebling within a decade, private investors, aided by generous governments, laid two more transcontinental railways and countless branch lines across the West, erected warehouses, elevators, and abattoirs everywhere on the plains, and dammed and bridged its rivers. No project was too large, no scheme too visionary, no plan too expensive. Villages grew into towns and cities, frame houses replaced tarpaper shacks, irrigation ditches distributed water to parched land. The pioneer era was over and farmers and ranchers felt the full weight of municipal organization, the herd and pound laws, the fencing of road allowances — in sum, the transformation of a wild region into an ordered land. It was an age of progress, of growth, and of boundless optimism.

Lethbridge was not immune to this spirit of optimism. As in the rest of Canada, immigration was the basis of the unprecedented exuberance. At first settlers were slow to come to the semiarid Lethbridge area but the introduction of dry-farming techniques, especially summerfallowing, to southern Alberta early in the twentieth century opened the gates. Lethbridge's first major land rush occurred on 1 September 1908. More than a thousand eager settlers besieged the government land office to secure homesteads or to redeem land certificates. At the Lethbridge land office, applications for dryland homesteads peaked in 1910 with 4,952 entries. The last major land rush occurred on 1 May 1912 when applicants lined up two abreast for four city blocks in the hope of getting homesteads in the Del Bonita area.

The initial success of dryland farming owed much to technological innovations. In some instances, huge steam tractors, pulling 20-bottom plows, broke the sod for the new farms. Although these slow-moving, smoke-belching monsters bankrupted many of their owners, they never replaced the horse on western farms. Mechanization of farms in the Lethbridge area actually began during the First World War. The bumper crops of 1915 and 1916,

high war-time prices, and the removal of tariffs on small tractors entering Canada from the United States allowed farmers to purchase less costly and more efficient gasoline-powered machinery. In 1918, one local dealer sold well over 200 small gasoline tractors to neighbouring farmers.

Of great significant to the success of dryland farming was the introduction of Marquis wheat, a hard red, early maturing spring wheat of excellent quality. The Marquis variety was so well suited to the prairies that it soon replaced winter wheat. In 1912, a Raymond farmer, Henry Holmes, took a sample of this exceptional grain to the Seventh International Dry Farming Congress and on the basis of its colour and plumpness won the grand championship and a $2,500 Rumley Oil-Pull tractor.

Unfortunately, dry farming technology suffered from a serious drawback. The practice of summerfallowing caused major soil erosion. Every summer local farmers cultivated some of their fields but kept them free of crops and weeds, thereby conserving about 20 percent of the rainfall from one season for use in the next. But, after 1910, the ever-present winds began to erode the loosely cultivated, dry soil. Conditions continued to deteriorate badly until the local farmers developed effective conservation techniques. Norman Grier of Macleod tried cover cropping, the Koole brothers of Monarch used strip farming and Otto Wobick and the Erdmans of Barons, and Charles Noble of Nobleford, experimented with blade type cultivators. Farmers around Raymond and Magrath perfected the idea of trash-cover or stubble-mulch farming and shallow cultivation. As a consequence of the new techniques, sales of plowshares in Lethbridge fell from several tens of thousands in 1910 to a few hundreds by 1925.

The negative side effects of dryland farming aided the promoters of irrigation. Lethbridge's city council, its newspaper, and its board of trade worked ceaselessly to promote and encourage the expansion of the existing irrigation works. They were successful and in 1917 the Taber Irrigation District was established, followed in 1919 by the Lethbridge Northern (first called the Old Man River

Project), in 1923 by the Mountain View, in 1924 by the Magrath, and in 1925 by the Raymond irrigation districts. By encouraging mixed farming and by providing conditions for the growth of speciality crops such as sugar beets, irrigation stabilized local agriculture and made it less susceptible to the vagaries of weather and the international grain market. Two indefatigable workers for irrigation were George R. Marnoch, president of the board of trade, and George W. "Old Man" Pearson, a farmer from Iron Springs. Marnoch was an irascible, hard-working Scot, Pearson an easier-going man of the soil. But both were united in their single-minded pursuit of irrigation development, particularly of the Lethbridge Northern.

The rapid settlement of Lethbridge's environs had a dramatic impact on the community. Real estate fever gripped the city from 1907 to 1913. Prices soared and city lots were traded on markets as far away as Europe. Properties on 5th Street South, which sold for $1,000 per front-foot in August 1912, went for $1,200 in September. One realtor bought 40 acres (16.2 ha) near Queen Victoria Park for $40,000, subdivided the estate and sold portions of it in Lethbridge, Calgary, Toronto and Detroit. The licensing and registration of real estate agents in 1907 deterred the most dishonest of the speculators but the wheeling and dealing continued unabated until the bubble burst in 1913.

Caught up in the optimistic spirit of speculation and unbridled growth, Lethbridge's councillors permitted uncontrolled, even frantic subdivision of the properties surrounding the city. The earliest subdivision included the Village of Stafford (west of 13th Street between 9th and 14th Avenues North), the southern portion of the North Ward (east of 13th Street between the railway and 14th Avenue North), and North Lethbridge (west of 13th Street between the railway and 9th Avenue North), which was further subdivided for industrial purposes after the completion of the 9th Street Overhead Bridge in 1911 enchanced its value. Between 1908 and 1912, developers created Duff, Alexander, Barnsley, Gibbons, Parkdale, Sunnyside, Arico Park and perhaps another fifteen subdivisions on the south side. And, west of the river, eager speculators carved out West Lethbridge and Westmount.

In 1912, the Alberta Town Planning Act tried to stem the rampant growth of subdivisions by outlining steps whereby municipalities could plan orderly growth. An amendment to the Land Titles Act required cities to obtain provincial approval before

82

subdividing their land. This belated government action came too late to stem the subdivision explosion. Finally, the collapse of the real estate boom in 1913 torpedoed the unrealistic development plans. Lethbridge, meanwhile, anxious to get tax dollars from those receiving its services, annexed most of the surrounding subdivisions; most reverted to the city for tax arrears and few were settled until the 1950s and 1960s.

Part of the reason for Lethbridge's unbridled expansion was the spirit of boosterism which dominated the first decade of the new century. Boosterism incorporated pride, greed, publicity seeking, and gross exaggeration in an unmitigated quest for growth. One of Lethbridge's greatest boosters was William A. Buchanan, publisher of the *Lethbridge Herald.* Buchanan scorned the sceptics or 'knockers,' and constantly reiterated the "Boost Southern Alberta" theme. He was not alone for in May 1907 a group of enthusiasts formed *The 25,000 Club* with the avowed and unchallenged purpose of boosting the city's population from 7,000 to 25,000 by 1912. Fully equal to the club's optimistic goals was the board of trade's letterhead which in 1910 boasted that Lethbridge had the advantages of:

Most up-to-date water system, finest climate
Mildest winter, most productive soil
Purest water, most progressive city
Most trees, most sunshine
Cheapest fuel, widest sidewalks
Best electric power, best schools, prize wheat
Of any place in Western Canada.

One effect of the booster's unrelenting campaign for economic growth was the early incorporation of the City of Lethbridge. Shortly after Alberta's formation as a province in 1905, the town council applied for city status. The new legislature granted it willingly and Lethbridge became a city on 9 May 1906. At first, seven councillors — one of whom was elected mayor by the others — governed the municipality but an admendment to the city charter created a commission type of government. On 1 January 1914, a commissioner of finance, who was also the mayor, a commissioner of public works, and a commissioner of utilities took office. These positions were held by W. D. L. Hardie, out-spoken, mercurial and business-like; A. M. Grace, a land surveyor who laid out the Raymond townsite and later owned a coal mine in the city; and Arthur Reid, an unimaginative but sound, dependable

Piche & Miron butchershop on Round Street (5th Street South) in 1908.

administrator. In 1917, the city abandoned its offices in the No. 1 Firehall (then called the Municipal Public building) and several nearby buildings and moved into the Chinook Club premises on the corner of 4th Avenue and 7th Street South.

The new city administration, driven by the prevailing spirit of optimism, launched the most expensive expansionary program in the city's history. In 1906, for example, it adopted the costly policy of replacing the existing three-foot (1.0 m) wide wooden sidewalks with those of four-foot (1.2 m) and then with those of eight-foot (2.4 m) widths. Less than a year later, the councillors decided to build cement walks in the downtown area. Then, in 1910, when home delivery of mail appeared imminent, the city authorized the renaming of all streets to numbered streets and avenues. This

policy, like that of the sidewalks, was council's attempt to imitate its prairie rivals.

Although agriculture was the real mainstay of Lethbridge's prosperity, its council eagerly joined the wild scramble for industries. Competing with other prairie towns and cities for the favors of the businessman, the city offered generous concessions. Its councillors usually granted free sites to developers, water and power at cost, and one or more decades of tax exemption. The first business to take advantage of the generous offer was the Lethbridge Foundry established in 1898 and reincorporated as the Lethbridge Iron Works in 1900. Following suit were the Lethbridge Brewing and Malting Company in 1901; Ellison Milling and Elevator Company, Taylor Milling and Elevator Company, and Lethbridge

TO THE MAYOR AND ALDERMEN OF THE CITY OF LETHBRIDGE

GENTLEMEN:-

WE THE UNDERSIGNED RESIDENTS OF THIS CITY,
TO PRESENT TO YOUR NOTICE THE FOLLOWING PETITION:-

WHEREAS IT IS A MATTER OF COMMON KNOWLEDGE THAT CERTAIN
HOUSES OF ILL- FAME ARE SAID TO EXIST IN OUR CITY NOTABLY
IN THE VICINITY OF THE ISOLATION HOSPITAL AND GALT HOSPITAL
SUCH A STATE OF AFFAIRS WE CONSIDER TO BE A DISGRACE TO
OUR CITY

THEREFORE WE WOULD HEREBY PETITION YOU TO DO ALL IN YOUR
POWER TOWARD CLOSING UP SUCH HOUSES AND SUPPRESSING THE
SOCIAL EVIL TO THE FULL EXTENT OF YOUR LEGAL POWER .

[Signatures follow, largely illegible handwritten names, including: Alex M Gordon, William Reid, W. S. Galbraith, Joseph Tuff, J. L. Clarke, Elizabeth McKillop, Howard Cox, Frank Chaddenew, W. A. Buchanan, C. Ross Talt, A. E. Humphries, J. S. Stewart, Jas Fisk, E. B. Hill, W. Simmons, W. R. Dobbin, J. W. McKean, James Dalrymple, J. W. Crofts, A. T. Rosain, Wm. Hansford, William Scott, John D. Higinbotham, S. J. McDiarmid, Geo. L. Vrooma, G. J. Tuff, W. Stanley Tuff, Robt M. Boak, Edwin W. Huntington, Andrew Tilley, A. McNally, A. C. Fife, Edwin Johnson, J. Rochon, A. E. Carter, D. A. Taylor, Fred Fleck, J. D. McKenzie, E. A. Sherman, Father Van Tighem O.M.I., Jos Head & Co Ltd, J. W. Davidson, F. R. F. McKitrick, and others]

Part of a 1909 petition from the Moral Reform League to City Council.

84

The Moral Reform League

The organization of the Moral Reform League in 1909 sparked greatly increased efforts to control prostitution in Lethbridge. An investigation by the Rev. W. T. Perry of Wesley Methodist Church showed that there were at least five brothels operating on The Point, with 30 inmates. Twenty-two of the women were prostitutes, while eight were female servants. There were six or seven Chinese cooks and waiters. The inmates, according to Perry, were of the hardened type, mostly foreigners. Several were blacks. Their customers were the married men of the city and not the unmarried men. Over a period of three months the number of prostitutes had increased from 18 to 22 while the larger part of the colony had changed. Perry added that no more than one-third of the prostitutes operating in the city were in the restricted area.

Mayor Elias Adams and Police Chief Joseph Gillespie believed in segregation and control of prostitution. They argued that any attempt to break up the segregated area would simply result in the prostitutes being scattered all over the city.

Perry described the problem in this way: "I have it from people living off the street leading to the district that the drunken rowdyism, obscene language, and fighting there is almost more than they can bear. It is depreciating the value of their property to say nothing of the abomination of the thing. With my own eyes in broad daylight I saw an automobile filled with half-drunken men go down Round Street [Fifth Street] and turn down Redpath [Third Avenue South]. Their loud brawling conversation was such that the men, women and children on the streets could not help but know where they were going."

In order to lessen the social evil, Mayor Adams offered:
- to make the street leading to The Point the most brilliantly lighted street in the whole city and to station a policeman there to take the names of any men going to that quarter;
- to forbid completion of a bordello then in process of construction and to prohibit the building of any additional houses of prostitution;
- to pursue a policy of discouragement toward these houses and their inmates, giving them no assurance they would escape drastic action at a later date;
- to prohibit prostitutes from other places from entering and residing in the city.

It was all illusion. The Segregated Area operated relatively unmolested for another 35 years.

Woolen Company in 1906; Lethbridge Sash and Door in 1910; Frache Brothers, Terrill's Floral, Columbia Macaroni Company, and the Purity Bottling Works in 1913; and, the Hygienic and Crystal dairies in 1914. The obsession with factories was partly due to the abundance of coal buried beneath the soil but more influential was the generally held belief that only industrial economies could be truly wealthy.

Lethbridge signed its largest incentive agreement in May 1905. To lure the CPR's divisional point from Macleod to Lethbridge, the city offered the company a 20-year tax exemption on 120 acres (48.6 ha) of land, and 200,000 gallons (756 800 L) of water daily at cost. In return the CPR agreed to spend at least $50,000 on a union station, railyards, roundhouse, machine shops, and freight sheds. As an outgrowth of this deal the CPR commenced construction on a railway viaduct across the Belly River. Completed in 1909, this structure became the longest viaduct in Canada. It reduced the length of the Crownest line between Lethbridge and Macleod, eliminated excessive curves and steep grades into the valley, and enabled the railway to carry full loads.

In making these generous industrial concessions, Lethbridge seriously weakened its financial position. Because the city was centrally located in an agricultural area, it probably would have attracted the processing factories and the divisional point anyway. The woolen mill was the only real catch, a prize taken from Medicine Hat. While the policy may have occasioned the growth so ardently desired, it came at a heavy cost to the home owner and small businessman. By 1913, one-third of assessed city property was tax exempt. This erosion of the tax base was accompanied by heavy spending on facilities for the new industries. The growing gap between revenues and expenditures eventually caused serious financial difficulties.

The rapid expansion of industrial and rail facilities, for example, strained the city's water supply. The pumps, installed in

Opium

In the early years of this century, the drug of choice among street people was opium or laudanum, an infusion of opium in alcohol. Opium was used by some members of the Chinese community while the prostitutes of The Point tended to use laudanum, occasionally by overdose for suicide.

Opium was smuggled into the city by courier. For example, in December 1910 a headline read: "Detective Pat Egan Grabs Suspicious Celestial Who Lands in Lethbridge With Seven Tins of Opium."

The news item reported, "Seven tins of opium were found in the possession of a Chinaman named Wong who arrived in the city on the 12:35 train last night from Vancouver. Wong got off the train carrying a small grip. Detective Pat Egan of the city force, who was standing close by, immediately became suspicious of the grip, and walking up to the Chinaman asked if he might see what was in it. The Chinaman refused and the detective, showing him his authority, demanded to see what it contained. Wong immediately thrust his hand into his pocket, found the key and threw it away, whereupon Detective Egan immediately arrested him . . . Wong is a big Celestial, nearly six feet tall, and a rough house was started outside the depot inside a few minutes. He was very game, and put up a hard fight for freedom, but the detective in the end overpowered him and started for the police station. On the way Sergeant Silliker joined them and Wong was soon in the cells . . . The usual search being made, both of Wong and the bag, seven tins of opium each weighing about half a pound were found in the grip, while Wong had $95 on his person, besides the drug which is worth $15 a tin . . . The Celestial is an isolated smuggler. As far as the police can ascertain, he has no relatives in Lethbridge to whom he was bringing the opium but it is thought that he would not have had any difficulty in disposing of his goods if he had escaped the police.

"All Chinks Must Move"

"The Chinese laundrymen in Lethbridge feel as if they have been ordered off the earth, for all of them that don't move from their present locations to the part of the city west of Smith Street [4th Street South] some time during the next eight days will be violating city by-law No. 83. The Celestials are much wrought up over the matter and have banded together to see if something cannot be done to amend the present by-law, which reads as follows:

" 'And for the better regulation of laundries and insuring their location in places having adequate sewer connection it is hereby provided that no laundry shall be hereafter established in that portion of the city which lies in the south of the north side of Courtland Street [6th Avenue South], to the east of the west side of Smith Street or north of Baroness Road [1st Avenue South], and any such laundry now established on any of the said streets shall cease to be maintained thereon from and after the 31st day of December, A.D. 1910.'

"This is a part of the city by-law which is 'respecting the erection and removal of buildings, fire limits and prevention of fire,' and the part noted above was passed by the city council some months ago, at the request of residents who do not desire to have laundries in close proximity to their residences.

"The by-law means that there can be no laundries in the North Ward and that there can be none in the greater portion of the city to the south of the tracks. The designated district is not very extensive unless the Chinamen want to set up business in the coulees.

"The [white-owned] Lethbridge Steam Laundry is a few yards outside the proposed limits and will not be affected by the by-law. Practically all the Chinamen will have to move unless the by-law is amended."

--Lethbridge Daily News, 23 December 1910

Students and teacher on the steps of a Chinese school in Lethbridge in the early 1900s.

Eugene B. Ely

The first "airport" in Lethbridge was the small, grassy field enclosed by the racetrack at the Exhibition Grounds. Only two aircraft ever flew from this location, the first being operated by Eugene B. Ely in 1911, the second by Miss Katherine Stinson in 1918.

There was considerable excitement in Lethbridge on 13 July 1911 with the local paper telling citizens to "Watch Ely Fly Tomorrow At Henderson Lake Fair Grounds."

The next day the paper reported that, "Ely flew a heavier-than-air Curtiss biplane. The spot chosen for starting and landing the plane was a level spot of about 200 yards in length in the middle of the race course. Though somewhat rough in spots, it served the purpose and, by keeping the crowds back to the track, provided ample space to get the biplane started and stopped after landing. At 12 minutes to three, the crowd awaited the flight of the plane, something most of them had never seen. Many had witnessed balloon ascensions and parachute drops, which for years had been one of the big attractions at the local fair, but the sight of a man sitting in a frail aeroplane was new and interesting. Ely circled the racetrack at a height of about 400 feet, remaining in the air seven minutes on the first flight. The landing was thrilling to the crowd as Ely lined up the place, shut off the eight-cylinder motor, and glided in to a perfect landing. He said the air was 'jumpy' although at ground level all one could detect was a slight breeze from the northwest. He went on to explain that the 'air was full of holes'. The second flight lasted 13 minutes and he flew over the city this time at a speed of 40 mph."

Ely died in a plane crash in Georgia three months later.

The Village of Stafford

In 1890, the Galt company sunk a shaft on the prairie level and called it No. 3 coal mine. A settlement sprang up near the entrance and the community, called "Number Three," was brought under the Village Ordinance in 1900 as the Village of Stafford. This was done at the instigation of Dr. L. George DeVeber, Medical Health Officer, because the settlement was without a governing body or restraining influence, quarantine regulations could not be enforced, and provisions of the Health Ordinance were not properly observed.

Almost from the beginning, villagers wanted to be annexed by Lethbridge. City Council was not enthusiastic, pointing out in 1913 that bonded indebtedness of the village was about $25,000 against an assessment of only $200,000.

A series of errors and a little bluff made annexation possible. In 1908, the city amended its charter to extend city limits. A mistake was made in printing the legislation, the city being shown in township 10 instead of in township 9. When the first mistake was corrected, a line of type was left out in printing the second amended charter and, hence, 80 acres (32.4 ha) of North Lethbridge were not included in the city limits. Nevertheless, taxes were collected on this property, some $7,000 in all. The village council discovered this and, when their 1912 annexation bid was rejected, persuaded residents to demand a refund. Also, the village threatened to apply to the province to add 3,600 acres (1478 ha) to its land area; successful applications in 1901 and 1911 made the city believe it might happen. Because the city had little money for tax refunds, and in view of the administrative headache of an enlarged village on its northern limits, Mayor W. D. L. Hardie decided to support annexation. Consequently, at the 1913 sitting of the Legislature a new charter was requested as well as an amendment to the old, city limits were changed, and the Village of Stafford became part of the City of Lethbridge.

GEO.O.KERR D.J.WHIVEY J.F.RODGERS W.B.BURNELL E.A.CUNNINGHAM T.S.MACKENZIE GEO.HOOK GEO.HATCH J.W.MCNICOL W.H.FAIRFIELD W.OLIVER W.A.HULTON

CHIEF ONE-SPOT CHIEF LITTLE-PLUME CHIEF BULL-PLUME CHIEF MANY-WHITE-HORSES CHIEF BULL HORN CHIEF LITTLE EAR CHIEF OLD WOMAN HEAD-CHIEF CROP-EARRED-WOLF HEAD-CHIEF BUTCHER CHIEF RUNNING-ANTELOPE

Fair Board directors and Blood and Peigan Indian chiefs at Lethbridge in 1910.

89

George "Steamboat Bill" Messmer

George "Steamboat Bill" Messmer, a well-known character of early Lethbridge, got his nickname from working on the Missouri River steamboats. He was born in Sun River, Pennsylvania, in 1848 and came west to Montana in early manhood. After his stint in the river boats, he came to southern Alberta in the early 1880s and got a job as a bull whacker with I. G. Baker and Company, freighting out of Fort Macleod. He gained the reputation of being one of the best drivers on the trail and could handle a team of ten span of oxen with ease. From the early 1890s, he worked in the mines at Lethbridge or, more often as he grew older, as a sheepherder. He owned a succession of sheep dogs, all named "Ring," which accompanied him everywhere.

From the 1890s into the 1910s, Steamboat, as he was usually called, often indulged a king-sized thirst and frequently appeared in magistrate's court on drunk and disorderly charges. He was usually jailed overnight and paid a $5.00 fine in the morning. However, in November 1903 and likely on other occasions, he was jailed for 40 days on an assault charge. On 10 December, the day of his release, he got drunk, got into a fight, was escorted to the station by the police and was put aboard the first departing train. But like the bad penny, he soon returned. What got Steamboat Bill into trouble was a wild temper and a willingness to take on anyone anywhere, regardless of size or numbers, whenever he had a few drinks. His remedy for the cuts, scrapes and bruises he received in these encounters was to daub them with axle grease, an abundant commodity at the time, which could be obtained from "Curly" Whitney's Livery Stable on Redpath Street (3rd Avenue South).

Steamboat Bill died in April 1927 at age 79, his earlier escapades forgotten. All Lethbridgians mourned the death of yet another pioneer, one who was typical of a West that was passing — rough, rugged, big-hearted, and independent.

1904 at a cost of $130,000, were soon inadequate, resulting in several incidents of dangerously low water pressure. In 1906, the city engaged a night shift of workers to fill a 160,000-gallon (0.6 million-L) standpipe after midnight. It also installed higher capacity pumps and another standpipe. A year later, council asked the city engineer to study the feasibility of building a dam across the river but nothing came out of his report except a series of experiments with gravel dikes, wells, and diversion weirs. In 1910, the city improved the water intake and built a filtration plant. By 1916, the new facility proved so faulty that the city had to replace it with a 3.0 million-gallon (11.5 million-L) plant. To combat a persistent typhoid epidemic, the city also installed a chlorinator in the new facility. Despite these improvements not all Lethbridgians enjoyed running water. Horse-drawn tank carts delivered water to householders on the eastern outskirts, on the north side, and in Hardieville. In addition, a wagon standpipe was located on Westminster Road (13th Street) where water was sold for 50 cents per tank.

The city also had to improve its sewage disposal system because the existing plant did not conform to the provincial health act. In 1910, the city hired T. Aird Murray to design an improved facility. Murray's design did not meet the approval of provincial authorities because the storm pipes, which were separated from the industrial and domestic sewers, emptied directly into the river. However, Murray eventually won approval of his design and supervised the construction of the new system during 1911 and 1912.

The construction of three-storey buildings in the downtown core and the expansion into subdivisions strained the city's firefighting capacity. In December 1907, Fire Chief A. E. Humphries resigned because he feared that a fire department designed for a small village could not cope with fires downtown or in North Lethbridge. City council, shocked by the sudden resignation, permitted the firemen to elect their new chief, purchased new fire hoses, improved water pressure, and placed a hose and reel in a shed at Westminster School. In 1910, it enlarged Firehall No. 1, originally built in 1890, and later began construction of No. 2 Firehall on 13th Street North.

Better garbage collection also occupied the attention of city councillors. In 1908, they signed a contract with E. J. Cook as the city's first scavenger. Cook cleaned and limed about 44 outdoor privies, regularly picked up garbage, and buried or burned the dead

The Lethbridge Fair in 1912; the Seventh International Dry Farming Congress was held here in October 1912.

A bird's-eye view of Lethbridge in 1912, from a real estate brochure.

92

93

Belly vs. Oldman Rivers

Much confusion has arisen over the name of the river which flows through Lethbridge. Until 4 August 1915, it was known as the Belly River, the name being a translation of the Blackfoot *Mokowanis,* meaning paunch or belly, so-named from the resemblance of the Belly Buttes in outline to a buffalo's paunch. Around 1907-08, hydrological surveys were conducted in southern Alberta and the flow of the rivers was measured. The surveys revealed that the Oldman River, rather than the Belly River, was the main stream and the name Belly eventually was assigned to a tributary. But as early as 1886, Lethbridge citizens met to protest the name "Belly," which they said they could not use in genteel company. They wanted the river to be called either the Alberta River or the Lethbridge River. These protests continued, led by the Board of Trade, from 1909 to 1914. The protests, plus greater knowledge of streamflow, caused the Geographic Board of Canada to approve a name change from Belly to Oldman. The name was assigned because of long usage. The name of the Oldman River is a translation of the Blackfoot, *Naw-pew-ooch-a-tay-cots,* which, according to Peter Fidler, meant "The river the Old Man played upon." This changed gradually to "The Old Man's River," "The Old Man River," and finally became "The Oldman River." The literal translation of Oldman River is *Napi-tahta.* The Old Man was *Napi,* a Blackfoot deity who was the well-known trickster in legends of the tribe. He miraculously constructed a playing field near the river in the Livingstone Gap; the playing field exists and its location is known to modern archaeologists.

animals found in the coulees or around the city. Gradually, garbage collection became the city scavenger's main function. Although council had discussed an incinerator plant as early as 1901, garbage was generally deposited in various 'nuisance grounds' in nearby coulees. After 1912, the favourite was a coulee immediately south of the brewery, today a roadway called the Third Avenue Extension.

The rapid growth of Lethbridge in the first decades of the century also forced the city to expand its electrical generating facilities. In July 1908, the city bought the plant and distribution facilities of the Lethbridge Electric Light Company, a private utility. This plant burned down on 1 January 1910 causing a lengthy blackout in the city. Fortunately, the AR&ICo's generators from Galt Mines Nos. 3 and 6 could be connected to the city's water pumps and the domestic water supply was quickly restored. The fire was not a serious loss because the city was already building a new power plant on the river bottom next to the pumphouse, but it did have to order a new boiler and generator. The move was particularly wise because a year earlier the city had opened two drift mine entrances on its coal properties near the projected power plant. The City Mine, which operated until 1941, supplied the powerhouse generators with cheap fuel enabling the city to sell electric power for as little as two cents per kilowatt-hour or at flat rates of $13 to $21 per horsepower per year and still earn a profit.

Not all of city council's expenditures had such beneficial results. Sometimes the spirit of optimism beclouded their practical judgment. Although the city was blessed with an abundance of cheap coal, councillors desired the convenience, cleanliness and reliability of natural gas. In July 1906, council signed a contract with the Lethbridge Electric Light Company to drill for gas. The electric company hired James Peat & Sons to drill a 2,000-foot (610-m) well in the yard of the Music Conservatory on 5th Avenue South. Peat commenced the work in December 1906 and by the following September reached the 1,375-foot (420-m) mark. At 2,935 feet (620 m) the company had still not found any gas and it abandoned the effort. Instead, the city asked Calgary's Canadian Western Natural Gas, Light, Heat and Power Company to supply Lethbridge with natural gas from the Bow Island field. Work on the high pressure gas lines began on 13th Street in the summer of 1912.

The most flagrant way in which the city councillors allowed the prevailing spirit of optimism to affect their better judgment was in the matter of a street railway system. Talk of constructing a streetcar system first surfaced in 1906 and re-emerged in 1909. By 1910 the project had reached committee stage and by the end of the following year tenders worth almost $200,000 were being called. The proposed system consisted of five lines radiating from the downtown core: the Blue and Red lines to North Lethbridge and Henderson Park respectively, the White and Orange lines to the southside residential area, and the Yellow line to a small downtown area. On 16 August 1912, Mayor George Hatch opened the first 11 miles (17 km) of track. The ceremony coincided with the annual fair being held at the new Exhibition Grounds at Henderson Park. But, on an early trip with street cars, half way to the fair, a temporary generator burned out and the system ground to a halt. Fortunately, CPR trains were able to take over and transport the revellers to and from the fairgrounds every half hour.

The first day's misfortunes were prophetic. Lethbridge's small population could not support the expensive transportation system and as the city's growth stagnated after the collapse of the great boom, the council had to take drastic economizing measures. It discontinued the Yellow Line almost as soon as it was built and in 1917 abandoned the Orange Line, one of the southside residential arteries. Earlier, in 1914, it had reduced the staff in each car from two men to one man and several months later dismissed all the remaining streetcar employees, then rehired them at lower wages. Unhappily, the firings coincided with other civic layoffs and sparked considerable unrest. Vandals cut several cables at the power plant and caused other damage. The happy days of growth, prosperity, and optimism came to a rude and harsh end.

The last fling of the era of optimism was the Seventh International Dry Farming Congress. Held simultaneously with the Second International Congress of Farm Women and the International Conference of Agricultural Colleges, it was, according to the Alberta department of agriculture, the largest gathering of agricultural experts and farmers ever assembled in North America. Representatives came from 15 foreign countries, including China and Persia. All hotel rooms, private billets, temporary dormitories and even tents were required to house the 5,000 delegates in the city of 8,400 citizens. It was the ultimate exercise in boosterism.

The Dry Farming Congress, which had as its aim the promotion of dry farming through lectures, exhibits, and interchange of ideas, generated much publicity for the city. As early as November 1911,

Major Alvin Ripley, postmaster, and his family in 1914. Ripley was C.O., 20th Field Battery CFA. and was killed in action in May 1917.

Congress staff arrived in Lethbridge and for the next 11 months churned out more than 800 items and feature articles on dry farming to newspapers and magazines all over the world. The advance publicity and the conference popularized the name of Lethbridge and fulfilled the wildest hopes of the city's boosters.

The Congress did not come without a heavy cost, however. Although local businessmen, surrounding municipalities, the

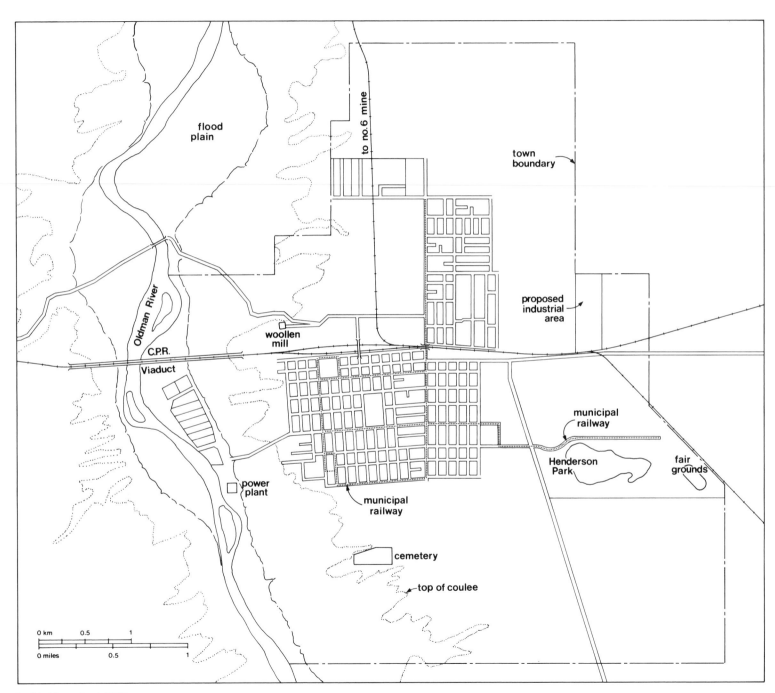

flood
plain

to no.6 mine

town
boundary

Oldman River

C.P.R.
Viaduct

woollen
mill

proposed
industrial
area

municipal
railway

Henderson
Park

fair
grounds

power
plant

municipal
railway

cemetery

top of coulee

0 km   0.5   1

0 miles   0.5   1

Lethbridge, about 1915.

railways, and the governments of Alberta, Saskatchewan, Manitoba, and Canada contributed to the expense, city council assumed a heavy financial burden. Lethbridge spent about $1.5 million on various civic improvements, including the paving of downtown streets, the construction of the 9th Street overpass, the streetcar system, the water filtration plant, improvements to the sewage disposal system, and landscaping and building of several structures and a grandstand at the Henderson Park Exhibition Grounds. These heavy financial commitments aroused considerable opposition. Worried that a small city could not afford the extravagance of such a large conference and could not possibly successfully organize it, a former mayor, six-foot four-inch Elias "Shorty" Adams, lashed out at the city engineer, charging him with incompetence and inefficiency. As money bylaw after money bylaw came before city council, uneasiness spread throughout the city and tempers flared. City councillors even threatened to sue each other. The Municipal police force went on strike — probably the first police strike in Canada — just before the Congress, but Pinkerton detectives and management managed to maintain law and order.

Boosterism, fueled by the aura of optimism, produced unprecedented growth and expansion. It greatly enlarged the boundaries of Lethbridge, sparked a huge public works program, and attracted industry and railways. It also encouraged reckless deficit spending teamed with lenient tax exemptions. The consequence was an unmanageable municipal debt. While in 1906, the burden stood at $175,000, six years later it had mushroomed to $2,515,676. Repayment of this staggering debt was virtually impossible for the small community, especially after the economic downturn in 1913. Within two years, city debentures dropped to 75 percent of their face value and often could not be sold at all. The Bank of Montreal even refused to extend credit to the school board. Meanwhile the city held more than $600,000 in uncollectable bills, all of them eventually discarded. These financial problems were not resolved until 1928 with the establishment of a city manager form of civic government.

Although costly, the optimistic expansionism transformed Lethbridge from a single resource coal town into a railway, service and distribution centre. By the end of the first decade, CPR spur lines connected the brewery, wholesale houses, plants and mills, and farm implement dealers, as well as the coal mines to the central mainline. An overpass at 9th and a level crossing at 21st Street,

both built in 1911, and a subway at 13th Street, completed in 1915, provided access to the industries and residences of North Lethbridge. Also in 1915, the CPR yielded its old Crowsnest right-of-way to the city enabling it to replace the Six-Mile Coulee Road, the main south and southeastern approach since the 1880s, with the Southeast Entrance road. A year later, the railway and city swapped their right-of-way on the Macleod road so that the city could build a better road crossing under the second span of the CPR bridge and then down a different coulee to the river. These major transportation arteries completed the transformation of Lethbridge into a commercial and marketing centre. By 1915, the wholesale district was in place, the downtown core was completed, and industrial development was at an end. Not until after the Second World War would Lethbridge experience an equally exuberant period of expansion and optimism.

Just before the economic boom, which marked the first decade of the twentieth century, collapsed, the federal government commenced construction of an imposing post office. The building of the post office owed much to C. A. Magrath, Member of Parliament from 1908-1911, who engaged in bitter debate with the Hon. W. Pugsley — "the unspeakable Pugsley" — minister responsible for post offices, forcing him to agree to build a post office at Lethbridge even though the city was represented by a member of the Opposition. The west and north elevations of the new edifice were expensively faced with stone cut from quarries at Tyndal, Manitoba. Completed late in 1914, the building provided space for post office, customs and other federal services. In 1916, the government installed a clock in the tower. The elaborate structure, grandiose in design, became a prominent landmark and a source of pride to Lethbridgians. It was a fitting symbol of the prosperity and optimism which had dominated the previous 15 years.

Downtown Lethbridge in 1921.

Chapter Six

Portents of a City

Undoubtedly, the first few years of the twentieth century were happy years for Lethbridgians. Bounteous crops, plentiful jobs, and good wages created prospects of a bright future which seemingly would never end. As Lethbridge continued to grow beyond all expectations, its boosters took great pride at the appearance of city trappings. "We have outgrown town clothes," the Lethbridge *Herald* asserted in 1906, "and are sufficiently certain of future growth to don the garb of a city and strut about in the company of Calgary and Edmonton." The *Herald's* statement embodied the confident, swaggering optimism so typical of the early decades of the twentieth century. It also reflected the vibrant dynamics of a young society wishing to be mature and grown-up. Lethbridge, the editor implied, had entered the century of urbanization and industrialization. Although he may not have been fully aware that the portents of the city he so proudly noted also signalled the start of a dramatic period of change and transition, nevertheless, his optimistic claim indicated that Lethbridge was no longer a small isolated coal town; it displayed some of the marks of a city. Modern means of communication tied it into the culture and commerce of the outside world. Being part of the world community would profoundly affect Lethbridge society.

A clear signal that Lethbridge had stepped into the modern industrial world was the miners' strike of 1906. The rising prices which were a natural outgrowth of the overheated economy, caused considerable discontent among a large majority of Lethbridge's workers. In February, believing that their earnings were not keeping pace with inflation, the miners of the Galt and Ashcroft collieries sought to increase their earnings and decrease their working hours by joining the United Mine Workers of America. Only a month later, they presented the AR&ICo with a list of demands. The company rejected them and on 9 March 1906 the union called a strike. Initially, the strike was peaceful but when the company hired about 100 men to keep the mine operative, the situation deteriorated rapidly. Several times during the hot summer, angry miners and their wives attacked policemen protecting the strikebreakers; on two occasions explosives damaged the homes of workers.

By the end of the summer, the strike had reached a stalemate and intervention was necessary to prevent a coal famine later that winter. Lethbridge's city council and its board of trade tried to arbitrate but met with little success. Next the government of Saskatchewan, fearing a fuel shortage, pressured the dominion government to act. The federal government was receptive to intervention because a coal famine would seriously hurt immigration to the prairies. It sent its senior mediator, W. L. Mackenzie King, to find a settlement. By alternately cajoling and bullying the workers, King brought about an accord and the mines reopened on 6 December 1906.

The long and bitter strike resulted in few immediate gains. The men won a small wage increase and the right of collective bargaining, but because the company refused to collect union dues from the men's wages, they failed to win union recognition. The disappointment left a bitter legacy; similar lengthy strikes broke out in 1922 and 1924, lasting five and seven months respectively.

Another of the marks of urban status was the racial discrimination which reared its head after 1906. Sometimes it took a subtle form as in January 1909, when city council ordered its engineer to employ English-speaking workers in preference to foreigners. At other times, racism became more ugly and violent. On Christmas Day 1907, for example, Harry Smith quarreled with a Chinese waiter in the Columbia Restaurant. The waiter, greatly provoked, attacked Smith with a hammer. Although the police managed to end the matter before anyone was hurt, the rumor that Smith had been killed spread like wildfire. A mob descended on the restaurant and wrecked it. The rioters were about to vandalize adjoining property when Mayor W. S. Galbraith arrived and, with the aid of the mounted police, dispersed them. Later, in an open display of racial feelings, North Ward ratepayers and Round Street merchants asked city council to ban Chinese laundries and restaurants from their neighborhoods. Anti-oriental feelings crystalized in November 1910 with a by-law restricting Chinese laundries to an area west of Smith (4th Street) and south of Ford (2nd Avenue), a district which became known as the Restricted

The Chobator Case

Harold G. Long, general manager of the Lethbridge Herald, once said that *The Lethbridge Daily News* ran into trouble over a story about Lethbridge's first hanging — one Wasyl Chobator — and had to close up.

We have not been able to determine what the *Daily News* wrote about the Chobator case that was instrumental in its demise. The case seemed straight-forward enough. On a night in May 1910 Chobator lay in wait for Alex Lazaruk, whom he knew would pass there on his way home from work at Galt No. 6 mine. Lazaruk was shot three times but lived long enough to identify his assailant. The motive was Chobator's infatuation with Lazaruk's wife. Chobator readily confessed to the crime and, at the October 1910 sitting of the Supreme Court of Alberta, was found guilty of murder by Chief Justice H. Harvey and sentenced to be hanged on 14 January 1911. Chobator was confined in a cell in the RNWMP Barracks Square and was hanged on a gallows erected in one of the barns. His execution went off without a hitch, Chobator walking unassisted the 150 yards from his cell to the gallows. The body was placed in a coffin in quicklime and was buried in the seven-foot pit already dug under the gallows to permit adequate distance for the drop.

It was Lethbridge's first and only execution. The Provincial Gaol was built five miles east of the city in 1911 and the next hanging, that of James Carlson on 15 June 1912, took place there. Seventeen more men followed Carlson to the gallows at Lethbridge before capital punishment ended in 1976.

Area. The racial by-law remained in force until 1916. By then, the First World War had changed the target and people of German descent suffered from physical assaults and verbal abuse.

The Great War had an enormous effect upon Lethbridge society. It was the first industrialized war, a vast slaughter house made possible by modern factories, railways and machine guns. Men were killed almost as fast as they could be replaced. Canada, which prided itself on its loyalty to the British flag, the British king, and the British empire, immediately rallied to the cause. More than 66,000 Canadians died and 155,000 were wounded, the greatest proportional sacrifice of any combatant nation. The war, with its terrible casualties, affected all of Canadian society: it transformed the country from an agricultural, rural society into an industrial, urban nation. It forced Canada into greater maturity; the country took a major step toward nationhood at Vimy Ridge.

Lethbridge had been the headquarters of the 25th Battery, Canadian Field Artillery (CFA), since 1908 when Major John Smith Stewart raised the unit. Major Stewart, who had served under Colonel Sam Steele in the Boer War, rose rapidly in rank to become a Brigadier General, the most senior military officer to come from Lethbridge. At the outbreak of the war, the 25th mobilized as the 20th Overseas Battery CFA under Major Alvin Ripley, the local postmaster. Other artillery units raised in Lethbridge were the 39th Battery CFA under Major A. B. Stafford; the 61st Battery CFA; and the 78th Battery, a depot battery which did not leave Canada. Still other groups raised in Lethbridge included "A" Company of the 31st Alberta Battalion, and elements of the 50th Battalion and the 13th Canadian Mounted Rifles. Also recruited locally was the 113th Battalion, Lethbridge Highlanders. As well, the city established a home guard, whose chief responsibility appeared to be to guard the CPR bridge.

Lethbridge paid a high price in the war. Many of its citizens were British-born; consequently, many young men volunteered for active service. By November 1916, 1,875 Lethbridgians had joined the armed forces, representing about 20 percent of the city's population — the largest percentage enlistment for any city in Canada. In total, about 2,600 men and some women served in the armed forces during the war; 261 of them died in action. All young, healthy, and active, they left a gaping hole in Lethbridge society.

A large number of organizations in Lethbridge tried to ease the soldiers' return to civilian life. When the wounded began to come back to Lethbridge in 1917 from the Battle of the Somme, for example, a variety of Soldier's Welcome Home Committees sprang up. As early as 1917, the Great War Veteran's Association, later the Royal Canadian Legion, asked city council for clubrooms. In June 1919, the city obtained title to the old Dominion Land Office and leased it to the legion at a token rate.

Despite the many organizations, integration into civilian life remained a difficult task. The government treated the veterans poorly. Volunteers had been promised back their jobs upon

Union Station, Lethbridge 1906. Built to serve the Canadian Pacific, Alberta Railway & Irrigation Company, and Great Northern railways.

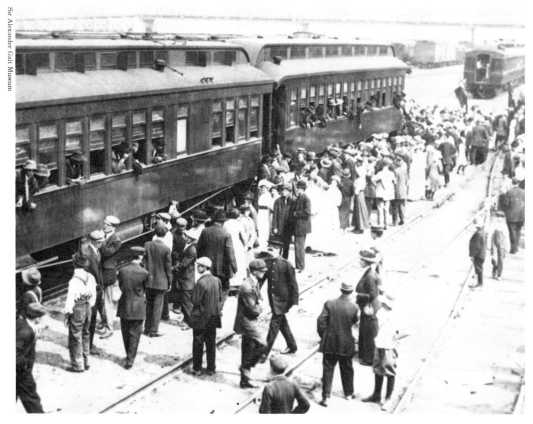

Volunteers embarking at Lethbridge for service overseas in the First World War.

The first flight in Lethbridge: Eugene B. Ely's 14 July 1911 exhibition at the Fair.

demobilization but few were that fortunate. When discharged, veterans were allowed to keep their uniforms but were given only a $35 clothing allowance. They were also given a gratuity averaging about $240 to find jobs, a far cry from an expected cash bonus of up to $2,000. The Soldier's Home Tax Exemption Act forbade the eviction of wives and widows of soldiers for unpaid taxes. More helpful to those willing to farm were the various land settlement plans, such as the CPR's ready-made farms in the area east of the city, still known as the Readymade District. Those who remained in the city were less fortunate. Lethbridge's veterans and their families did not share in the prosperity from 1916 to 1919 and the late 1920s, but they participated fully in the intervening depression. Little wonder that veterans played active roles in the labour unrest in the post-war years.

The war had a profound effect upon Lethbridge society. The absence of loved ones and the appalling casualty lists created a spirit of sacrifice and community on the home front. The theme was "Patriotism and Production," which meant voluntary rationing when goods ran low or growing gardens on vacant lots when food supplies dwindled. Sales of victory bonds became frequent events with lots of hoopla and flag-waving. The Exhibition Grounds came to play an important role. It served as a bivouac for troops awaiting transfer, and from September 1914 to November 1916 as a

detention camp for civilians of German and eastern European background.

Part of the sacrifice that those at home were expected to make was abstinence from alcohol. The Women's Christian Temperance Union had great success in convincing the public to institute prohibition. Alberta went dry on 1 July 1916 and remained so for the next seven years. While prohibition reduced the number of drunks and alcohol-related illnesses, curbed convictions for alcohol-related offences, and lessened wife and child beating, it did not stop the consumption of liquor. Local rum-runners and operators of speakeasies made fortunes supplying a thirsty and determined public. Eventually, the open flaunting of the law, the loss of tax revenues and public pressure, especially from war veterans, forced governments to change their minds. Lifting prohibition in 1923 was greeted with great pleasure by Fritz Sick who had been forced to rent his brewery's cold storage facilities to wholesale grocery houses during prohibition. The madams of the Point also cheered the end of prohibition. Although they had continued to operate illegal speakeasies, their supply of bootlegged liquor was often uncertain, usually of dubious quality, and always overpriced.

While the advocates of moral reform had successfully used wartime patriotism to introduce prohibition, they had failed to stamp out prostitution. By 1920, Lethbridge's brothels had

No. 1 Firehall in May 1914, called the Municipal Public Building until 1917.

103

gradually moved from the infamous Point to an area bounded by 1st and 5th Avenues and 1st and 4th Streets South. Known as the Segregated Area, the district was wide open, it represented the golden age of prostitution in Lethbridge, and it was the main tourist attraction in the city until 1944.

Chlorination of Domestic Water Supply

The first waterworks in Lethbridge, built in 1903, consisted of a pumping station, a few miles of pipe, and two 160,000-gallon (605 000-L) standpipes to give adequate water pressure. Water was taken from the river in a raw state, charitably described as "gravel strained". The system worked well enough until February 1916 when a persistent typhoid epidemic broke out in the city.

It was later determined that there had been about 20 cases of typhoid in Macleod in November-December 1915. Macleod dumped its raw sewage into the Oldman River, where it settled to the bottom of the slow moving stream or froze on the surface of the ice. In February, after an unseasonably warm spell, the river rose, the ice broke up and the winter sewage, containing billions of typhoid-causing "colon bacillus," headed towards Lethbridge.

At Lethbridge, it was pumped into the domestic water supply and, in about ten days, people started coming down with typhoid fever. By 3 March, there were 60 cases and new cases were being reported at a rate of two per day.

By 9 March, there were a few cases of typhoid among troops of the 113th Battalion, then recruiting in the city, in barracks at the Exhibition Grounds. The Medical Officer, Captain G. W. Leech, was sufficiently concerned to convert the vacant Dominion Land Office building into a military hospital and to obtain 30 hospital gowns from the IODE for use of patients at the barracks.

The immediate response of city officials was to chlorinate the domestic water supply, the first such treatment in the city's history. Later, a 2.8 million-gallon (10.6 million-L) filtration plant was built, becoming operational in 1917.

The prostitutes managed to thwart the attacks by moral reform groups because they enjoyed the support of the business community, city council, and the police. As early as the 1890s, the mounted police had insisted on a segregated red light district as the only way to control prostitution in a masculine mining and ranching society. City council reaffirmed this position in 1909 when a large delegation of citizens representing the Social and Moral Reform League asked for a ban on houses of ill-repute. Council replied that, "we cannot suggest any remedy at present for the state of affairs supposed to exist, but the matter will have consideration in due course." With variations, this remained council's stock answer for the next 35 years. The reason for its stand was clear. On New Year's Eve 1912, Chief of Police W. B. Davis led the first raid of any consequence on the red light district, closed the houses, and ordered the prostitutes out of town. Within days, local businessmen complained that trade had suffered; the prostitutes were soon back in operation. Mayor W. D. L. Hardie, an apologist for the policy, later explained that as long "as regulations were not broken and it was of benefit to the town, [segregation] helped to keep the rest of the city clean." The only effect of the pressure from the Ministerial Association and the Moral Reform League was the institution of regular medical check-ups for the prostitutes and control of their movements and visibility. The ladies were permitted downtown only on one day per week and delivery boys had to bring them toiletries and medicinal supplies and mail their letters.

Inevitably, the segregation policy sparked charges against Lethbridge's small police force. In August 1912, Police Chief Joseph Gillespie, Inspector Leslie Silliker, and Detective Pat Egan were suspended for improperly receiving money from keepers of disorderly houses. Although a judicial inquiry exonerated Gillespie, the city nevertheless dismissed him and Silliker. Mayor Hardie noted in the margin of the September council minutes, "There is nothing very serious against Mr. Gillespie in Judge Winter's report. All that is proved could happen to the most honest and honourable of men." Authorities continued to insist that there was no problem and in 1915, the police commission dismissed out of hand charges that, "police PROTECTION was afforded to women of easy virtue for $300 to $350 [per house] per month." (Rumors in 1908 set the price of protection at $50 per house per month.) Despite local confidence in the honesty of the police force, Alberta's attorney general several times expressed grave reservations about the force, notably in 1917. That year, an undercover policeman, hired by the

His Royal Highness, Edward, Prince of Wales, with Mayor W. D. L. Hardie in Lethbridge in 1919.

mayor on the recommendation of the Royal North-West Mounted Police, located 40 active prostitutes where city police said there were none. On 18 May 1918, however, Hardie assured the board of trade that there was absolutely no truth to "insinuations of graft by the Mayor and Chief of Police."

Despite the high visibility of prostitution in Lethbridge, it was by no means the only means of public entertainment. Theatres proliferated, starting with the first crude moving pictures shown in Oliver's Hall in 1901. By 1920 the city had three theatres: the Empress, the Colonial and the Phoenix. Of these the Phoenix was the oldest, first opened in 1908 and renovated and reopened under several different names. The Empress, which had opened its doors first in 1913 in the former Salvation Army Citadel was the most popular of the three theatres, its prices were the highest, and it deliberately appealed to the women of the city. The Majestic, opened in 1910 as Griffith's Theatre, featured live performances, with such artists as Harry Lauder, the Dumbells, and other highly-rated European and American troupes. At $2.50 for a box seat and an age restriction of 16 and older, the Majestic was exclusive; it was the first theatre to show the new talkies. It frequently featured boxing and wrestling cards.

The first Chautauqua in Canada was held in Lethbridge on 7 August 1917. Chautauqua was travelling live stage performances of professional singers, actors and lecturers, all under canvas because few towns had large halls. It brought drama and glamour to rural communities until better roads and radio brought about its demise in the 1930s.

Lethbridge also hosted several dances every weekend and often in mid-week. The most popular dance hall was the Knights of Pythias Hall which held a dance every weekend and admitted ladies free of charge. It often featured Lethbridge's favorite band, the Cannoneers, a jazz group. Other dance spots included the new Exhibition Hall and the Masonic Hall. Other forms of entertainment, such as the radio, lessened the popularity of public dances and by the end of the decade their frequency had begun to dwindle.

Amateur entertainment remained an important feature of Lethbridge society. By 1910, the city had a Music Conservatory and in 1916, Edith Fanny Kirk, a graduate of the Royal Academy, who emigrated to Canada at age 60, became Lethbridge's first instructor in the visual arts. Gladys Attree, an exceptionally tall woman who had to dance male roles after training with the Russian ballet, taught dance classes. Ernest G. Sterndale-Bennett founded the Lethbridge Playgoers Club in 1923, and the Alberta and the Dominion Drama Festivals by 1932. Southminster United was a popular location for amateur variety and musical shows.

The library became an important social institution in Lethbridge. Plans for a library dated back to 1886 and in 1890 the Alberta Railway and Coal Company's Employees' Reading Room and Library Society was formed. Two totally different organizations grew out of this society, the Lethbridge Miners' Library Club, a social club, and the Lethbridge Public Library.

Radio revolutionized communications and entertainment in the 1920s. Jock Palmer experimented with radio equipment in Lethbridge in the early 1920s and, on 9 January 1925, made his first formal transmission with Harold G. Long as announcer. Palmer obtained a licence for radio station CJOC in April 1926. By 1928, the radio station had been taken over by H. R. Carson, a local businessman, for $250 and was managed by W. W. Grant, a flawed radio genius, in a penthouse atop the new Marquis Hotel. Only then did the station begin regular programming. The station became a popular form of family entertainment, playing a variety of programs from drama to jazz. Along with the phonograph, radio permitted people to find more diversion at home, thus lessening the need for public entertainment. It tied Lethbridge into the contemporary world and hastened its modernization and Americanization.

Another successful means of keeping Lethbridge in touch with the world was the newspaper. Lethbridge's oldest paper was the weekly *Lethbridge News* published continuously since 1885. Southam Limited bought the paper in 1910 and converted it to the daily *Lethbridge Morning News*. The company stopped publishing the *News* in 1914 and substituted a weekly called the *Telegram*. (All were supporters of the Conservative party.) This paper folded in 1918 leaving Lethbridge with only one paper, the *Lethbridge Daily Herald*. F. E. Simpson, of the *Cranbrook Herald*, had founded the *Herald* in 1905 and within a month sold half an interest in the paper to William A. Buchanan. A year later, Buchanan became the full owner and the paper began to be referred to as "Buck's Bible." He turned the *Herald* into a daily evening paper in 1907, but also published a weekly edition for the next ten years. Throughout the 1920s, therefore, Lethbridge's newspaper

Grade Three, Central School, 1919.

was the *Herald,* a strong supporter of the Liberal party. For much of this period its publisher, William Buchanan, served as a senator in Ottawa.

The pages of the *Herald* reflected the quiet lifestyle of an agricultural service centre. Lethbridge was a pleasant place to live, a small city where no one needed to lock their doors, where lawyers only drew up wills, mortgages, and business agreements. Doctors made house calls and policemen walked their beat with dignity and were treated with respect. Monday morning was washday and, while some housewives might own a new-fangled electric washing machine, most made do with tub and scrub board. All of them dried the wash on clotheslines in the back yard. Meanwhile, on the dusty streets in front of the homes, small children played their seasonal games of hide-and-go-seek, kick-the-can, anti-i-over, and other

107

Frank Hamilton Mewburn

One of the most colourful figures in early Lethbridge was Dr. Frank Hamilton Mewburn, who was born at Drummondville, Upper Canada, in 1858. He was a slightly-built man, only five-foot-six and one hundred and forty pounds, skinny of limb, with a chest flat to the point of being concave. The only thing physically big about Dr. Mewburn was his magnificent walrus moustache. The spirit of the man, flashing from his steel grey eyes and crackling occasionally with eloquent abuse, more than made up for his lack of size.

Dr. Mewburn arrived in Lethbridge in December 1885 and accepted a post as Medical Officer with the North Western Coal & Navigation Company. Working from a three-bed hospital on the banks of the Belly River, he served the medical needs of the town of Lethbridge as well as the scattered farmers and ranchers of surrounding regions. He was company physician, and medical officer for the various railway and other projects of the Galts.

Although a general practitioner, he never lost his fascination for surgery. He read, studied, and made periodic trips to one or another of the great medical clinics of the time. In 1893, he performed the first successful appendectomy west of Winnipeg. Meantime, Lethbridge hospitals progressed from three, to 35, then 100 beds, the name changed from the Terrace Hospital to the Galt Hospital, and the Galt School of Nursing was established.

In 1913, Dr. Mewburn decided to move to Calgary and to specialize in surgery. However, the First World War broke out in 1914 and he enlisted as a major, later winning promotion to lieutenant colonel. In 1921, he was called to Edmonton and asked to head the newly-created Department of Surgery at the University of Alberta. He died in January 1929.

Lethbridgians enjoyed informal sports like football, cricket, tennis, lawn bowling, and lacrosse. The city also fielded several excellent local football teams, including the Sons of England, Caledonians, St. Andrews, and the Overseas Club. A composite team was runner-up in the Dominion championship in 1912, losing to Fort William. In the 1920s, football tended to give way to baseball, a reflection of the large numbers of Americans moving into the area and the influence of such stars as Babe Ruth. Although the first annual five-mile (8.0-km) Herald Road Race was run on 11 May 1913, it soon became an annual Thanksgiving Day event and was reduced to three miles (5.0 km). Other annual sporting events included the Trades and Labour Council's sports day and those of the various schools.

Traditionally, Lethbridgians used the Square, today's Galt Gardens, as the sporting grounds. But, in 1906, the city plowed and seeded grass on the square, planted spindly trees around its periphery, and constructed cinder paths. On 7 November 1910, it formally acquired all of the property, except for a 200-foot (61-m) square reserve, from Elliott Galt with the stipulation that it be maintained in perpetuity as a park. Successive councils tried vainly to get title to the reserve as a site for a theatre, courthouse, post office, city hall, or a war memorial. In 1926, the CPR finally transferred its title to the city, which built a war memorial there in 1931.

Sporting activities shifted to the Athletic Park, later called Eckstorm Park, at 3rd Street and 7th Avenue South. A second park was located at 10th Avenue and 13th Street South. Called Queen Victoria Park, it served as the Agricultural Fair grounds from 1897 to 1910. In 1910, the city bought 10 acres (4.0 ha) from the AR&ICo in North Lethbridge and turned it into Adams Park.

On the same day in March 1910, Lethbridge purchased 280 acres (113 ha) of AR&ICo land surrounding Slaughterhouse Slough, southeast of the city limits. This tract became Henderson Lake Park, the linchpin of the city park system. In 1911, the Exhibition moved there and in 1912 it hosted the Seventh International Dry Farming Congress. The city commenced an aggressive building program including a grandstand, race track, and other facilities. It dammed the slough, built a footbridge near the west and, and enlarged, levelled, and eventually concreted some of the shoreline. To encourage swimmers, the Rotary Club built an artificial beach

impromptu activities. The older ones were busy with homework and chores. Crime and juvenile delinquency was rare and when discovered was quickly and decisively punished.

Boys skinny-dipping at the "Old swimming Hole," Oldman River, ca. 1920s.

John Ender (Jock) Palmer DCM, AFC, about 1918.

later Lethbridge's showman mayor, and J. B. DeGuerre, known as "D the Tailor", in 1924, located their pavilion and dance hall in the park. As a result of all these activities, the park became a major recreation facility and popular gathering place for the community. All the school sports days, for example, were held in Henderson Park.

The park and the sports scene reflected the growing sophistication of the city's society. The more affluent Lethbridgians began to play golf in 1906, and in 1913 organized the Country Club Syndicate, which built the first golf course east of the provincial jail at the corner of the Coaldale and McLean School roads. About 1916, the Hudson's Bay Company Athletic Club surrendered its course south of Henderson Lake to the city. The new facility, called Henderson Lake Golf Course, was still relatively exclusive. To control trespassing, council leased the course to club members and the Hudson's Bay Company boathouse became part of the first clubrooms. In 1919, the Sunshine Golf Course was located in the vicinity of the modern Collegiate Institute.

A much less successful facility was the YMCA, which was dedicated to the physical and moral fitness of all classes but especially young single men. Established in Lethbridge in 1910, the YMCA had a very checkered career; it was taken over by the city and other organizations on several occasions for failing to pay tax, water and light bills.

Still close to its agricultural roots, Lethbridge enjoyed its annual rodeo, holding the first one in 1904 as part of the annual fair. Although Lethbridge had a regular racetrack from 1891, horse racing had been a popular diversion from the early 1880s. Pari-mutuel betting machines, or "Iron bookies" began to be used at the fairgrounds in 1914.

Winter also presented many opportunities for sport. In 1893, Lethbridge curlers played on two sheets of ice near the boarding houses north of the railway, and in 1906, Lethbridge Curlers Limited moved the sport to four sheets of ice off 4th Avenue near 13th Street South. In 1923, the city helped build the Lethbridge Ice Arena, at 2nd Avenue and 12th A Street South. An open-air skating rink, the Crystal Rink, was located on 3rd Avenue between 12th and 13th Street South.

Just as Lethbridge paid close attention to pleasant recreational facilities, it also built a good public health system. Under the

while the city erected changing rooms. For some years, council maintained a small zoo which featured two bears in a pit and an eagle in a cage, but in 1915 the city shipped the bears back to Banff National Park — or so the authorities said! (Actually the bears were shot and skinned in the city.) In 1913, Joseph Gillespie, ex-chief of police, built a teahouse, docks, and other conveniences. Boaters organized an active aquatics club and in the summer of 1914, regular band concerts began and continued until the 1930s. The Lethbridge Amusement Company, organized by A. W. Shackleford,

GREETING

via the First Canadian Air Mail Plane

from LETHBRIDGE, ALBERTA

The Little City With The Big Future

Capt. J. E. Palmer
Ottawa
Ont.
Can

Aviator on Airplane
"Lethbridge"

A war surplus Curtis JN4, or "Jenny," only equipment of the Lethbridge Aircraft Co. of Harry Fitzsimmons and J. E. (Jock) Palmer, July 1921. This plane was used in an abortive international air mail flight in June 1922.

Official opening of Rotary Beach, Henderson Lake Park, 16 June 1926.

112

leadership of Mayor Galbraith, a physician, council passed a public health by-law in 1907 which served as a model for later provincial legislation. The by-law was essential to help curb the endemic outbreaks of virulent contagious diseases such as smallpox, typhoid, measles, diptheria, chicken pox, scarlet fever, and whooping cough in the pre-antibiotics and immunization period. Tuberculosis was a dreaded illness; child mortality was high and old age a privilege attained by few. Dr. Galbraith established the first isolation hospital in rented quarters on the Point but subsequently moved it into a house near the public cemetery. In 1929, the hospital moved to a 16-bed brick building at 1902-7th Avenue South, where it remained until no longer needed in 1955. Galbraith also established a Municipal Board of Health.

Galt Hospital provided regular hospital facilities. Founded in 1891 by Sir Alexander Galt, on the site of the 1886 three-bed Terrace Hospital, it had been managed by the city since 1903. In 1909, Elliott Galt donated $30,000, matched by the city, for the construction of a brick addition, bringing the capacity of the hospital to 65 beds. Sir Wilfrid Laurier opened the new addition in September 1910. That same year, the hospital established a training school for nurses. In 1912, Elliott Galt turned the hospital over to the city, which incorporated the institution, and became a permanent trustee to oversee the election of a board of management.

Galt Hospital did not treat all the sick in Lethbridge. The chronically ill, tuberculosis patients, mentally handicapped children and emotionally disturbed adults were usually transferred to specialized institutions elsewhere in the province. In 1909, Mrs. Elizabeth Van Haarlem set up a two-bed maternity hospital in her home, and in 1910, Grace Dainty operated a small private hospital at 244-15th Street North. Another private facility was the Wimpole Private Hospital, established in 1911. A nursing mission, formed in 1914, distributed mothers' allowance, provided home care, sheltered neglected children, and distributed milk and hampers among the needy. A children's shelter was set up in 1921.

These various institutions still could not cope with the pernicious contagious diseases which periodically swept through the community. Late in 1918, a killing influenza (popularly called the Spanish 'flu) devastated the country: the disease affected 2,578 Lethbridgians, killing 129. It was the city's most traumatic peacetime experience. In desperation, Lethbridge banned all public gatherings, allowed stores to open only in the afternoons, and compelled citizens to wear cheesecloth masks on the street or job. The city borrowed a 50-bed tent hospital from the militia and set up another temporary hospital in Wesley church hall.

Similar measures were used to fight tuberculosis. In 1914, the Women's Civic Club petitioned council to enforce the bylaw against spitting on the sidewalk as it believed that to be one way in which the disease was spread. That same year, council called on the veterinary director-general to better control bovine tuberculosis and, in 1920, asked provincial authorities for compulsory milk pasteurization.

Like health, education remained a primary concern of Lethbridge. The school board opened the first publicly funded kindergarten in 1907 near the Central School. To accommodate

The Human Spider

An act billed as "The Human Spider" thrilled Lethbridgians in September 1921. It consisted of Texan Bill Strother, the human spider, and a couple of helpers.

Strother's speciality was to climb the walls of tall buildings. On 13 September, a report in the local newspaper said, "While thousands stood aghast last night before the Sherlock Block, Bill Strother scaled Lethbridge's tallest building and, not satisfied with that, rode a bicycle around the edge of the roof. The bicycle stunt was the last word in recklessness . . . It was a magnificent feat of courage and physical strength and skill. On two nights the Spider made pretty climbs, electrifying the crowds with the chances he took in performing acrobatic stunts en route up the brick wall . . . Last night he climbed the Colonial Theatre building also, and later he and his manager put on an act in connection with the regular program . . . How does he do it? Here is one secret of the Spider's marvellous skill - he keeps fit by simple, clean living. 'I live as near like nature wants us to live as I can, and that is how I can do it,' said the Spider."

The Spider left Lethbridge on the evening train for Calgary where he intended to climb the Herald building.

Galt Gardens with Bandstand-Board of Trade Building, ca. 1925.

the rapidly increasing population, the board added four rooms to the Westminster School, demolished the original section of the Central School and added a new wing onto the still standing four-room Barford Addition. Two one-room, frame schools, the Bailey Street and Courtland Street schools, served the outlying areas of the city. In 1911, the board opened the eight-room Fleetwood School in Duff Addition, and, in 1912, completed a two-room, frame structure in Hardieville, the larger, eight-room, brick Galbraith School on 9th Avenue North, and yet another brick building on 5th Avenue, called the Manual Training School. The latter became a high school in 1916, and eventually Bowman Elementary in 1929. Garbutt Business College operated in Lethbridge from 1909 to 1967.

The Roman Catholics also expanded their facilities. They added rooms to the separate school at the corner of 9th Street and 2nd Avenue South in 1902 and 1911 and they opened a second school, St. Basil's Catholic School, on 12th Street B near 7th Avenue North. Meanwhile, St. Aloysius Convent, at 116-9th Street South, taught 22 female boarding students music, stenography, and other subjects.

In sum, Lethbridge in the 1920s sported many of the trappings of large urban centres. Many automobiles appeared on its streets. Elliott Galt's 20 HP gasoline-powered Wilton, which he brought to the city in the summer of 1903, had been the first automobile in the city. Several years later, in 1907, there were sufficient car owners to form the Lethbridge Automobile Club. The city commemorated the event by passing By-law 232 which required owners to register their cars and set the speed limit at eight miles (13 km) per hour. For a few months that year, Lethbridge even had its own automobile manufacturing company, the Lethbridge Motor Car Company, which may have produced one car. The city purchased its first automobile in 1910 and bought several more in 1912, including a patrol wagon for the police and an ambulance for the fire department. People who owned a car limited its use to summer weekend outings to relatives or countryside parks. Most owners removed the battery from their cars, drained the radiator, and put the vehicle on blocks for the winter months. Travel around the city was largely by foot, bicycle or streetcar.

The automobile affected the urban landscape. In 1913, the city passed a parking by-law and paved 13th Street. In addition to the

115

Corner of 3rd Avenue and 5th South in 1912.

*Corner of 3rd Avenue and 5th Street South in ca.
1925.*

Courthouse, Lethbridge, ca. 1925.

Courthouse and city offices (formerly the Chinook clubrooms), ca. 1925.

117

inevitable gasoline stations, the Prairie City Oil Company installed storage tanks on 2nd Avenue near the railway tracks. After vigorous lobbying, Lethbridge became the centre of three major highways. The Black Trail, or Sunshine Trail, ran from Butte through Great Falls and Lethbridge to Calgary via Vulcan; the Red or the All-Red Trail traversed southern Alberta in an east-west direction; while the Yellow Trail connected Lethbridge to Cardston and Waterton Lakes. These trails, marked with coloured bands on telephone poles, were blade-graded dirt roads with some of the low places Fresno-filled and most of the small streams diverted through wooden culverts.

Most of the city's traffic consisted of various tradesmen making their daily deliveries. Usually the first on the road was the milkman, making his rounds with horse-drawn wagon. If he arrived at the door early in the morning he took his orders and money from the empty bottles on the front step and left fresh, pasteurized milk, cream, and other dairy products. The bakery van usually came next with fresh bread and other baked goods. The postman delivered mail door to door twice a day. Several times a week, a Chinese market gardener sold organically-grown, fresh vegetables, and sometimes British Columbia fruit from a wagon or small truck. Housewives usually phoned in their grocery orders, which were quickly delivered by a young boy on a bicycle. Twice a week, the iceman came around and left a 25-pound (12-kg) block of ice in the icebox. The ice had been cut from the river or Henderson Lake in January and stored in sawdust in icehouses.

The church was an important institution and in the 1920s almost universally attended. Except for the Salvation Army and the Church of Jesus Christ of Latter-day Saints, the churches in Lethbridge belonged to the mainline religions: Roman Catholic, Anglican, Presbyterian, and Methodist. In 1923, the Church of the Nazarene rented the old Methodist Church at the corner of 3rd Avenue and 8th Street South and conducted a month-long evangelism campaign, the first of many such efforts in Lethbridge. By 1925, Lethbridge supported 12 churches and its reputation as the buckle of southern Alberta's Bible Belt was firmly established.

Equally reflective of the piety and uprightness of the majority of Lethbridgians was the legion of fraternal organizations. The era of optimism and boosterism also spawned a plethora of secret and benevolent societies such as the Ancient Order of Foresters, Loyal

Canned Heat

In the 1980s, Skid Row alcoholics often mixed Lysol disinfectant spray and cooking wine and drank the mixture to obtain the oblivion they sought. In the 1920s and 1930s, it was canned heat that they used.

"Canned Heat" was a trademark for a solid fuel, which was sold in small containers and used for heating as in portable stoves. The actual fuel was alcohol, as boozers of the day soon discovered, which could be separated from the solid medium by straining or sucking it through a sock or handkerchief.

In May 1927, Lethbridge city police responded to a complaint and noted that "canned heat was the cause of a hot jag." The complaint involved a party in a downtown hotel. The police investigation revealed that there were nine men in the room and that they had consumed 25 tins of canned heat. Two men, released from the provincial jail only the day before, were so hopelessly intoxicated that they were taken to the police station to sleep it off. They were assessed $20 fines or 30 days when they sobered up. The registered occupant of the room, one Andrew Lane, also was jailed until being put aboard the first departing train by the police.

Addiction to canned heat was a great problem for the police at the time. There was no restriction to its sale, and the habit of taking it was common among alcoholics. Canned heat sold for two tins for a quarter and anyone could purchase it. Its legitimate purpose was to heat a kettle quickly, or to be used by picnickers and campers to heat food. Its internal use was very dangerous, a report stating that five men in British Columbia earlier had died from imbibing the poison.

An alcohol-based shoe polish was often used by men desperate for a drink around the same time. They could be spotted instantly by the black ring around their mouths caused by sucking the alcohol from the shoe polish through a cloth container.

The Purcell-Akers Affair

On 3 December 1893, David E. (Dave) Akers rode over to Tom Purcell's ranch on Pothole Creek, south of Lethbridge, to have it out over a continuing disagreement involving cattle. Akers, on horseback, crowded Purcell, who was afoot, and slashed at him with a quirt. Purcell managed to reach a rifle, which was leaning against the fence, and, after warning Akers to back off, killed him with one shot.

Both men were old frontiersmen and both had been deeply involved in the whiskey trade of 1869-1874. Akers, born around 1835 in Bedford, Pennsylvania, had operated and managed several whiskey trading posts, one in partnership with John "Liver-eating" Johnston, and was at Fort Whoop-Up when the NWMP arrived there in 1874. Purcell, born in Cincinnati, Ohio, in 1829, had known Akers in California in 1856. When he came to Canada about 1870, he found Akers already at Whoop-Up and wintered with him for several years.

The two old traders got into farming and ranching, and had an interest in a coal mine. Purcell, particularly, continued to run in liquor from the United States, likely with the backing of Akers. Their business arrangements led to bitter disagreements so that, by fall 1893, they were both uttering threats to solve their problems in the old way — with guns!

The shooting of Dave Akers by Tom Purcell led to the first murder trial in Lethbridge's history. It was held in the Building Company's Hall, also known as the Opera House, now the location of the downtown Safeway store. Purcell, who had turned himself in following the shooting, was found guilty of manslaughter and was sentenced to three years in Stoney Mountain Penitentiary. (He commented that he had once received a longer sentence for stealing a calf.) Purcell served his time and went to live on the Baldwin Ranch on the Little Bow River. He died there about 1910 and was buried at Carmangay.

Order of Moose, Canadian Order of Chosen Friends, Modern Woodsmen of America, Federated Order of Eagles, Brotherhood of American Yeoman, Dramatic Order Knights of Khorastan, Benevolent and Protective Order of Elks, Knights of Pythias, Masonic A.F. & A.M., and the Sons of England Benefit Society. Their rituals and hierarchic order, their uniforms of royal colours, their secret ceremonies, and their para-military marching drills represented more than a night out with the boys. The secret societies were a throwback to days gone by, to an era of mystery and romance, to a period when the city was not yet born and the portents of a new industrial age not yet visible.

By the end of the decade, the city had implemented a new form of government. Mayor Hardie, who had always been a strong supporter of the commissioner system, reluctantly raised the issue of reform in a 1927 plebiscite. The commissioners had become unresponsive and dictatorial despite addition of three advisory commissioners in 1922. Dissatisfaction continued and, on 27 October 1927, another plebiscite approved a council-manager form of civic government. The following July, the six commissioners simply left office and a new council installed itself. The councillors elected Robert Barrowman as mayor and in September hired John T. Watson, the power plant superintendent, as city manager.

When still in office, Mayor Hardie had made the civic administration much more representative of the city's population. In 1927, he began to place representatives from labor on such city boards as health, the library, and Galt Hospital. At the same time, the Civic Employees Union (later the Canadian Union of Public Employees or CUPE) began to assert itself; no longer would it permit supervisors to fire its members on a whim or in a fit of anger. The union negotiated a medical contract with the city and periodically renewed it with increased benefits. By 1935, it had gained a group sickness and accident plan, by 1941, a pension scheme, and was well on its way to becoming the most powerful union in the city.

Unemployed mens' protest march — one of many marches and protest meetings — on 5th Street South, in the early to mid-1930s.

Chapter Seven
Depression Mentality

On 28 October 1929, four days after panic selling swept the New York Stock Exchange, Lethbridge's city council met to discuss the already alarming numbers of unemployed in the city. Councillors called upon the provincial and federal governments to accept some of the responsibility for relief and not leave the burden entirely with the municipalities as had always been done in the past. Local politicians also asked for a conference of federal, provincial and municipal authorities, as well as labor leaders, transportation companies, and manufacturing associations to deal with the crisis.

The hurried meeting dramatically illustrated the suddenness with which the devastation of the economic crisis reached Lethbridge. It exposed the city's vulnerability to economic and political events far removed from the city. For years, Lethbridge had been dependent upon the coal mines whose operations reacted instantaneously to outside demand and whose output affected employment, wages and business in the city. The gradual settlement of the countryside had alleviated this dependency somewhat, but world food markets and prices still affected the income of Lethbridgians. This situation became particularly evident in the late 1920s and early 1930s. At first, a general boom, reminiscent of the first decade of the century sent prices soaring and wages rising. Optimism and speculation reached unprecedented proportions. But, inevitably, the bubble burst and late in 1929, the Wall Street crash sent the world and Lethbridge into dizzy descent toward poverty, distress, and hunger. The decade-long depression, which followed the orgy of spending and speculation, was not merely an economic phenomenon. Its tragic privations created a special depression mentality, a frame of mind, which pervaded all of society.

The predominant characteristic of the great depression of the 1930s was deflation, the steady and ominous decline in prices of everything. In 1929, for example, the price of one loaf of Holsom's Bakery bread was 12 cents; in 1931, it dropped to two for 13 cents; and in 1933, it fell to three for 14 cents. Wheat, the source of much

of Lethbridge's wealth, earned $60 million in 1928, $21 million in 1930, and only $9 million in 1933. A good steer could fetch $10.50 per cwt in 1929 but barely $1.75 by 1933. To those who enjoyed a steady salary or had a safely invested income, the years of uninterrupted price erosion meant a comfortable existence. But, for the unemployed and for the farmer, it was a sad and desperate time.

Luckily, farmers in the Lethbridge area escaped the most devastating effects of the great depression. The relentless, desiccating winds which elsewhere on the southern prairies scorched the landscape, blew away the soil, and ruined thousands of farms, skirted the Lethbridge region. Local irrigation works also provided an agricultural and economic security not experienced elsewhere in the southern prairies. Moreover, the sugar beet industry contributed to economic stability. The acreage under sugar beets expanded from 12,000 acres (4,845 ha) in 1930 to 21,500 acres (8,692 ha) in 1939. The completion of a second sugar factory in 1936 stimulated increased production; its expansion was limited only by the industry's inability to persuade housewives that beet sugar was as sweet as cane sugar. Many continued to use imported cane sugar in making preserves. Nevertheless, Lethbridge agriculture expanded during the depression and many hard-hit communities looked upon the city with some envy as one of the fortunate survivors of the economic collapse.

Coal miners and other workers were not quite so fortunate, however. The largest coal producers at the time were the CPR's Galt No. 6 colliery at Hardieville and the North American Collieries' Imperial Mine at Coalhurst. From 1926 on, coal production declined steadily. In 1935, at the depth of the depression, the CPR closed the No. 6 mine and sold its remaining Lethbridge interests to a newly formed company, Lethbridge Collieries, itself a merger of North American Collieries and Cadillac Collieries. The latter firm had come to Lethbridge in 1927, when it opened the district's first completely electrified coal mine, called the Standard, at Shaughnessy. Although the new company opened Galt No. 8 on the west side of the river near the CPR railway bridge, the industry continued to falter throughout the depression. Unemployment remained high among miners for the entire decade. Late in 1935, an explosion rocked the Imperial Mine at Coalhurst, killing 16 miners and destroying its operations. Some of the surviving miners moved to the new No. 8 Mine but most of them lost their jobs. The company, meanwhile, renamed the Standard mine as Galt No. 10, to take advantage of that good name in the West.

Lethbridge also lost the corporate headquarters of a major brewing chain. Lethbridge Brewery Limited, started by Fritz Sick in 1901 as the Lethbridge Brewing and Malting Company, grew steadily throughout the twenties. In 1928, Fritz Sick and his son, Emil G. Sick, organized Associated Breweries of Canada Limited, a $5 million holding company with plants in Lethbridge, Edmonton, Prince Albert, Regina, and Vancouver. In the early thirties, the Sicks expanded into Montana and Washington and, in 1933, moved their head office to Seattle.

Although the Sicks' move did not have a dramatic effect upon Lethbridge's workers, the ailing coal-mining industry continued to dismiss its laborers. Consequently, Lethbridge shared the misery of its counterparts elsewhere in the country. Her unemployed could not find any job, any place, at any rate of pay. One of the few occupations that remained was domestic help. The affluent could afford to hire poverty stricken women as domestic helpers or maids for long hours and hard work at low pay. Numerous delegations appeared before city council pleading for help, but all that the city could do was to provide limited welfare, or relief as it was then called. In June 1931, 1,000 individuals out of a total population of 13,400 received relief payments from the city. The numbers reached a staggering 2,110 in 1934, remained at those levels for several years, and did not decline significantly until the outbreak of the Second World War.

The city government bore the brunt of the cost of relief. Not until 1932 did the senior governments begin to contribute sporadically to the cost. By then, Lethbridge's annual relief bill had climbed to an alarming $79,000. From 1932 to 1938, council spent a total of $664,000 on welfare payments; in those same years, the provincial and federal governments combined granted only $731,000. Lethbridge's 51 percent proportion of relief spending compared favorably to Calgary's 40 percent, Saskatoon's 20

Night Flight, 1931
by BILL HAY

I had the pleasure of being the first southbound passenger on the new Calgary-Lethbridge air mail link and can truthfully state that it was one of the most pleasant journeys I have yet made. Under the skillful guidance of Pilot Hollick-Kenyon, the powerful Boeing biplane landed in the glare of the Lethbridge airport floodlight in about 57 minutes after the take-off from Calgary airdrome.

Being the lone passenger, I was ushered into the front seat of the cabin, which will accommodate four passengers in comfort. My baggage was stowed away in a forward compartment along with the sacks of mail. The pilot, clad in fur-lined garments, mounted the two steps into the outside cockpit of the idling plane. The motor was then "revved" up to an ear-splitting roar, which was plainly audible inside the cabin and the machine began to move. Taxi-ing to the far end of the Calgary field, the Boeing was turned round and with gathering speed rose off the ground out of the rays of the floodlight, over the spectators' heads. A sharp right bank and with the city's myriad of twinkling lights fading behind us, we were on our way.

One of the first things to attract the attention after leaving Calgary is the glare of the gas flares at Turner Valley. The night was clear and visibility was good for many miles. The ruddy glow of the flames lit up the countryside and the reflection played against the wings of the plane. Towns and farmhouses all along the route could be picked out by the lights and flashing off in the distance could be seen the revolving beacons of the emergency landing fields. In the semi-darkness the ground could be seen but it was difficult to determine at just what altitude the plane was travelling. Unless one has travelled the route several times and has a map, it is impossible to tell which town one is passing over. The emergency landing fields are laid out in two directions, in order that any planes forced to land can do so with the wind in the proper direction. The ground lights of the field give the pilot the assurance of a good landing and the landing

Lethbridge Municipal Airport at 23rd Street and 5th Avenue North. Planes were part of the National Air Tour, which visited Lethbridge on 19 September 1930.

lights on the underside of the wings could be switched on to take the place of the floodlights installed at the stopping points.

The air was calm Sunday night and the plane speeded along without the least bump or jar. The cabin of the Boeing is most comfortable, the leather upholstered seats and the hot air register giving one the impression of sailing along in a huge motor boat. There is a metal knob on the floor of the plane near the register which, when opened, permits cool air to enter and there is no chance of the cabin becoming too stuffy.

When nearing Lethbridge, the air apparently had a few "holes" in it for the plane bumped around now and then, but nothing to upset even the most nervous of passengers. The flashing beacon of the city port could be seen plainly before the lights of Lethbridge itself were visible. Crossing the river, the roaring motor was idled down and the landing lights flashed as a signal to the ground crew awaiting the plane's arrival. Immediately the surrounding countryside was illuminated from the city floodlight, every depression and trail being shown up clearly. Circling the field and gradually losing altitude, the pilot brought the huge plane around in a gradual left bank and dropped down to earth without jar or bounce in full view of the floodlight. The plane was taxied to the hangar where passenger and mail were delivered — all in the remarkably short time of 57 minutes!

The "fly-by-night" experience was interesting and enjoyable and as the days go, more and more travellers will come to look upon the plane as the only means of safe and speedy travel.   --*Lethbridge Herald, Jan. 19, 1931.*

percent, and Vancouver's 16 percent. Moreover, Lethbridge paid all the relief costs out of current revenues; it capitalized none of it. The enormous burden, however, ate up more than a quarter of the city's average 40-mill tax rate for the decade.

City authorities could not cope with the insurmountable problems of unemployment and relief. Cost continued to rise but, as the tax burden mounted, so did Lethbridgians' inability to pay. By the end of 1936, tax arrears in Lethbridge stood at $429,965 and many citizens had lost their property. By 1937, 8,064 out of 14,721 undeveloped town lots had reverted back to the city, 60 homes were up for tax sale, and caveats had been filed against another 753 residences.

Decreased revenues forced city council to look for cuts in its expenditures. In 1935, for example, it terminated the garbage collection contract and assigned the job to the public works department. A year later, it sold the arena, which it had acquired in 1929 through default of a loan, to the Lethbridge Artificial Ice Company which agreed to provide a satisfactory hockey and skating rink by the winter. The company installed an ice-making plant but the arena continued to be a marginal operation at best and the city eventually reassumed control.

Other recreational facilities also suffered from the parsimonious city council. Throughout the thirties, various groups sought the construction of playgrounds and swimming pools, but council thwarted all these efforts. In 1938, it finally resolved to end a confusing series of resolutions by moving that "the program of work for a swimming pool be rescinded, and bathers and swimmers reconcile themselves to use of temporary pools until the City or Service Clubs or other organizations can finance a concrete pool with such accessories as may be necessary."

City administrators also took a hard look at the inefficient and expensive street railway system. The street cars had continuously lost money since 1911 and had accumulated a sorry labor relations history. By 1927, the equipment was worn out and needed to be replaced. Simultaneously, the city was negotiating an electricity interchange with Calgary Power Ltd. which then served Hardieville and the area north of the city. The city power plant, which had access to its own coal mine, had always been a profitable venture. Nevertheless, the commissioners decided to offer the power plant for sale along with the street railway.

The city received a number of attractive offers, including one for $1.2 million from the Canadian-United States Development Office of New York. The finalists were bids by Calgary Power and International Utilities of New York. But, after lengthy negotiations, a thorough investigation by an outside consultant, and an exhaustive study by the city manager, council concluded that it

A share in the Lethbridge Arena Limited, the company that built an ice arena at 12 Street A and 2nd Avenue South in 1923.

was in the best interest of the city to keep both the street cars and the power plant. It repaired and maintained the street cars until buses replaced them in the late 1930s and early 1940s.

Health expenditures also ended with the economic crisis. By the mid-1920s, Lethbridge had several small private institutions, including Van Haarlem's Hospital, which had a capacity of 27 beds, and included an operating room, a bio-chemical laboratory and physio-therapy room. In June 1929, the Sisters of St. Martha purchased the hospital and renamed it St. Michael's. Two months before the stock market crash, a delegation to city council obtained nine town lots at 9th Avenue and 13th Street South on which to build a 100-bed hospital. The new $300,000 St. Michael's Hospital, a four-storey building with five operating rooms, opened its doors on 8 September 1931. Equally fortunate timing benefitted Galt Hospital. Just two weeks before the Wall Street collapse, city council approved a $75,000 by-law for improvements to the Galt Hospital, including a 35-bed addition and an elevator, both completed in 1930. It was the city's last major expenditure on health facilities for the next decade and a half.

The fire department received considerable criticism in the late 1920s and early 1930s. The first instance involved the Dainty farm in the river bottom. Instead of dispatching equipment to the fire, the chief sent a couple of officers to assess the situation. By the time they had completed their inspection, the building was destroyed. In May 1929, council asked for an investigation into the slow response to the Dominion Laundry fire. And, in February 1931, the department simply refused to fight a fire in the tipple and power house of the Federal Mine because Chief Wm. Hardie feared his equipment would "sink to the hubs" in the river bottom, thus endangering other properties should fire break out elsewhere.

School boards were also affected by the depression. Until the economic crash, both the separate and public systems continued their building program, but sharply curtailed their spending afterwards. In August 1926, Rev. Father Michael Murphy, in whose honour St. Michael's Hospital was named, arranged the exchange of some separate school property for city land and a year later opened a four-room, two-storey high school, eventually named St. Patrick's. In September 1927, the public board added a $40,000 addition to Westminster School and, a year later, completed a new high school called Lethbridge Collegiate Institute. It also converted

126

"FASCIST MOB"
ATTEMTS TO TERRORIZE Beet Workers
ON LETHBRIDGE NORTHERN.

We Beet Workers of Southern Alberta, after being driven to a starvation level thru out after out in the price of our labor, have organized, as the only means of resisting further depths of misery, and regaining some measure of a decent standard of living.

enemy   From the outset we have regarded the Sugar Company as the enemy of both the worker and the Farmer, and have formulated our demands, and approached the whole question of struggle from this angle. We not only organized united front meetings between the workers and growers and proposed unity on the basis of struggle against the Company but we chose a correct time for such a struggle. Had we wished to direct our attack against the grower we would have chosen a much more advantageous time, (say: the beginning of the thinning season.) On each occasion when we approached the central executive Board of the Growers Association to negotiate a working agreement we were met with a decided atmosphere of hostility, usually the police, and a representative of the Sugar Company were present. As soon as the Sugar Company and the Central Board saw that we were determined to increase the price of our labor they rushed to Attorney General Lymburn and were assured plenty of police, and the militia if necessary to smash any attempt to increase the price of our labor. Not being satisfied with this guarantee of violence, such members of the Central executive Board as Mr. Jim Nelson and Gibbons, organized a mob of over a hundred Fascist Hooligans on the Lethbridge Northern, including Reverend McInnis of Iron Springs, and a number of other people who are more interested in mob violence than in working 16 hours a day in beet fields and along with a few of the actual Beet Growers of the district burst into turn our shacks while we were at a meeting, seized our meagre furnishings and personal effects and after legalizing this mass House breaking act by obtaining the assistance of two members of the R. C. M. P. dumped suitcases, bedding, etc., into the road allowance where our meeting was taking place.

THUS ATTEMPTING to carry through a mass eviction of all Beet workers and their women and children, despite the fact that a large number of Growers were against having their workers evicted. This act of turning women and children onto the road allowance, had the double purpose of striking terror into the hearts of the workers, and at the same time working a riot, to pave the way for flooding the strike area with the R.C.M.P. (Lymburns promise) and bringing about another "CORBIN" to club the workers into submission. Both purposes were defeated. The R.C.M.P. took a ballot to see if the workers were terror striken enough to sign contracts for $19.00 per acre. The workers stuck to their demands voting for $20.00 per acre. A second vote was taken with the same result.

AT present approximately 40 workers, some with families, are being housed in the unoccupied buildings of sympathetic Farmers. Altho it is almost certain according to threats, ominating from people like Jim Nelson, and Gibbons that a more vicious attack will be launched at the workers in the near future, nevertheless the workers are 100% solid around their minimum demands which are:

1. $20.00 per acre Cash Contract.
2. All contracts to be signed in the presence of a field committee elected by the workers.
3. No contracts to be signed until all Beet Grower's locals agree to the above demands.

We sincerely appeal to all people who are in sympathy with the right of workers to organize and strike for improvement in living standards to send resolutions of protest to Attorney General Lymburn at Edmonton, and to the Secretary of the Growers Association at Taber, Alberta and Sendal, &co.

Issued by ARM WORKERS INDUSTRIAL UNION.

Fifth Street South, Lethbridge, in 1931.

Studio of CJOC Radio ca., 1928 in the penthouse of the Marquis Hotel. CJOC was established by J. E. (Jock) Palmer but never broadcast with any regularity until acquired by H. R. Carson and managed by W. W. Grant in 1928.

the Manual Training School, which it had been using as a high school since 1915, into an elementary school called Bowman. Unfortunately, early in 1929, a fire gutted Lethbridge Collegiate and the board had to send its students to Bowman Elementary and to the old Barford Addition until repairs were completed.

During the 1930s the board followed a very cautious policy. At various times it reconsidered the matter of technical education, which it had discontinued in 1915, but did very little. The board renovated the physical education building on the grounds of Westminster School, rented a garage, and refurbished some of the old equipment which had been in storage for years. In October 1935, the makeshift school began to teach domestic science, motor mechanics, and electricity classes. Four years later, after voters turned down a $15,000 by-law to continue the program, the board closed the technical school.

128

Lethbridge Orchestra, 1930-1931. L-R, upper row: C. Gerbrandt, N. Taylor, F. Delay, Mrs. Longrove, J. Blockside, M. Little, W. Galdzinski; bottom row: Paul Pherson, Sylvia Keel, Phyllis Raworth, Milton Edwards, and Ralph Laycock.

129

Chinese Freemasons, Lethbridge, 1924.

The Ballplayers

For the first 60 years of its history, Lethbridge permitted a wide-open red light district to operate on its western limits. The district was called "The Point" from the mid-1880s until about 1920, then, when the bordellos moved a few blocks to the east, as "The Segregated Area" from 1920 until 1944. The number of prostitutes involved ranged from 22 in 1909, around 40 in 1918, to probably 50 or 60 in 1944, when the provincial department of health forced the closure of the district.

From the early 1900s, local authorities tried to exercise some control of the district and of the prostitutes. This took the form of insisting on regular medical check-ups, for which the madams retained the same doctor assigned to the Provincial Jail, and on very low visibility. The latter was accomplished by restricting movement of the girls by limiting their shopping expeditions to one day a week and by not allowing them to wear all their finery even then. Delivery boys of the 1920s and 1930s made a lot of money off the prostitutes as they tipped well for getting goods delivered or letters mailed.

By and large, the prostitutes were all reasonably healthy young women, even if they were known to Moral Reform Leaguers as "soiled doves." On Sundays in summer, they were in the habit of visiting a nearby farm, choosing up sides and organizing a ball game, and working off a lot of surplus energy in the fresh air. "The man who ran the girls" was known to everyone in Lethbridge. He owned a small farm on the southeastern outskirts of the city and it was to this farm that the girls went on Sunday mornings for a bit of fresh air and exercise.

Only one new school opened in the depression years. In 1932, the Central Church of Christ instituted Alberta Bible College. By 1937, this private institution had 39 pupils.

Restraint affected the churches and none started new buildings in the 1930s. The Lethbridge Hebrew Congregation, which had been meeting in the former Conybeare house on 6th Avenue South since 1911, did plan a new meeting place but in 1935, city council refused to donate a building lot. Rebuffed, the congregation bought the old Baptist Church on 3rd Avenue South.

Most of the modern downtown core was in place prior to the depression. Garish electric lights and signs, profuse in their shapes, colors, and guy wires, brightened the downtown at night. In the late 1920s a few new structures had been built downtown, including the McFarland Building, the Marquis Hotel, and TECO stores; a new pavilion was completed at the fair grounds to replace the one destroyed by fire.

An aerial view of Galt Gardens and downtown Lethbridge in 1930.

All the major structures completed in the 1930s were utilitarian and directly related to agriculture. The largest was the government elevator, later Alberta Terminals Limited, a $1 million structure, finished in 1931. That same year, the CPR moved its stockyards from the fair grounds to a site just east of the city. Hill & Bates, livestock dealers and feeders, later W. T. Hill Farms, relocated their premises opposite the new stockyards. In the late 1930s, O'Loane, Kiely and Company built a modern seed cleaning plant near Ellison's flour mill and contracted with local farmers for specialty crops such as peas and beans. George W. Green Company, long involved in the processing of alfalfa meal, expanded into the production of breakfast foods and other processed cereals, and the Logan-Knit Garment Factory established a factory producing ladies wear from locally-grown wool.

The poor economic conditions slowed the development of transportation into the city. In aviation, for example, Lethbridge remained on the fringes of air routes across the country, even though it had a relatively long association with flight. The first planes visiting Lethbridge belonged to stunt fliers, like Eugene Ely and Katherine Stinson. Captain Ernest C. Hoy landed at Lethbridge on 7 August 1919 after an historic first flight across the Rockies from Vancouver. In 1920, John Ender (Jock) Palmer and Harry H. Fitzsimmons formed the Lethbridge Aircraft Company and barnstormed throughout the region for the next three years.

As early as 1922, Palmer and Fitzsimmons introduced commercial aviation to Lethbridge. They attempted an international airmail flight from Lethbridge to Ottawa but crashed at Minot, North Dakota. From 1926, they and other early Lethbridge aviators, like Charles Elliott, Charles Tweed, and Wilfred Rutledge, flew out of a crude airfield in North Lethbridge, known as Fairmont Subdivision, bounded by 1st and 5th Avenues and 22nd and 28th Streets North. In September 1927, after extensive lobbying by city council, the federal government licensed the field as a formal air harbour for daytime public traffic.

Increased traffic and commercial operations forced the city to improve the air field. In the late 1920s, Emil G. Sick of Lethbridge Breweries recognized and promoted the commercial possibilities of air service. At about the same time, Charles Elliott founded Lethbridge Commercial Airways Ltd., primarily a pilot training school but on occasion a carrier of passengers on chartered flights.

By 1928, its successor company, Southern Alberta Airlines, persistently badgered council to lease the airport, install telephones, and make other necessary improvements. In January 1930, the post office approved Lethbridge as a point of call on the trans-prairie airmail service just inaugurated. As a result of these pressures, council spent about $20,000 in June on a floodlight, fences, and a hangar. In addition, the department of transport placed a meteorological station and beacon at the airport. On 15 January 1931, a crowd of 4,000 watched pilot Herbert Hollick-Kenyon land a Canadian Airways Fokker monoplane on the floodlit municipal airport inaugurating airmail service into Lethbridge.

The new airport did not attract the traffic its proponents had anticipated. The first scheduled air service commenced on 15 September 1930, linking Lethbridge with Edmonton. Planes owned by Rutledge Air Service of Calgary and Commercial Airways Limited of Edmonton carried only passengers on the three and a quarter hour trip. The service was short-lived, however, because the companies failed to secure either an airmail contract or an extension of passenger service into the United States. Similarly, for less than a year, Lethbridge was the chief divisional point on the Edmonton-Lethbridge-Winnipeg airmail run. But low volumes and high costs prompted the federal government to end the service.

The failure to attract passenger and mail service doomed the airport to primarily recreational use. One popular attraction was gliding and in the early thirties the Lethbridge Gliding Club was formed. Its members built many gliders and logged thousands of flights. The enthusiasts established a number of records and two members, Evelyn Fletcher Smith and Arthur L. Larson, became the first Canadians to qualify for gliding certificates from the Federation Aeronautique Internationale. Another club member built one of the first gliders capable of soaring.

With airplane travel still judged uneconomical, Lethbridge had to content itself with buses. Canadian Greyhound Coaches established a bus stop at the Alexandra Hotel (today's Alec Arms) in the late 1920s and in February 1930 asked council for special permission to park along 4th Avenue between 5th and 4th Street South. The city's hotelmen opposed the request and, in 1939, the company built a bus depot and restaurant at 411-5th Street South. Subsequently, Northern Bus Lines Limited (presently, Canada West Transportation Limited), founded in 1927 in Shaughnessy, moved its headquarters to Lethbridge.

City water standpipe, installed in 1904 at 5th Avenue and 9th Street South, ca. 1930.

Part of 4th Avenue South in 1935 with Knox Church in the background.

Lethbridge city council continued to concern itself with transportation problems throughout the 1920s and 1930s. The first auto show in Lethbridge, held in March 1926, symbolized the increasing popularity of cars and trucks. The province reacted by modernizing its road system. It replaced the color-coded road markers with the modern system of numbered highways, graded and sometimes gravelled the main arteries. The growth in traffic also saw a proliferation of gas pumps and service stations in the countryside and city. Used car lots appeared and the city had to concern itself with new traffic problems — speeding, joy-riding, abandoned derelict cars, parking restrictions and stop signs. In September 1935, the city considered but abandoned the idea of a new highway entering the city from the southeast. The depression-ravaged budget permitted few public works.

The economic crisis of the 1930s, with its radical curtailment in government and business spending, also affected the frame of mind of the people. Many, not just the unemployed, believed that they were witnessing the breakdown of the capitalist society and fear of Communism pervaded the community. To be sure, a few Communist agitators were active in the relief camps and among the unemployed. Two such agitators, both well-known in Lethbridge, were Malcolm L. Bruce and Sam Cohen. In 1931, officials identified Robert Scott as "the head of the Reds in Lethbridge" and deported him to Scotland, a common prescription for such suspects and easily carried out under an amended Criminal Code. Later, police reports listed George Anderson as the head of the local "Reds". He was eventually jailed a year for "uttering seditious words". Despite the fears expressed by authorities, no Lethbridgians attempted a Communist revolution.

The economic crisis also produced right-wing reaction. Late in 1929, city council received a letter from the head of the Ku Klux Klan of Canada, protesting the employment of Orientals in the city. Council neither condemned nor praised the request but filed it away without comment. The Klan organizers did not make much headway in the city. Among its targets were eastern Europeans most of whom were strong supporters of the United Mine Workers and other unions. Consequently, labor actively opposed the Klan in Lethbridge.

The fear of violence caused by the depression prompted some repressive action from the provincial and federal authorities.

Ottawa strengthened the RCMP and applied the Criminal Code in its severest form. The provincial government even toyed with press control. The UFA government passed its first newspaper legislation in 1934 in an attempt to dampen the sensational press coverage of the sexual scandal surrounding Premier John E. Brownlee. In 1937, Social Credit Premier William Aberhart muzzled the press with his "Act to Ensure the Publication of Accurate News and Information." Popularly called the Press Gag Act, the legislation was declared *ultra vires* by the Supreme Court the following year. The *Edmonton Journal* won a Pulitzer prize, shared by the *Lethbridge Herald,* for severely criticizing the measure.

Radio came into its own in the 1930s. Its exciting mixture of music, comedy, drama, and news held audiences spellbound. Church attendance dropped dramatically when Amos and Andy came on the air on Sunday evenings. The possibility of radio was recognized by some preachers and by the mid-1920s, William Aberhart of Calgary had become a household name in Lethbridge. The city's CJOC expanded quickly and in 1928 moved to permanent studios on top of the Marquis Hotel, broadcasting a mixture of music and commentary. A frequent visitor to the penthouse station was Henry Viney, who had his heart set on a career in sport broadcasting. Lacking an education and a good vocabulary, and to improve diction and pronunciation, the station manager made him read aloud from a dictionary for hours on end. Eventually, Viney became CJOC's sports announcer, then moved to CFCN Calgary, where he became Alberta's top sportscaster on both radio and later on television.

The late 1920s and 1930s were a golden age for movies. The improved wages and shorter working hours, won during the heady 1920s, caused a revolution in leisure activities and movies became a popular attraction. In 1928, A. W. Shackleford joined forces with Famous Players and a year later opened the opulent Capitol Theatre, resplendent with its gold and silver trim, its satin curtains, and its loge seats reserved for notables for an extra ten cents.

The depression mind, suffering from poverty and lack of employment, thrived on movies. It hungered to see Fred Astaire dance his way beside floodlit pools set in front of huge mansions. It sought momentarily relief from its problems and worries in Walt Disney's "Snow White and the Seven Dwarfs." Exploiting this desire, Famous Players expanded rapidly in Canada. In Lethbridge, Shackleford purchased the only air-cooled theatre, the Empress, and renamed it the Roxy. The Odeon chain took an option on a

Typical 1930s dust storm at Pearce, Alberta.

town lot but postponed construction of a new theatre until better times. The entrance of the American theatre chains into the city demonstrated that, in a subtle way, the new electronic media — radio as well as movies — were carrying Canadians into American culture, gradually dissolving their northern distinctiveness.

Jukeboxes, sometimes called Wurlitzers after a manufacturer, accelerated the Americanization of Canada. These coin-operated record players blared American hits through every restaurant,

coffee shop, pool hall, and games arcade in the country. Pinball and slot machines enjoyed great popularity in the mid-1930s, replacing an earlier fad for miniature golf. Dances remained popular with the favorite places including the Henderson Lake Pavilion and the Trianon, the former Hudson's Bay Company store at the corner of 5th Street and 1st Avenue South. The famous band, Mart Kenney and His Western Gentlemen, appeared often at the Henderson Lake hall in the 1930s and used it to premiere their theme song "The West, A Nest And You, Dear."

James Stanley Kirkham

James Stanley Kirkham was born in Lethbridge in 1888. His father, Thomas F. Kirkham, was the town's first tinsmith, with a shop at 3rd Avenue South. In 1911, James Kirkham married Jessie Walton, secretary to W. S. Ball, solicitor. And in 1917, with three children, Kirkham went back to complete his high school, then read law with W. S. Ball. He was admitted to the Alberta Bar in 1920.

From 1909 to 1919, Kirkham partially supported his family by writing sports for the *Lethbridge Herald* and, in the 1920s, by writing a regular column called "Mrs. Iama Peach." He published a semi-weekly called *The Square Shooter* in 1923 and was involved with a weekly called the *Canadian Advocate* later in the decade.

Kirkham became interested in the repeal of prohibition because one of his first important clients was Fritz Sick, the local brewer. Kirkham worked through the Moderation League of Alberta. After repeal in 1923, Kirkham became known as the man to see in southern Alberta if one wanted a liquor license for a hotel. By 1925, tired of obtaining licenses for ex-bootleggers and other such entrepreneurs, he decided to get one for himself and established the Garden Hotel in the former Kirkham business block. He became active in the Alberta Hotel Association and was an executive member from 1925 until his death in 1941.

He was an important figure in the establishment of the modern Country Club Golf Course in the early 1930s at its riverbottom site.

Kirkham was very interested in local and regional history and in the contribution of the oldtimers of the region — the "Builders of Yesterday," as he called them. With lawyer A. B. Hogg, he reorganized the Lethbridge Historical Society in 1935, previous organizations of the body having been made in 1888 and 1923. The purpose of the third reorganization was to sponsor the 50th Anniversary celebration, held in Lethbridge on July 23-25, 1935.

Despite the poor economic conditions, the Lethbridge Country Club managed to make some modest improvements on its riverbottom property. The 1933 annual meeting decided to purchase the former Courtland School from the school board for $750, move it to the river valley, and convert it into a clubhouse. The club also began to irrigate its fairways, bought a power mower and arranged with city council for easement of a road to its property and closure of a former road allowance.

By 1935, Lethbridge was fifty years old. It had retained much of its small town atmosphere and continued to value its relatively slow-paced lifestyle. Saturday nights were firmly established for the traditional shopping expedition. Despite the lack of money, it seemed everyone from the city and its surroundings flocked to the downtown stores, more to meet and mingle than to shop. Fifth Street South, the main shopping street, was crowded with people, surging between the main stores, Kresge's and the Metropolitan. The Salvation Army played on the Alexandra Hotel corner, while the ladies used their tambourines to collect offerings. The music appeared an appropriate omen for the quiet Sunday that was to come.

This sign was erected in front of the Courthouse at 4th Avenue and 6th Street South; Lethbridge citizens raised about $11 million in eight Victory Bond campaigns in 1939-1945.

138

Chapter Eight
The Second World War

The depression years highlighted Lethbridge's vulnerability to outside forces. Its coal mines, service industries, and surrounding farms suffered from the world-wide economic stagnancy. While the outbreak of the Second World War ended the era of despondency, the global conflict reinforced the city's reliance on world conditions.

Lethbridge failed to capture a share of the lucrative munitions and arms production, but it did provide food, fuel, and military training facilities. These contributions stimulated economic activity and produced population growth. But, perhaps a more significant result of the total war, and its resultant anxiety, was that it allowed governments at all levels to expand their powers, to increase their economic activities, and to strengthen their curbs on the freedom of their citizens. Lethbridge did not escape this pervasive impact of the global war on its society.

One of the most visible effects of the war on the Lethbridge economy was evident at the airfield. Well before war's outbreak, the old municipal airport proved to be too small while several surrounding structures created a safety hazard. Early in 1937, the city purchased 730 acres (295.6 ha) of land south of the city from the CPR and commenced construction of two hard surfaced runways, a hangar, a radio and meteorology facility, and a radio range station. The new airport, named Kenyon Field in honour of Herbert Hollick-Kenyon (something it shared with the Hollick-Kenyon Peninsula and Plateau in Antarctica), was opened in June 1939. A crowd of 35,000 people attended the ceremonies, creating the most monumental traffic jam in the city's history.

By the mid-1940s, Lethbridge enjoyed fairly good air-passenger service. Western Air Express provided two daily north-south flights while Trans-Canada Airlines included the city on its east-west trans-continental routes. The latter service was largely due to Lethbridge's position on the eastern edge of the Rocky Mountains. The propellor aircraft then in use cruised most efficiently at about 10,000 feet (3000 m) and relied on radio beacons for navigation. Trans-Canada preferred to fly the passes west of Lethbridge and, hence, logically stopped at Kenyon Field.

The Second World War radically changed the nature and scope of the airfield as the military became the predominant user. Kenyon Field became the site of No. 5 Elementary Flying Training School, operated by the Lethbridge Flying Training School, Limited, under Royal Canadian Air Force supervision. It was part of the vast British Commonwealth Air Training Plan. Soon the field was a beehive of activity; the RCAF brought in 35 officers and, with 65 civilian instructors to staff the school, erected several buildings and shipped in a number of Tiger Moth aircraft. The influx of people and money pleased the business community but began severely to strain local school, housing, health and other facilities.

Lethbridge's constant winds, however, proved to be too strong and too gusty for the trainee pilots and the light Tiger Moths. In June 1941, after training about 900 pilots at Kenyon Field, the RCAF moved the facility to High River. The airport did remain the base for a local Air Cadet League under the leadership of George Watson; youths drilled and received instruction from resident experts. It was an important program because a significant number of the 1,750 enlistees from Lethbridge joined the RCAF.

Despite the loss of No. 5 EFTS, Kenyon Field continued to grow. Late in 1941, the RCAF opened No. 8 Bombing & Gunnery School at the airport to train wireless air gunners and air observers in night flying and advanced aerial bombing and gunnery techniques. To support the program, the air force launched a $620,000 construction project to lengthen and strengthen runways, to build a parade square, as well as to build additional huts, hangars, and a hospital. Eventually, establishment strength reached about 1,600; many local civilians were employed at the base, much to the benefit of the community.

In addition to No. 8 Bombing & Gunnery school, the base accommodated for a time No. 133 Fighter Squadron and No. 124 Ferry Detachment. Barracks were built on the east side of the highway across from the main base to accommodate the extra staff. As a result of all the military activity, Kenyon Field became a fairly large, modern airport, eminently useful for post-war commercial traffic.

Aerial view of Kenyon Field, Lethbridge, in 1942. The airport was the location of No. 5 EFTS and No. 8 B & G School, RCAF.

Original flying instructors and their Tiger Moths, No. 5 EFTS: Joe Patton, Homer Thomson, Bill Roy, Jock Palmer, Bill Smith, Ken Piper, Frank Hawthorne, and Fred Lasby.

Indian Chiefs

The air firing and bombing ranges of No. 8 Bombing & Gunnery School RCAF were located on the north end of the Blood Reserve, near Lethbridge, in 1942-44. Blood tribal leaders took a keen interest in these activities as young men and women from the tribe served in various theatres of the war. On 22 July 1942, several chiefs visited the air base.

"A unique good will inspection of the Station was held this afternoon when chiefs of the Blood tribe were guests for a few hours and had dinner in the officer's mess. Chief Shot-in-both-sides, Chief Cross-child, and Chief Owns-different-horses were flown over their own reserves by Group Captain W. A. Jones. Other chiefs who visited the Station were Fred Tailfeathers, honourary chief Chief Mountain Rev. Canon S. Middleton, the principal of St. Paul's Indian School, and honourary chief Chief Brave Rock A. McMillan, Indian Agent from Cardston. Following the air flights the chiefs and their guests were entertained at dinner in the Officer's Mess. Prior to dinner and in a very surprise ceremony, Group Captain W. A. Jones was honoured by the visiting chiefs with feathered head-dress and full regalia, and in a befitting ceremony they named this School's Commanding Officer "Chief Heavy Shields." Chief Shot-in-both-sides presided at the ceremony, with Chief Percy Creighton acting as interpreter. The honourary title given to Group Captain Jones is particularly fitting as the original Chief Heavy Shields, who died several years ago, was a noted warrior in the early days and took part in many raids. He was an outstanding Medicine Man of authority, and was the owner of several ritualistic charms which have been handed down from the past. He was a kindly chief of good judgement, and was the last of the surviving chiefs to sign the original Indian Treaty. The chief was a great friend of St. Paul's School and of the white man. It is interesting to note that No. 8 Bombing & Gunnery School now possesses two honourary Indian chiefs, Barrack Officer A. C. Russell, the former manager of the Lethbridge Exhibition, having been made an honourary chief some years ago in recognition of his kindly relations with the Indians at the annual Exhibition."

In 1943, Group Captain W. Kennedy, then Commanding Officer of No. 8 Bombing & Gunnery School, was inducted into the Kainai Chieftainship, as the honourary chiefs are called, as honourary chief Flying Chief.

--*Commanding Officer's Daily Diary, 22 July 1942.*

Other military activities affected Lethbridge as well. At the start of the war, the city was headquarters of the 18th Field Artillery Regiment of the Non-Permanent Active Militia. In September 1939, the regiment included the under-manned 20th, 39th, and 112th Field Batteries, Royal Canadian Artillery. Initially, the 20th was called upon to guard the local power plant, armouries, CPR Bridge, and the airport, but in September was mobilized as the 20th Anti-Tank Battery. In October, the 108th Howitzer Battery from Kimberly was transferred to Lethbridge and trained with the 20th as the 108th Anti-Tank Battery. Both units moved to Shilo in May 1940 and proceeded overseas in September as part of the 2nd Anti-Tank Regiment under Colonel W. E. Huckvale. Huckvale eventually became the highest-ranking Lethbridgian in the Second World War, serving as a Brigadier and Commander of Royal Artillery during the Italian Campaign.

Other troops from Lethbridge included a contingent of the 55th Light Aide Brigade and the 6th Field Park Company, both mobilized early in 1941. The 39th Field Battery was mobilized in September and served in the Aleutian Campaign and as an NRMA artillery unit on the west coast. The 112th Light Anti-Aircraft Battery also mobilized late in 1941.

Women played a more important part in the armed forces than they had in the First World War. In November 1940, a branch of the Canadian Auxiliary Territorial Service (CATS) was formed in Lethbridge and 125 women received training in a variety of military subjects. When the Canadian Women's Army Corps was formed in September 1941, 18 of Lethbridge's CATS answered the first call including Major Leona McIlvena, Lethbridge's highest-ranking woman officer. Other local women joined the RCAF (Women's Division), the Canadian Army Nursing Service, and the Women's Royal Canadian Naval Service. Lillian M. Parry, subsequently Lethbridge's first female councillor, was commissioned a Nursing Sister in the Royal Canadian Army Medical Corps.

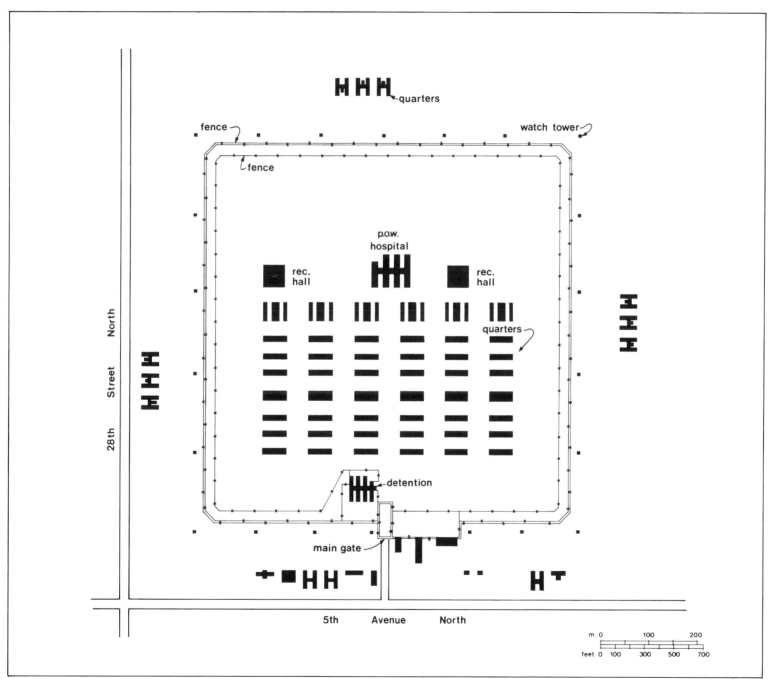

Plan of Internment Camp No. 133, Lethbridge, which operated from November 1942 to June 1946.

143

Main gate to prisoner-of-war compound, Internment Camp No. 133, Lethbridge, in 1943.

Prisoners-of-war, Internment Camp No. 133, Lethbridge, in 1943.

144

Prisoners-of-war "behind the wire" of Internment Camp No. 133, Lethbridge, in 1943.

The civilian population felt the impact of the war in many ways. In order to prevent profiteering and the creation of artificial shortages, the Wartime Prices and Trades Board controlled prices, beginning in September 1939. For the first time in their history, Canadians suffered the inconvenience of compulsory rationing and were issued ration books for sugar, canned milk and fruit, tea, coffee, meat, jam, honey, and maple syrup. Gasoline and tires, also rationed, were sometimes difficult to obtain, while automobiles, household appliances, and radios disappeared from the marketplace.

Government influences became all-pervasive. The reimposition of the War Measures Act gave the Dominion government dictatorial powers. Under the Act, for example, the federal government forbade coal miners from striking, set their wages, and severely curbed their freedom to change jobs. In June 1940, the National Resources Mobilization Act (NRMA) initiated a national registration program, which at first authorized the call-up of men to serve only in Canada but, after a national plebiscite in 1941, permitted mobilization of NRMA soldiers, called "Zombies" by General Service troops, for overseas duty. Other legislation imposed Daylight Saving Time. The government increased taxes, especially income tax. Application of an Excess Profits Tax caused Lethbridge theatre owner A. W. Shackleford to comment that never before had he seen so much money coming in while being allowed to keep so little of it.

Local governments also increased their powers. Faced with a critical housing shortage, Lethbridge city council sought and received authorization from the Wartime Prices and Trades Board for a local rental board, which effectively imposed rent controls in the city. The board failed to solve the problem and, on 27 September 1943, it had on hand 115 applications for light-housekeeping suites, 53 applications for unfurnished rooms, and 15 applications for unfurnished houses but not a single listing of available space. Not until Wartime Housing Limited began building a substantial number of houses in 1945 was the drastic shortage eased.

As in the First World War, citizens were encouraged to invest in the war effort. Eight Victory Bond loan campaigns netted well over $11 million in Lethbridge alone, while sale of War Savings Certificates added $1 million more. Sold with much fanfare and display, the war bond campaigns became a form of public entertainment.

Perhaps the most visible presence of the war in Lethbridge was an enormous prisoner-of-war camp, called Internment Camp No. 133, which was designed to hold 12,500 POW. The camp was located on the N½ of section 4 and the S½ of section 9-9-21-W4 consisting of 638 acres (259 ha), an area that, in 1984, was bounded by 5th and 14th Avenues and 28th and 43rd Streets North. The land was purchased by the federal government for $35,000 in February 1942. Completed in November 1942, the $2 million camp consisted of six sections each containing six two-storey barracks, mess halls and administration buildings. In addition, the camp included two large recreational buildings, a dental facility, mortuary, hospital and detention barracks. All were enclosed in a barbed wire compound. Housing of Veteran's Guard of Canada personnel required the construction of four sets of barracks outside the wire — Headquarter's Company on the south and A, B, and C companies on the remaining sides of the compound.

The first prisoners arrived on 28 November 1942. Many of the men, captured in North Africa, still wore tropical issue uniforms. They were unloaded from trains east of the government elevator and were marched in columns of four between two long rows of armed Veteran's Guards to the camp. The POW lived well in Lethbridge because the Geneva Convention called for prisoners to receive the same rations as Canadian troops stationed at home. Consequently, carloads of sugar, jams, meat and other rationed foodstuffs poured into the camp throughout the war, causing much local resentment.

The POW helped to ease the critical shortage of farm workers. A few of them worked on the 1943 sugar beet harvest. The plan proved to be so successful that the Departments of Labour and National Defence drew up a formal agreement whereby local farmers employed 1,200 POW in the 1944 harvest. Although paid only in canteen credits, the POW eagerly volunteered for the freedom to work in the fields. Sometimes accommodated in temporary, lightly-guarded camps for days on end, about 6,000 prisoners worked on southern Alberta farms until the camp's final evacuation in June 1946.

Ironically, the farm labor shortage was also eased by the paranoia directed against the Japanese living on the British

Japanese-Canadian evacuees arriving in Picture Butte, Alberta, in 1942.

Columbia coast. Fears of Canadian Japanese began on 7 December 1941 with the bombing of Pearl Harbour. The thought that Japanese residents might join in an attack, coupled with British Columbia's long history of racism, led to the forced evacuation of about 23,000 Japanese from their homes to internment camps in the interior.

On 16 March 1942, Councillor J. A. Jardine, later the author of many anti-Japanese resolutions passed by Lethbridge's city council, represented the city at a Vancouver meeting called to discuss the movement and control of Japanese residents in Canada. One of the subjects of discussion was the employment of Japanese as beet workers and one of the conditions drawn up to govern such

147

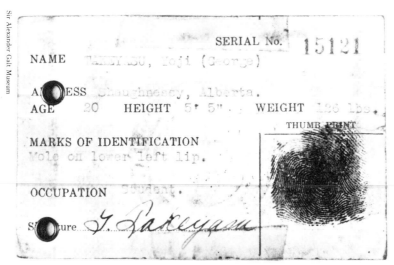

Wartime Japanese-Canadian identification card.

a scheme was "that any Japanese so moved remain domiciled on the farms to which they are allocated, and that they will not move to and reside in the City of Lethbridge."

A physically-fit, adult male Japanese with help from his family could thin and hoe about 12 acres (4.9 ha) of sugar beets, for which he was paid $30 per acre or only $360 for the season. As a result, the individual, or members of his family, simply had to find work in the off-season in order to survive. Jobs tended to be in Lethbridge, hence, the Japanese beet workers found themselves on a collision course with the B.C. Security Commission, which governed their movements, and the City of Lethbridge, which did not want them as residents.

The result was endless harassment of Japanese by city officials. They were forbidden to patronize local beer parlours. In August 1942, council complained that some Japanese were working in Broder's canning plant although the Foods Administrator, concerned at a labor shortage, wanted them to continue. Next, council protested that "Jap" girls were working as domestics and reiterated that "council is positively opposed to employment of these Japanese in any capacity in the City of Lethbridge." In September 1944, James Shimbashi wrote a poignant letter to council. His daughter had been refused permission to train as a

148

nurse at Galt Hospital "on account of the city policy which barred Japanese." Shimbashi explained that he had been a resident of Alberta since 1910 and had been wounded while serving overseas with the 50th Battalion in the First World War. With some shame, the city dropped its opposition to Miss Shimbashi's application. About the same time, council reserved certain plots in the local cemetery for Japanese, a racist acknowledgement of their presence in the city.

Even as late as 23 April 1945, four Presbyterian ministers pleaded with council for some Christian understanding. They charged that the city had been guilty of much racial discrimination and asked that Japanese be allowed to work in the city and that their children be allowed to attend its schools. It was an ironic plea in light of the bloody war against repression and dictatorship being fought in Europe and the Pacific islands. But the harassment of the Japanese in Lethbridge continued well into 1946.

The extra powers accorded to governments during wartime finally brought an end to the segregated area in Lethbridge. The solution to that hoary perennial was closely linked to the emergence of venereal disease as a major social problem. The situation was so serious that at least one military VD lecturer ranked Lethbridge second only to Montreal as, proportionally, the worst source of VD in Canada. Obviously, in Lethbridge, the segregated area with its six to eight bordellos, each with four to six inmates, was a prime target for the war against VD.

Previous campaigners had been unable to eradicate the segregated area in Lethbridge and the current effort initially ran into similar problems. Repeated letters from, and meetings with, Dr. Harold Orr, of the provincial health department, and officials of the attorney general's department, met with city council's polite assurances that the police were doing all they could and that council would study the matter. Finally, after four year of fruitless efforts, the provincial government delivered an ultimatum: clean up the segregated area or the province would send in the RCMP. This sparked a special meeting of council at which the policing of the city using the RCMP was discussed but finally rejected. Instead, council hired George Harvey, an RCMP staff sergeant then nearing retirement, as its new chief of police.

George Harvey took over command of the Lethbridge police force on 1 November 1944. By Christmas, the segregated area had

The 20th Battery leaving for Shilo, Manitoba, and further training in May 1940. The unit went overseas in August 1940.

Adoption of a City in USSR, 1943

Once upon a time we were friendly with the Russians. The Soviets destroyed the cream of the German Army, some two million men, before the first Allied soldier stepped ashore in Normandy on D-Day. Thus, the USSR saved our collective skins in the Second World War and, in the process, took appalling losses. Much of the country was systematically destroyed by the invading Germans, while some seven millions soldiers and 12 million civilians were killed.

This was the background when, in 1943, the National Council of Canadian-Soviet Friendship called upon Canadian cities to adopt a Soviet town or city and help to restore its devastated economy. Lethbridge's city council adopted Timoshevskaya, called Timo for short, a city of about 16,000 in the southern Ukraine, near Krasnador.

Council must have forwarded a letter to Timo through the Soviet Embassy in Ottawa. An undated reply was received from "Chernenko, Chairman, Executive Committee of Soviet Working People's Deputies, Temashevsky District, Krasnador Territory." It said that Timo had been occupied by the Germans for six months. During those six months, the Nazis shot 115 men, women and children and plundered property to the extent of 8,606 cattle, 7,136 hogs, 6,650 sheep, 14,000 chickens, and 5,584 horses. Field crops, orchards and vineyards on 33,800 hectares were destroyed, as were three machine and tractor stations, 144 dwellings, four libraries, and one large stadium. All schools and hospitals in the district were ransacked. The railway station, locomotive roundhouse, grain elevator, hydro power station, cold storage plant, oil extracting plant, flour mill, foodstuffs factory, printing plant and other enterprises were burned. Total damage inflicted on the district by the Germans was estimated to be 157,955,000 rubles.

Chernenko expressed gratitude that Lethbridge had already raised $5,000 for rehabilitation of "our native village."

And that was the last we heard of Timoshevskaya. Likely there were a few contacts until the end of the war. But the Cold War started soon afterwards. By 1948, the North Atlantic Treaty Organization had been formed and the Berlin Airlift (to counter a Soviet blockade of that city) was in operation. A long era of mutual distrust and fear had begun.

Adoption of HMCS "Lethbridge"

In March 1941, following receipt of information that the city had been honoured by the Navy in naming one of its new corvettes "Lethbridge," the Mayor and Council arranged a public banquet, to which Lieutenant W. Mahan, then the commander of the ship, was invited.

During the evening Lieutenant Mahan was presented with a sterling silver tea and coffee service, with a suitably engraved tray. At the same time, the members of the local IODE Chapters advised that they were preparing parcels of comforts for the crew, and would continue to do so as funds and time permitted.

Parcels were sent at Easter 1941 and 1945, and at Christmas from 1941 to 1944, inclusive. At each mailing, there were 54 parcels, each containing such things as knitted articles, records and needles, stationery, pocket editions, playing cards, candy, cigarettes, shaving material, jig-saw puzzles, chocolates, Oxo cubes, nuts, gum, handkerchiefs, socks, games, toothpaste, and magazines. Money was donated by the chapters to the Local War Services Council to assist in the purchase of a radio and subscriptions to various magazines.

HMCS "Lethbridge" was decommissioned in 1946. As was customary, the ship's bell was presented to the sponsoring city. Thus, on March 25, 1946, the bell from HMCS "Lethbridge" and a scroll from the Minister of National Defence for Naval Services were presented to Dr. H. A. Arnold, Office Commanding HMCS "Chinook," the local naval cadets. A photograph of the corvette, and her brass nameplate, were presented to the Lethbridge Branch of the Royal Canadian Legion.

Looking east from the west side of the CP Rail High Level Bridge about 1945.

been closed and prostitution was no longer a problem. Harvey was totally honest, a strict disciplinarian, and anxious to professionalize a police force that, before his take-over, had been called a "Police Farce." The innuendos, the suspicions of graft and corruption, the concerns of Alberta's attorney general about policing in Lethbridge, and the periodic judicial investigations of the police force or of individual officers all ended with the appointment of George Harvey.

The city administration was streamlined and professionalized in the war years. One of the reforms was the appointment of assistants to the heads of key city posts. Alfred W. Shackleford, who entered civic politics in December 1939, concerned himself with reforming the civic administration. He argued that while Lethbridge may not have been able to afford a bureaucracy in the past, it could in 1945 when its financial position was one of the best of any city in Canada.

Seventh Street South about 1938 with the Post Office in the background.

Organization also encroached into sporting activities. In 1926, city council had appointed a baseball commission, later expanded to a baseball and athletic commission, with the task of running the ball parks. It also named a boxing commission to regulate a popular city sport and, in 1940, placed Henderson Lake ball park under the parks department. Recreation in Lethbridge gradually changed from an unorganized, spontaneous activity for youngsters to an organized, structured activity dominated by adults.

Brigadier W. E. Huckvale, shown here as a civilian about 1960, commanded the 1st Canadian A. G. R. A. during the Italian campaign and was the highest-ranking military officer from Lethbridge to serve in the Second World War.

Brigadier General J. S. Stewart, C.M.G., D.S.O., E.D., C.R.A. 3rd Canadian Division, the highest-ranking military officer from Lethbridge to serve in the First World War.

A Thanksgiving Observance on 7 May 1945 at Victory Square (corner 6th Street and 4th Avenue South) to celebrate the unconditional surrender of the Axis forces earlier in the day. V-E Day was proclaimed and celebrated on 8 May.

One Lethbridgian, Jack Patey of Art Signs Limited, made curling more efficient. Hired to paint the one-inch (2.5-cm) circles then used to delineate the scoring rings of the house at the first Shirtsleeve Bonspiel (the first bonspiel on artificial ice in Western Canada), Patey decided that masking of all the narrow circles was a waste of time. He used solid red and blue colours to make two wide rings, the white ice making up the third circle and the button.

Masking of the wide circles was easy and colors were applied from a spray can. The idea spread and became popular everywhere.

The quest for efficient administration extended to charity. The United Way began in Lethbridge in 1941 as the Community Chest and replaced literally dozens of annual tag days and individual appeals. The board of trade was solidly behind the move and, for years, provided office space for the Community Chest.

154

The cityscape changed somewhat during the war years. Broder Canning Company built a plant in Lethbridge to process sweet corn, peas, beans and other specialty crops grown under irrigation. In 1942, Purity Dairy constructed a plant at the corner of 8th Street and 5th Avenue South, now a parking lot.

A major change occurred in the downtown area. After years of negotiations, the city and RCMP concluded an agreement whereby the city purchased the north half of the Barracks Square for $6,841 and leased the south half for 99 years at a dollar per year, provided that it was used for recreational purposes. In 1943, Fritz Sick marked his 83rd birthday by donating $100,000 to the city to build a swimming pool in the old barracks square, by now being called the Civic Centre. In 1944, the city hired the architectural firm of Meech & Meech to prepare a Civic Centre plan. The plan envisaged a city hall, war memorial, and library-museum-art gallery fronting on 4th Avenue South; a civic auditorium and playground-wading pool behind city hall; a Fritz Sick Memorial swimming pool fronting on 11th Street South; and tennis courts, soccer field, baseball diamond, and skating rink fronting on 6th Avenue South. In 1945, the first phase, the swimming pool, was started.

Downtown underwent another, albeit minor, change in 1944 when the board of trade abandoned its Galt Gardens headquarters building. The structure, built by the city as a bandstand-publicity building in 1909, had become a hangout for drunks and idlers. Walter Gurney asked permission to rent and renovate the building in order to house and display his natural history and gunnery collections, as well as other curios. The city agreed and, in October, Gurney opened his museum to the public.

Another cosmetic change was the city's purchase of the remainder of the public cemetery from St. Augustine's church. The move gave the city full title to the cemetery. In January 1945, with input from citizens, the more euphemistic name, Mountain View Cemetery, replaced the old name, the Public Cemetery.

Daily life changed little in Lethbridge during the war. While Canada was rapidly becoming an industrialized country, agriculture increasingly dominated the Lethbridge economy. The coal industry revived momentarily, but the frequent condolences sent to those who lost loved ones overseas served to underscore the fact that the city's new economic prosperity was fragile, based on temporary wartime activity. Symbolic of the rural, conservative nature of Lethbridge society was the beer parlour. Invented by the provincial government as a means of discouraging public drinking by removing all joy, these barn-like places, dark and smelly, the tables awash with spilled beer, with boozed patrons segregated by sex, replaced the earlier saloons and brothels. Yet the appearance of zootsuiters in the city showed that Lethbridge was in tune with fads elsewhere. The zootsuiters, with duck-tailed haircuts, baggy pants with tapered bottoms, and long jackets with padded shoulders, violently protested the straight-laced formality of the wartime establishment. In October 1944, several zootsuiters armed with lead pipes, knuckle dusters, heavy metal finger rings, and blackjacks, attacked a group of LCI students as they snake-danced through downtown streets. The police moved in quickly, restored order, and arrested several of the assailants.

To everyone's relief, the tensions engendered by a wartime society began to ease late in 1944. War's end was in sight and Canada began to prepare for the post-war reconstruction. In Lethbridge, D. G. Oland chaired the Regional Reconstruction Committee, a part of the provincial Post-War Reconstruction Committee. Oland's organization combined the efforts of several older organizations and became a model for smaller committees established by every major business and public institution in the city. In addition, Wartime Housing Limited was set up by the federal government to build houses for veterans, many accompanied by war-brides.

The war in Europe ended on 7 May 1945. Church services and other celebrations were marred by a ferocious dust storm that blackened the city for several hours. With little warning, a dark wall of rolling turbulence, carried by 70 mph (115 km/hr) winds, swept into the city and forced the cancellation of the main celebrations for a day. Thus, on 8 May, proclaimed V-E Day, an outdoor church service attended by 2,000 people opened the festivities, and fireworks and a bonfire, witnessed by 10,000, crowned the day of thankfulness. The war had ended and Lethbridgians could welcome back their fighting men and women and begin to resume a normal life.

Railway yards, Galt Gardens and vicinity about 1950, looking east.

Chapter Nine

Age of the Consumer

At the end of the Second World War, Canada did not suffer the serious economic dislocation it experienced after the First War. The baby boom and the pent-up desire for homes, appliances, and cars created an insatiable demand for consumer goods. Canadians had saved money during the war and they wanted to spend it on goods denied them the previous five years. At the same time, the country shared in the business of reconstructing the shattered economies of war-torn Europe. Consequently, Canada's factories boomed and her exports surged. As an added bonus, weather conditions were relatively stable and favorable for the next three decades. Although yearly fluctuations in yield and quality continued, crops, on the whole, were good and plentiful. With the exception of a minor recession in the late 1940s, the post-war years saw little unemployment and economic hardship. They were good years.

Lethbridge, whose wealth came from the rich, irrigated agricultural lands surrounding the city, participated in the economic boom. Towards the end of the war, the provincial and federal governments gave top priority to the 300,000-acre (121,000-ha) St. Mary River irrigation project and, by 1946, construction on the St. Mary River Dam was well on the way and the Jensen Reservoir was started. The two governments spent about $21 million over the next ten years to complete the scheme and in 1951 the federal minister of agriculture, Hon. J. G. Gardiner, opened the St. Mary River Dam. The subsequent completion of the canals and levelling of the lands, doubled the irrigated acreages surrounding Lethbridge and added to the rapid growth of the city.

Immigration also contributed to post-war prosperity. The war in Europe uprooted many thousands of civilians and the first of these displaced persons, sometimes disparagingly called "DPs", arrived on district farms in 1948. Others came voluntarily. Perhaps, the revelations of Nazi genocide sickened and horrified them. Certainly, they worried about the overcrowding in their countries and the lack of opportunity for their children, or they feared the threat of Communist invasion. In southern Alberta, most of the immigrants were Dutch but they also included Poles, Italians and various other nationalities. For all of them, Canada beckoned and they were willing to accept the fact that the only way to enter the country was as menial laborers, which in southern Alberta meant working in the beet fields. They cheerfully moved into the delapitated shacks recently vacated by the Japanese and, buoyed by the hope of one day owning a farm, they eagerly took on the backbreaking work of the beet fields.

Lethbridge's acceptance of the immigrants was markedly different from earlier years. In 1948, a city councillor described someone who had driven a car over Galt gardens as a Bohunk, a term he had probably used unthinkly all his life. But this time, the miners' union confronted him and demanded an explanation and an apology. In 1956, the city welcomed refugee Hungarians driven from their country by Russian repression. Julia Fischer, a tough but compassionate and caring woman — one of the city's unsung heroines — who operated a boarding house on 3rd Street South, temporarily accommodated up to 80 of these young men.

Immigration, post-war reconstruction, and good weather, then, combined to create a level of growth and prosperity not experienced since the boom at the turn of the century. Growing at an average rate of over five percent, Lethbridge's population exploded in only one decade by 78 percent while school attendance nearly doubled. The city expanded its boundaries, doubled its retail sales and commercial activity, and extended its street network.

The rapid growth severely strained the ability of municipal resources to provide adequate services. By war's end, the Lethbridge housing situation was desperate. A few houses had been built during the war and by 1946 every shed and shack was rented out and occupied. Even the old RCMP barracks in the city centre and the RCAF huts at the airport were in use. To help, the city sold returning veterans serviced lots in designated areas for one dollar. It was not enough, however, and more direct government involvement was necessary.

Only the federal government had the resources to cope with the housing problem effectively and after the war it became very influential in the city's housing situation. In 1945, the veteran affairs department bought a number of lots in the 1912 Parkdale subdivision just east of the city and constructed 30 houses. The city serviced these lots and graded the streets, naming them after campaigns in which Canadians had fought and died. Also, in 1945, Wartime Housing Limited erected 50 houses elsewhere in the city. The houses were cheaply built, many without basements, and the tax rate was set so low that the city was slow to provide curbs, gutters and sidewalks. Although some critics feared that the new district might become an instant slum, Wartime Housing completed 150 more units in 1946, 100 in 1948, and 50 in 1949. Central Housing and Mortgage Company took over Wartime Housing in 1948 and two years later, in the face of strong opposition from city council, began to sell the houses to veterans.

The federal government's program did not solve Lethbridge's housing problem. As late as 1948, nearly 500 veterans and numerous other families wanted homes. The demand stimulated the construction industry. The city opened a major subdivision, called Lakeview, in southeastern Lethbridge. One of the first private contractors into the subdivision was M. L. Fengstad, who applied under the Integrated Housing Plan of CMHC to build 28 units in 1948 and another 100 in 1949. A second contractor was Arthur L. Batty, who, by 1954, was constructing 30 units or more per year. In 1959, Lethbridge Housing Corporation built Rideau Court, a low rental housing project consisting of 156 units in 20 blocks attactively set on spacious, grassy fields. By then housing starts had peaked and a period of tight money and slackened demand produced a slump in house construction. One casualty of the recession was a housing project designed for North Lethbridge called Dominion Square — first proposed in 1908!

The frantic pace of house construction prompted a judicial inquiry into allegations that elected civic officials had gained from policies set by council at its meeting of 13 July 1959. Allegedly, Keith Construction of Calgary had purchased land from Mayor Shackleford's Majestic Theatres and then received a higher subdivision priority than Art Batty Construction. The inquiry, conducted in 1961 by Judge R. M. Edmanson, found the charges groundless.

The housing crisis was not the only problem confronting city councillors. The rapid growth in population, the development of suburbs, and the tendency for children to remain in school longer than ever before created a shortage of classroom space. In 1950, the separate school board built St. Joseph's High School and, in

1951, St. Mary's, while the public school board built Fleetwood Bawden. The city constructed a pedestrian underpass in 1951 at 17th Street primarily for the use of students from North Lethbridge who attended Hamilton Junior High and the Lethbridge Collegiate Institute. Two years later, the public school board opened Westminster School in new quarters and, in 1954, Senator Buchanan, while the separate school board established St. Paul's. The rapid rate of school construction in the post-war era was but a presage of the more frenetic pace of the next decade.

The expanding population also required new or larger churches and several buildings were erected, renovated, or enlarged during the period. The long abandoned but still lovely old stone St. Patrick's, built by Father Van Tighem in 1888, was demolished and replaced with a parking lot. The Roman Catholics, meanwhile, completed a new St. Patrick's Church on a basement built in 1913. Another historical landmark, First Baptist, formerly Knox Presbyterian, burned to the ground in 1953. While it was building a new edifice at 16th Street South, the congregation met on Sundays in the Paramount Theatre. The church for the Church of Jesus Christ of Latter-day Saints, begun in 1941, was completed in 1949. The congregations of Southminster United and St. Augustine's Anglican considerably enlarged their places of worship. Others, like Our Lady of Assumption, McKillop United, and St. Andrew's Presbyterian built new churches.

Indicative of the immigrants moving into Lethbridge was the establishment of new congregations and their churches. One of the earliest of these was Christ-Trinity Lutheran, established in 1950. Lethbridge Hungarian Presbyterian followed in 1955 and Lethbridge Christian Reformed in 1956. Beth Israel synagogue served the Jewish, the Buddhist temple and Nisei Gospel church the Japanese, and Hope Reformed Church the Dutch community. Other churches erected during the period included Lutheran Church of the Good Shephard and Lakeview Mennonite Brethren church.

The city's rapid growth was reflected in the downtown core. Within a five-year period several major projects altered the townscape. In 1950, S. S. Kresge tore down the Hill Block to make way for a new store while Safeway constructed a modern supermarket at the corner of 3rd Avenue and 13th Street. Within a few years of each other, the former Chinook Club/City Hall was

Riverside, now called Indian Battle Park, on 10 June 1953. This flood forced evacuation of residents and conversion of the area to parkland-recreation.

demolished to make way for the Royal Bank Building; the Dominion Block was removed for the Eaton's store; and, the Court House was torn down for the Woolworth's edifice. In 1952, the provincial government completed a courthouse in the Civic Centre while the federal government finished a major extension on the Post Office. And, in 1955, the RCMP constructed a new headquarters on 9th Street South.

One major change in the downtown core was caused in part by an accident. On 9 June 1950, fire of unknown origin damaged the presses of the Lethbridge *Herald*, forcing the staff to issue a tabloid news sheet. It was the first time since the flood of June 1908 knocked out the power plant that the newspaper missed a publication deadline. Partially as a result of the fire, the newspaper constructed a new plant, called the Buchanan Building.

The advertising pages of the *Herald* chronicled the most dramatic change to affect the lives of Lethbridgians, the popularization of the car. Throughout the war and after it, cars were scarce and difficult to obtain. As late as 1948, an effective advertisement for local garages asked, "Is your car going to give you service until you are able to get a new one?" Car dealers placed prospective purchasers of new cars on long waiting lists for months on end and often required them to purchase options at exorbitant prices — $250 for a backseat blanket or $800 for a trailer. All that changed in the early 1950s. With production lines at full speed, automakers launched the automobile revolution. In the first half of the decade, thousands of Canadians acquired cars, many for the first time, so that by 1955 the car had become a social phenomenon, a status symbol with a culture all its own. Increasingly flashy with shiny chrome, bright colours, and wrap-around glass, the car came to represent the extravagance of a materialistic era.

For some years, Lethbridgians purchased the small, economical English cars: Austin, Hillman, and Morris Minor. But, as the supply of American cars became more plentiful, most preferred a Chevrolet, Ford, Pontiac, Hudson, or Studebaker. Those who could afford it purchased the larger and more prestigious DeSoto, Chrysler, Buick, Oldsmobile, Mercury or Monarch, while the very affluent displayed their wealth with Cadillacs and Lincolns. Like North Americans everywhere, Lethbridgians became totally dependent upon their autos, driving to the corner store for a package of cigarettes or, on weekends, hundreds of miles to

Sweetgrass, Shelby, or Great Falls to take advantage of cheaper prices and looser liquor laws. City teenagers viewed the car as a toy to be borrowed from their fathers or built from wrecks into fast, chrome adorned hotrods, to be driven from hamburger joints, to dairy bars and drive-in theatres. For the first time, too, large numbers of ordinary citizens came into conflict with the police over minor traffic violations and the former attitude of mutual respect became one of mutual suspicion.

Shocked Mayor

On Valentine Day, 1953, His Worship Mayor A. W. Shackleford was engaged in a duty dear to the hearts of all public officials: introducing beauty queens. This time, however, the duty became a shocking experience. Intending to introduce Teen Queen Donna Glock and runner-up Shirley Parkinson at a Valentine Dance in the Civic Centre, attended by 800 dancers, Shackleford took hold of the public address system microphone and, unfortunately, also grabbed the microphone of radio station CJOC. Instantly, an electric current flowed into His Worship's body and froze his hands to the microphones. The mayor, stuttering furiously, reeled backwards while radio announcer Joe McCullum and Alderman Cliff Black tried desperately to free him. But the microphones held the frantic mayor captive until someone turned off the electrical power.

A subsequent investigation revealed that the accident was caused by a difference of 50 volts in the grounding systems between the two microphones. When the mayor embraced both microphones he became a reluctant conductor.

According to a clipping service, a photograph taken by F. Orville Brunelle of the Lethbridge Herald at the height of the action appeared in 1,300 magazines and newspapers all over the world. It was "The Picture of the Week" in *LIFE* magazine on March 2, 1953, and appeared on the front page of the London *Daily Mirror,* with its five million circulation. It appeared in newspapers in Tel Aviv and Tokyo, in North and South America, and in Europe. It won for Brunelle the Canadian Press Picture Service "Best Picture of the Year" award for 1953. It was, and is, unquestionably the most famous photograph ever taken in the City of Lethbridge.

Mayor A. W. Shackleford frozen to two microphones by a 50 volt shock caused by improper grounding. Trying to assist him are CJOC announcer Joe McCallum (left) and city alderman Cliff Black.

Miss Margaret Hamilton, oldest practicing nurse in Lethbridge, cutting the ribbon to open the Municipal Hospital on 25 May 1956. L-R: Hospital board chairman A. G. Virtue, unknown, Deane R. Gundlock MP, Charles Parry, and unknown.

The proliferation of cars brought about many changes in the urban landscape. Enerson Motors established itself at the corner of 4th Avenue and 9th Street South. Local streets were improved and tourist facilities built. Motels, known since the 1930s as auto courts, became increasingly popular. The first in Lethbridge was the Blue Bird Motel and Auto Court built on 3rd Avenue South in 1946. By mid-decade, several motels sprouted along Mayor

Magrath Drive, creating what became known as Motel Strip. Parking became a major problem to the city and after much study and enforcement of parking regulations by police cadets and commissionaires, the city provided some off-street parking, a parkade and parking lots.

The automobile also altered entertainment. The most visible change was the drive-in theatre. Ideally suited for families and

Wartime Housing Ltd. bungalows in foreground; the Municipal Hospital, opened in 1955, in centre; and St. Michael's Hospital in the background. Ca. 1955.

The CPR marshalling yards and roundhouse about 1945. Part of the prisoner-of-war camp can be seen in the upper left of the photograph.

young lovers, the drive-in became a popular institution, particularly on warm summer nights. In 1950, Western Drive-In Theatres built a facility at the junction of the Coutts and Raymond highways. But within a year, the Shacklefords, anxious to maintain their movie monopoly, bought the drive-in. In the same year, they built the new 950-seat Paramount Theatre as mute testimony to the continuing popularity of film among Lethbridgians.

In the mid-1950s theatre attendance dropped rapidly as more and more families bought television sets. Lethbridge's CJLH-TV, owned jointly by Lethbridge Broadcasting Limited and the Lethbridge *Herald*, opened in November 1955. Soon Howdy Doody and Roy Rogers replaced children's matinees and Jackie Gleason and Country Hoedown supplanted adult fare. Hollywood reacted with colored films, cinemascope, and blockbusters like the Ten Commandments, the Guns of Navarone, and Sound of Music.

In 1947, city council surrendered its direct control over the annual fair. It signed a lease with the Exhibition Board under which the board took over the fair, rodeo, and other activities and agreed to operate the fair grounds on behalf of the city.

The divesture of the fair grounds was not typical for the period. In fact, the municipal government tended to expand its influence in most areas of recreation. In 1948, the city formed the Civic Playground Commission and appointed George McKillop as its first chairman. Subsequently, the city created a recreation department and named a recreation director. The new department became one of the first products of the prosperity of the city and indicative of the new concern with planning and organization. It organized recreational and cultural facilities and in 1951 conducted a complete parks program for children. The department, eventually reformed as a commission, also completed the Civic Ice Centre. By 1956, it operated nine playgrounds at various areas in the city and a year later was reorganized as the Parks and Recreation Department. It received considerable criticism from those who believed that the department was but a babysitting service for young children while it allegedly neglected school drop-outs, those not on school teams, and senior citizens.

Despite the criticism, the city continued to expand its interests in the recreation business. It repossessed Henderson Lake fastball stadium because it believed the lessees were not maintaining the facilities properly. In 1962, it also bought back the arena at 2nd Avenue and 12th Street South from Sick's Brewery, built a family swimming pool at Henderson Lake, and opened the Adams Ice Centre. At the same time, however, the city was sensitive to suggestions that recreational facilities in Lethbridge could be used more efficiently and by 1965, its playground and recreational program actively sought co-operation with school boards and service clubs.

The prosperity of the decade failed to spur the city to expand hospital facilities and it required a long political process to relieve the crowded buildings. Early in 1945, the Galt Hospital Board gained authorization to select a site and prepare plans for a modern 150-bed facility and in February 1947, voters approved a $700,000 by-law for a hospital immediately east of the existing building. Construction was commenced on a steam turbine plant to serve both hospitals but horrendous cost over-runs and an unstable slope doomed the scheme and the generator was never used. The problem seriously delayed the implementation of the plans for a new hospital.

In the spring of 1949, at the request of city council, the province established a municipal hospital district and appointed a provisional board for the Lethbridge area. Rural residents strongly favoured the idea but, on 9 November 1949, Lethbridge voters turned down a scheme for the purchase of the Galt Hospital by the district and for a $1.4 million loan to build and equip a 150-bed hospital. Two years later, when costs had escalated, Lethbridgians again defeated a money by-law, this time to borrow $1.9 million for a $2.5 million facility. The overcrowding at the Galt Hospital increased in 1952, during the polio epidemic, when the board took over the operation of the Isolation Hospital. The disease, which afflicted about 40 Lethbridgians and killed four, left the isolation hospital with a serious staff shortage and its matron pleaded for help.

Not until April 1952 did Lethbridge ratepayers approve a new municipal hospital district and a $2.8 million, 187-bed hospital for the city and environs. Fortunately, Dr. R. M. Hardy, using drilling results and old maps, demonstrated that old mine workings underlay the Galt Hospital site, hence, it could not support large buildings. Accordingly, the hospital board purchased 14 acres (5.7 ha) on 9th Avenue South for the new facility. In March 1953,

Construction of the St. Mary River dam on 30 October 1948; a sod-turning ceremony was held on 7 August 1946. This dam was the key to irrigation expansion in southern Alberta after the Second World War.

Cavalcade of cars passing over the main fill of the St. Mary River dam after opening ceremonies on 16 July 1951.

lawyer A. G. Virtue, chairman of the hospital board, turned the first sod for the new facility and, in May 1955, Margaret Hamilton, a 1914 graduate of the Galt School of Nursing, cut the ribbon to open the new Lethbridge Municipal Hospital.

The opening of the hospital signalled the end of Galt Hospital as an important health facility in Lethbridge. In 1955, the board transferred all patients to the new Municipal Hospital and closed the old facility. In August, at the instigation of A. W. Shackleford, the city decided to convert the hospital into a home for the chronically ill. The following spring, under the authority of the provincial government, a renovated 70-bed Galt Rehabilitation Centre opened its doors. In 1959 it became an auxiliary hospital and in 1964, when a new auxiliary was built, the old Galt Hospital became a nursing home, a role it kept for only one year. By then, the newly constructed Devon Nursing home took care of elderly patients.

The city also became involved with the care for the aged. Despite their material wealth, the families of the 1950s could no longer cope privately with the old. The trend toward small bungalows discouraged families from taking the elderly into their midst and, at the same time, improved mortality rates increased the number of senior citizens. Recognizing the problem, the Ladies Organization for Civic Improvement founded an Old Folks' Home Committee, soon renamed the Senior Citizens' Committee, to build shelters for the aged. It opened Senior Citizen Home No. 1, accommodating 12 patients, in October 1952 and Senior Citizens Home No. 2 for 16 patients in May 1954.

In 1958, Premier E. C. Manning announced a five-year, anti-recession program, part of which called for the construction of senior citizens' accommodation throughout the province. The types of shelters to be built varied from low-rental, self-contained units for independent couples to lodges with full nursing facilities. The government established foundations to administer the homes and asked communities to provide five-acre (2.0 ha) sites for each lodge or collection of cottages.

In 1960, Lethbridge created the Green Acres Foundation, which included representatives from the city and county of Lethbridge, Coaldale, Picture Butte, Nobleford, Barons, and Coalhurst. Green Acres Lodge, built, landscaped, and equipped by

168

the provincial government, was opened in September 1960. A second facility, Golden Acres Lodge, was completed in 1964.

Private individuals also became involved in the care of the elderly. In 1960, John and Elizabeth Paskuski took over Senior Citizen Home No. 1 and converted it into a nursing home for 31 patients. Six years later they closed it and transferred their patients to the new 100-bed Edith Cavell Nursing Home.

Public health services expanded in the prosperous post-war years. In 1948, a VD clinic was established, followed by a chest X-ray clinic in 1949, and a psychiatric guidance as well as a cancer clinic in 1954. The Victorian Order of Nurses also came to the city in the mid-1950s. In 1958, partly through the efforts of Councillor Lillian Parry, a public health unit was founded in Lethbridge. Among its problems were a rabies outbreak among local dogs and unsanitary conditions in community wading and swimming pools. It conducted a comprehensive spraying program to control flies and mosquitoes. The unit also monitored the manufacture of ice in local freezing plants, the practice of cutting ice from the river or Henderson Lake and storing it in sawdust for summer use having ended in the late 1940s.

Like many other cities, Lethbridge hotly debated the fluoridation issue. In 1957, in 1961, and again in 1965, the community defeated city fluoridation by-laws. Frustrated by the electorate, city council called on the public health unit to provide pre-school and older children with fluoride treatments. It asked the ratepayers to approve another fluoridation by-law in 1967 but they refused. Not until 1974 did Lethbridgians accept fluoridation of their water supply.

By the mid-1960s, then, Lethbridge enjoyed superior health facilities. Well over 100 physicians, dentists, chiropractors, and optometrists practiced in the city. Among them were specialists in all the major branches. Two hospitals, containing about 400 beds, symbolized a wealthy age which could afford and demand the best services available.

Post-war prosperity did not translate automatically into expanded cultural activities for the city. For many years, various citizens had tried in vain to organize a civic museum in Lethbridge. The efforts began in the 1920s, primarily to house the Fred

The first Dayliner to operate on the Lethbridge-Medicine Hat run on its arrival at Lethbridge on 24 April 1955. L-R: C. Frank Lawford, ticket agent; H. Layng, trainman; David K. Shorthouse, engineer; John B. Murray, conductor; and J. J. Merrick, road foreman of engines.

Lethbridge Exhibition, 26 July 1956.

City of Lethbridge street cleaning equipment in the 1950s.

City of Lethbridge dragline in the 1950s.

The first building on the modern Civic Centre, about 1955; it was financed by a $100,000 gift from Fritz Sick.

Botsford and, later, the Thyrza Young Burkitt Indian artifact collections. Unfortunately, these attempts failed, as did a 1951 campaign to have the RCMP include a museum in their proposed new building. In 1955, as part of the celebration of the 50th anniversary of Alberta, the Lethbridge Jubilee Committee unsuccessfully proposed to build a replica of Fort Whoop-up and a museum in Henderson Park. Three years later, Sven Erickson and the tourist committee of the Chamber of Commerce vainly pushed for the establishment in Lethbridge of a Provincial Museum but it too came to naught. Finally, in 1964, the Lethbridge Historical Society, reorganized in 1958, collected numerous artifacts and displayed them in three rooms of the empty Bowman Elementary School. By 1965, the Civic Museum had outgrown its facilities and the city granted it some space in the recently closed Galt Nursing Centre.

The city's library also suffered from neglect. In 1944, plans for a Civic Centre, including a library and art gallery, were prepared but the war postponed library expansion. Although the existing building in Galt Gardens was seriously overcrowded and inadequate, the city did not enlarge it until 1952 and even then did not expand it sufficiently.

The death of Deane Roscoe Yates in 1957 sparked the most important development in cultural circles in the history of the city. Deane Yates was a successful retail lumberman. He was a keen member of the Chinook Club and it was during discussions there that he came to appreciate the need for a good theatre-cum-cultural centre in Lethbridge. He and Mrs. Yates were childless and, as a memorial to his wife, Genevieve Easton Yates, he proposed to leave most of his estate to the city for a cultural centre. The estate consisted of parcels of property from coast to coast and conversion of assets to cash took years. But, in the end, the bequest to the city was $200,347, which appreciated to $266,896 before being used. Little did Yates realize the furore he unleashed by his generous action.

The bequest set off a heated debate on the best type, design and place for the proposed cultural structure. In May 1964, voters decisively rejected a $400,000 Yates Centre with an adjoining $200,000 Public Library. On 13 July 1965, city council ended a decade of sometimes bitter controversy by authorizing a start on the building. On 1 May 1966, the Genevieve E. Yates Memorial Centre opened its doors.

In the immediate post-war years, people sought peace and a return to normal times. That was not to be. The great prosperity of the era could scarcely mask the threat of a nuclear war whose devastation had been so horribly demonstrated in Hiroshima and Nagasaki. Shortly after the peace the Cold War reached its zenith and the fear of Russian expansion caused the western world to create the North Atlantic Treaty Organization. North Americans worried about the Berlin Blockade and some built bomb shelters. In November 1950, Lethbridge founded a Civil Defense Control Committee to identify adequate fallout shelters. The committee stressed evacuation as an escape mechanism, and encouraged the stock-piling of a year's food supply. In the typically naive contemporary view of nuclear devastation, it recommended such foodstuffs as honey and wheat germ but said nothing about drinking water. The strange illusions were fitting symbols of an age that loved ostentation and frills.

The post-war years were also preoccupied with a variety of psychic phenomena, including unidentified flying objects. While some people concerned themselves with reincarnation and the spiritual world, others saw strange craft in the evening skies and odd indentations made by landing gears of Martian spaceships in isolated pastures.

The obsession with extra-terrestrial things and the fear of nuclear war represented but a twinge in an otherwise untroubled era. With the end of the world war and the booming prosperity, people everywhere were concerned mainly with building new homes and fitting them with the latest in appliances and gadgets. The cleanly trimmed lawns which surrounded their pastel bungalows, the opulent cars in their driveways, and the roomy schools in their communities betrayed their ambition for ever-increasing material and social security. It was an age of material well-being.

A suburban street in Lethbridge around 1960.

Chapter Ten
A Planned Society

By the mid-1950s, the basic outlines of modern Lethbridge were apparent. The heavy industries envisioned by the founders of the settlement had not materialized; instead, the city had attracted only small plants which scarcely affected their physical and social environments. Lethbridge had become a pleasant service centre based on its agricultural hinterland, its inhabitants still aware of their natural environment and the vagaries of its climate. The city was still relatively small, its scale human and manageable. Traffic moved smoothly through its tree-lined streets; its parks provided a cool oasis on a dry and windswept plain.

The attractive character of the cityscape owed much to the careful planning and consideration initiated by the civic administration. The depression of the 1930s had demonstrated clearly that industrialized economies needed a large measure of government interference in the social and economic aspects of national life. Wishing to establish a measure of social security for its citizens, Canada introduced unemployment insurance, family allowances, and universal pensions. These programs not only served as precedents for subventions and subsidies to ailing industries and trades, but also allowed governments to play a much greater role in planning social and economic events in order to prevent the chaos and disasters of the past. The postwar prosperity enabled administrations to pay for such programs; consequently, the penchant for planning and orderliness became firmly established in Canada. It also came to prevail in Lethbridge.

As early as 1912, at the height of the real estate boom, the Alberta Town Planning Act had attempted to ensure orderly municipal growth through town planning, but the intervening war years and the depression had made such policies virtually redundant. After the Second World War, however, the demands for planning revived. In 1946, C. S. Burgess studied the need for town planning in Lethbridge and recommended the establishment of a planning commission. Appointed in 1947, the planning commission quickly became active and carefully considered proposed subdivisions and zoning by-law amendments. It sponsored

studies of parking needs, of tourist routes, of city highway approaches and markings, of advertising signage, and of uses for the riverbottom area. In 1950, the commission recommended the hiring of Gerald A. P. Carrothers to begin a master plan for the city. Carrothers submitted an interim report later in the year which called attention to the many problems plaguing the city. "Consideration should be given," he concluded, "to the establishment of a civic planning department with technically trained personnel to co-ordinate the planning activities of the city and to work with other civic departments and the Town Planning Commission."

One of the results of the commission was a 1947 city bylaw which prohibited the placing of signs along the highways leading into the city. At the same time, numerous signs of all shapes, colors, and sizes littered the sides of the roads within the city limits. The advertisers protested loudly against the bylaw, some persisting as late as 1954. Among the more vocal objectors were the local churches, accustomed to advertise their location to visitors on roadside signs.

Not unexpectedly, the attempts to implement orderly planning soon became embroiled in civic and provincial politics. In 1951, the Alberta government established district planning commissions designed to plan for entire regions. Lethbridge initially opposed the concept of district planning, as well as the idea of regional hospitalization, because it thought the costs excessive and it feared the dilution of its own power base. For some time, its opinion held sway and in 1953 its own town planning commission assumed the task of preparing a master plan for Lethbridge. In 1955, however, after the formation of the Lethbridge and District Planning Commission, the city authorized a district planner to prepare a master plan for the city. By then, there were few concrete results from these initial attempts at planning; nevertheless, the various departments and commissions had established the principle of orderly growth and careful planning.

These first attempts at town planning identified and established most of the basic principles which came to dominate

The Popcorn Man

Albert Edward Coulter, better known to generations of children as "Bert the Popcorn Man," operated a mobile popcorn maker at the corner of 3rd Avenue and 5th Street South from 1950 to 1976.

Born in Dundalk, Ontario, in 1902, Coulter came to Lethbridge in 1940. He worked for the Marquis Hotel for 10 years, then purchased a mobile popcorn stand and set it up opposite the Public Library, then located in Galt Gardens. After selling popcorn from the 3rd Avenue and 6th Street location for several years, he had a carpenter design and build a larger stand, painted it in gaudy colors and mounted a "Hot Buttered Popcorn" sign on top. It was this unit he operated at the southwest corner of Galt Gardens for many years.

Coulter's day began about 10:00 a.m., as it took about 30 minutes to get the popper warmed up and ready to go. He was open until noon, then took an hour off to have dinner. Afternoon and evening business was brisk and he usually stayed open until 10:30 p.m. or so. Before television, according to Bert, people stayed downtown longer and he was often busy until midnight. About half his daily business was with children, half with adults.

By 1984, the operation of colorful additions to the downtown scene, such as popcorn vendors, had become so enmeshed in red tape as to be impossible.

planning policies for several decades. The first principle was the recognition of the downtown area as the commercial core of the city. Consequently, the various plans promoted increased accessibility to the downtown area by a roadway, known as Scenic Drive today, and by an expressway along First Avenue, finally realized as today's Crowsnest Trail Corridor. Another long-term objective was to incorporate the river valley into the urban fabric by using its recreational potential and by preserving its natural characteristics. And lastly, early planners sought to balance city development by expanding west of the river so that downtown and river valley became centrally located and easily accessible. In all cases, the first planners wanted to strengthen and revitalize the downtown area and make it the commercial heart of the city.

In March 1956, council authorized the preparation of another master plan for the city. The general plan was to cover the next 20 years and provided for reviews at five-year intervals. But, in 1957, shortly after the Lethbridge and District Planning Commission was reorganized and renamed the Oldman River District Planning Commission, Lethbridge's own planning commission disbanded and transferred its task to the professional planners of the politically appointed regional body. The first working meeting of the new planning organization took place in September 1957 and, a year later, it assumed the function of preparing the city's master plan.

The Oldman River District Planning Commission, renamed the Oldman River Regional Planning Commission (ORRPC) in 1961, submitted the first phase of the city's master plan to council in January 1960. The study, which covered the background and growth of the city, formed the basis for a number of reports published in subsequent years. Late in 1961, ORRPC released the second volume dealing with population and economic activities, and, early in 1962, the third volume covering land classification, public utilities, residential areas, and education. In the next two years, the commission produced several more reports examining open spaces and recreation, parking, communications, commerce and industry. The seventh and last volume, completed in December 1963, discussed civic design and programming. In all, the master plan was a comprehensive attempt to control the growth and development of the city. It was studied in great detail by council and received much public input. On 2 November 1964, council enacted a by-law approving the general plan, becoming one of the few civic governments in Canada to do so.

During the years that ORRPC was developing the master plan, the city operated under a 1958 by-law which provided for the interim control of development. The by-law was amended in 1962 to conform with provincial legislation and to clarify the process of interim control. As a tool, interim development control was useful because it prepared citizens and businessmen for the strict zoning by-laws expected under the master plan. It also provided authorities with the opportunity to test planning concepts under local conditions unfettered by rigid zoning by-laws.

Interim control did create a conflict between town planners and developers. In the 1960s, for example, town planners were

Members of the Major Jack Ross Chapter IODE presenting Christmas gifts to a family of recent immigrants, called ''New Canadians'' at the time. Ca. late 1950s.

Fourth Avenue between 5th and 6th Streets South, ca. 1960.

convinced that far too much of Lethbridge was zoned commercial. *Ad hoc* committees and boards had permitted the spread of business establishments eastward on 3rd Avenue South, north on 13th Street North, and south along parts of Mayor Magrath Drive. The planners seemed determined to stop this ribbon development and objected to the construction of restaurants, motels, and service stations, rather than residences, along Mayor Magrath Drive. They also disliked the establishment of medical clinics and pharmacies on 9th Avenue South and on Mayor Magrath Drive.

The bitterest confrontation developed over a shopping mall promoted by Trident Development Corporation. The planners, backed by downtown businessmen, argued that such a mall would pose a real threat to the viability of the city centre and, in November 1965, they refused to recommend that council approve the $2 million mall. Their position was opposed strongly by lawyer W. E. Huckvale, who argued that the underlying policy of the planners was to prevent commercial development in the outlying

178

areas of the city. He argued that refusal to construct the Trident mall would stop all major developers from coming to the city. "How long," he concluded, "can the city continue to hold back development on a six-lane highway, such as Mayor Magrath?" Huckvale's views echoed the development voice in the city and his argument prevailed; city council eventually concurred and approved the Trident mall, subsequently known as College Mall Shopping Centre.

The controversies subsided somewhat with the appointment of an Interim Development Appeal Board, which also allowed a final appeal to city council. Consequently, other projects in which ORRPC was involved were less controversial. They included site selection for the junior college, replotting of the area that later included Scenic Drive, design of the industrial park, conversion from the old grid form of subdivision development to contoured plans, as well as a scheme for the redevelopment of the central business core.

Water tower near intersection of 3rd Avenue South and Mayor Magrath Drive in 1964.

Fundamental to the master plan was an efficient system of roadways. Central to this design was the street known today as Mayor Magrath Drive. Originating with the city's purchase of the right-of-way of the old CPR Crowsnest Pass branch line in 1916, the road was known as the Southeast Entrance in the 1930s and the Airport Road in the 1940s. The modern design owes much to Salisbury, Rhodesia (now Zimbabwe), where such thoroughfares are common, because Keith Driver, the planner in charge of the project, came from there. In May 1947 it was renamed Mayor Magrath Drive. In 1964, upon completion of the 21st Street underpass, it became South Mayor Magrath Drive, while the extension of the drive into northeastern Lethbridge and the industrial park was called North Mayor Magrath Drive. A recurring problem to the planners, who wanted the drive to be a main artery into the industrial park, was to maintain its 200-foot (61-m) width. They encountered constant pressure from businessmen adjacent to the roadway who wanted to eliminate the service roads and gain direct access to the highway from their establishments.

The other artery developed by the city was Scenic Drive. First proposed in 1948, this roadway was designed to connect a number of dead-end streets, provide a scenic by-pass route along the southwestern coulees between highways 3 and 4, and furnish easy access to the downtown core. Work was started on the project in 1958 and in 1963 it was named Scenic Drive. Once again, town planners had to fight local businessmen to prevent them from turning the road into a gaudy motel-restaurant-service station strip, a battle they managed to win.

Another important objective of the planners was the establishment of an industrial park in Lethbridge. Although the city had looked to the northeast section for an industrial park since the boom times at the turn of the century, the predominance of the free enterprise philosophy, the slow growth of its population, and a depleted treasury had prevented any concrete action. At the end of the war, however, council's attention was drawn to the land occupied by the prisoner-of-war camp and to its structures, both of which were ideally suited for industrial and educational purposes. In October 1947, the federal government sold the internment camp to the Alberta government which began to dispose of buildings and small plots of land through auctions and tenders. By the end of 1950, most of the buildings had been removed and several plots of land sold. Buyers of land included Charles O. Asplund, the

180

Lethbridge experimental station, Lethbridge Co-operative Packers Limited, and the Seventy-Seven Oil Company.

In addition to the internment camp, Lethbridge's industrial areas included the CPR trackage and yards, a strip two blocks wide on the south side of the tracks from 8th to 21st Streets, two sections on both sides of 9th Street North from 1st to about 5th Avenue North, a plot along the tracks east of the city limits, and a small triangle along the Coutts railway north of the Exhibition grounds. The old municipal airport was still vacant as was all of the land to the east of 23rd Street and most of the land to the north of 5th Avenue North. In the late 1950s, the city purchased several tracts in sections 4 and 9-9-21-W4 in order to round out the northeastern industrial park. In September 1965, council purchased hangars 2, 3, and 4 at Kenyon field and made them available to light industry. No. 4 hangar, for instance, was rented almost immediately to W. R. (Stubb) Ross, the manager of Comanche Aviation Limited.

The plans for an industrial park in the city's northeast coincided with the collapse of the western Canadian coal mining industry. The rapid conversion to natural gas for domestic heating and the dieselization of Canada's railways effectively destroyed the demand for coal. Galt No. 8 mine closed in 1957 and Galt No. 10, formerly the Standard Mine at Shaughnessy, became the last operating colliery in the Lethbridge field; it ceased operations in 1965. The closure signalled the end of an industry that had conceived Lethbridge and sustained it for three-quarters of a century.

The city sought to find alternatives. In 1951, it appointed an industrial development commission, and in 1957, coincident with the closure of Shaft No. 8, hired John Banfield as its first industrial commissioner.

The commission's effectiveness was difficult to measure. In some instances, its work may have been redundant. In 1948, before its establishment, for example, J. A. Jarvie founded Superior Cinder & Concrete Ltd., a highly successful manufactory producing cinder bricks and tiles out of slag from the worked-out Galt No. 3 colliery. (Jarvie, a double amputee as a result of service overseas, made a point of hiring handicapped persons while his success inspired all those with whom he came in contact.) Lethbridge's natural advantages attracted other small plants.

Most of the industries established in Lethbridge were closely related to its agricultural hinterland. Although one of the first

Lethbridge Parkade at 6th Street and 5th Avenue South in 1968.

companies to locate on a designated industrial site was Horton Steel Works Limited (today's Dresser Clark Division of Dresser Industrial Limited), most new plants involved the processing of agricultural products. More typical was Western Canadian Seed Processors Limited (today's Canbra Foods Limited) which built a plant on the old airport site in 1958. Initially, it produced oil from sunflower seeds but eventually it turned to safflower and rapeseed, the latter rapidly taking the primary place. The firm finally earned a profit in 1965 and by 1983, as part of Burns Foods, was the largest employer in the city. In 1965, another packing plant, Canadian Dressed Meats, established itself next to Canada Packers on No.

3 highway. By then a large poultry processing plant was in operation and a major freezing plant had started. Eventually, these modern food processing plants replaced the decaying coal mining industry.

The collieries were not the only victims of modern technology. Lethbridge had always been an important wholesale and retail centre for southern Alberta. Modern means of transportation and communication gradually shifted that business to larger centres like Calgary, Winnipeg, and Toronto. Nowhere was this transformation more obvious than in the farm implement business. All the major companies moved their parts depots to Calgary.

Above: A row of new bungalows in a new subdivision, Lethbridge, ca. 1960.

St. Augustine's Anglican Church, ca. 1960.

Southminster United Church, ca. 1960.

St. Patrick's Roman Catholic Church, ca. 1960.

Lethbridge also lost out in air transportation and her position as a regional air centre declined in the late 1950s. As passenger figures fell to 250 per month, Trans-Canada Airlines mounted a litany of complaints about Kenyon Field's short runways. Even after the runways were lengthened in 1958, the airline wanted to leave Lethbridge and that year it slashed its service into the city. Only a year later, Western Airlines began to overfly Lethbridge and land in Calgary instead. Convenient air service did not return to Lethbridge until one of its residents, Walter R. (Stubb) Ross, a president of the Flying Farmers of America, formed Lethbridge Air Service. This fledgling company was destined to become a leading airline in southern Alberta.

The increasing use of the automobile for intercity travel also destroyed passenger rail traffic. In 1954, the CPR stopped conventional passenger train service and the following year inaugurated dayliners between Lethbridge and Calgary, Medicine Hat, and Coutts. Rail travel continued to fall off, however, and by the late 1960s a dayliner sometimes left the city without any passengers at all. The railway cancelled the service entirely in 1971 and concentrated all its attention on freight.

Not all of the schemes proposed by the city planners were utilitarian. In the 1950s, they launched a policy to clear the river valley of houses and preserve it for parkland development. This policy was a radical departure from earlier practice. In 1912, the city had purchased 160 acres (64.8 ha) of river bottom lands and had subdivided them into small holdings called the River Bottom Tracts. From about six households in 1912, the population of the area, sometimes called Riverside, grew to about 84 households in 1953. Because the river flooded frequently, some of the floods of major proportions, the houses in the valley were small, frame structures of little value; consequently, the city encountered little opposition to its intentions to create a park in the river valley. In 1950, planners launched a program to remove people from the area, offering incentives which included the sale of prairie level lots at one dollar and financial help to move those houses worth moving. By 1959, all except one or two of the families had relocated and, in February 1960, the area was named Indian Battle Park to commemorate the battle fought there in October 1870.

The planners also developed a park at the west end of 6th Avenue North. The development of Mayor Magrath Drive in the late 1950s destroyed a baseball diamond at its intersection with the future Parkside Drive. Late in 1961, the city laid out a new baseball diamond and park on property it owned on 6th Avenue North and named it after Dave Elton, a former mayor.

Not all the city's plans were wise or popular. In 1956, for example, the city built an asphalt plant on an acreage in a residential neighbourhood near 9th Street and 4th Avenue North. It was a noisy, dirty and dusty facility and nearby housewives, reacting with anger and indignation, demanded that it be moved. After some bluster, city administrators realized their error and eventually moved the plant elsewhere.

In the mid-1950s, the city began a program to revamp its water supply system. In 1955, it constructed a four million-gallon (15 million-L) water reservoir at the corner of 3rd Avenue and Mayor Magrath Drive and laid plans for a 300,000-gallon (1.1 million-L) water tank at the same site. The completion of the reservoir meant that the old standpipes built in 1904 were redundant and the city removed them as well as a 1912 water tower which had never been used.

Also in 1955, Councillor C. J. Black, concerned about the uncertainty of long-term water supplies for the city, proposed the construction of a pipeline from the St. Mary Reservoir to Lethbridge. Black argued that the scheme was essential to Lethbridge because prospective food processing plants were refusing to locate in the city because of inadequate water supplies. Although his words went unheeded, the unreliability of water supplies and the frequency of muddy tapwater when river levels were low, were intolerable and, late in 1957, council completed a $500,000 river diversion weir.

To some extent, the initial emphasis on orderly planning can be attributed to the influence of local parties on civic politics. Prior to the war, the establishment party, then known as the Civic Government Association, dominated local affairs. But in 1947, A. Gladstone Virtue, a strongly opinionated local lawyer, broke the 60-year monopoly on civic politics by winning a seat on council as an Independent. That same year, the Civic Labor Organization, a creation of the city's labour unions, won two seats. Four years later, in 1951, several women's groups formed the Lethbridge Citizens Organization for the purpose of electing a woman to council, and

Prime Minister and Mrs. John G. Diefenbaker at Lethbridge station during the 1963 federal election campaign — the last of the railway coach whistle-stop campaigns.

the following December, Lillian M. Parry defeated Councillor W. E. Huckvale. The clustering of issues around political parties created identifiable platforms and provided voters with candidates committed to definite policies.

Lethbridge's civic political parties began to break down in the late 1950s and, increasingly, independent candidates ran for office and won elections. Rewards in city politics were few and parties found it difficult to maintain discipline. Unless businessmen and professionals could be guaranteed election, they refused to run under the Civic Government Association banner. Moreover, labour solidarity collapsed under the rivalry of competing interests. The result was that civic politics became a race between individuals each running for personal, disparate reasons.

Some of the new individualism in local politics carried over into civic organizations, for example, in the local civil defence committee. On 4 October 1957, the Russians placed into orbit a 70-pound (32-kg) satellite, Sputnik, an incident that frightened governments and citizens alike. The fear of a Russian invasion increased with the Cuban missile crisis of October 1962. For a short time the fear of nuclear war united the people, but by 1965, dissention and personality conflicts tore the Lethbridge civil defense organization apart and it lost its effectiveness. Eventually, an emergency measures organization took over its duties.

The Sputnik launch also caused North Americans to question their educational institutions. When coupled to the general prosperity of modern society and its increasing complexity, the belief that western educational institutions were inadequate spawned renewed emphasis on formal education. Students remained in school longer than ever before. Even as late as the early 1950s, only those preparing for university attended high school but within a decade nearly everyone completed high school and considered it the training ground for lifeskills. And a relatively large percentage of young people continued their studies at various post secondary institutions.

The consequence of increased interest in formal education, coupled with the baby boom, was an unprecedented school building program. In 1956, the public school board constructed three new facilities, Gilbert Paterson Elementary and Junior High School, General Stewart and George McKillop, while the separate school board built Assumption school. Only a year later, the Catholic board

built St. Francis Boys' High School and in 1960 St. Patrick's Elementary School. The Dorothy Gooder School for retarded children was established in 1959. The public system added Winston Churchill High and Wilson Junior High, and Lakeview Elementary in 1960, Agnes Davidson in 1962 and Hardieville in 1964. St. Francis' and St. Joseph's schools became part of the newly enlarged Catholic Central High School in 1966.

The city also witnessed the establishment of several private schools. The Church of Jesus Christ of Latter-day Saints founded a seminary in Lethbridge in 1953. The Glendale Seventh Day Adventists opened a private religious school in 1959, while the Christian Reformed Church founded the Immanual Christian School in 1962. In addition, several kindergartens opened and closed within the period. A Chinese language school, which taught outside regular hours, operated during the 1960s.

Very important to the development of Lethbridge was the increasing popularity of post-secondary education. The desire to build a community college first arose in Lethbridge at the turn of the century. Conceived in the United States, the community college taught students the practical skills needed on the farm or in the factory or business. Several small, specialized institutions emerged in Lethbridge during the next forty years but none ever remained long enough to become a permanent facility. The concept of agricultural or vocational training resurfaced in the late 1940s when the federal government abandoned the prisoner of war camp, an ideal site for a community college. But, by this time, a new idea, the junior college, had emerged. The junior college, unlike the community college, provided first and second year level university courses. Lethbridge educators combined both concepts and in the late 1940s developed the idea of an institution providing the first year of university as well as two years of vocational training.

Lethbridge's drive for a junior college encountered three major obstacles. The conservative-minded, Edmonton-oriented board of governors of the University of Alberta resisted all attempts to teach university courses outside their jurisdiction. Similarly, the provincial apprenticeship board wanted to retain full control over all vocational education in the province. Lastly, for some years, district school boards were decidedly unenthusiastic about the college and were unwilling to challenge Edmonton and Calgary's monopoly in post-secondary education.

Psychedelic designs, typical of the 1960s, on empty store fronts along 13th Street North; No. 2 Firehall, which was demolished in 1970, is in the background.

Lethbridge's oldest hotel, about 1960; the "Ladies and Escorts" sign is a reminder of the dreary, segregated drinking inflicted on a long-suffering public for decades following prohibition.

Despite these obstacles, several Lethbridgians persisted in their plans for a junior college in the city. Their leader was Gilbert C. Paterson, a consummate politician, who assembled a group of supporters with influence in crucial areas. Among them were the indomitable Kate Andrews, who was popular in rural areas; lawyer Alan J. Cullen, who was a skilled lobbyist with federal government connections; educator W. J. Cousins, who understood the academic community; and school superintendent L. H. Bussard, who worked among regional school administrators and boards. This group executed a carefully planned promotional campaign to popularize the notion of a junior college for the city. In 1949, Bussard undertook a study on the need for a college. His report, confirmed by a 1951 study conducted by Dr. S. V. Martorana from Washington State Univeristy, emphasized the rapid population growth in the city and surrounding region, the excessive high school drop-out rate, and, hence, the need for post-secondary education in southern Alberta.

By appealing to popular sentiment, and by winning the support of southern Alberta school boards, the proponents of the college idea overcame the outside objectors and eventually founded the first junior college in Alberta and, by some definitions, in Canada. On 17 April 1957, the Lethbridge Junior College opened with 36 pupils temporarily housed in the Lethbridge Collegiate Institute. Two years later, the college obtained an 80-acre (32.4-ha) campus south of the city and in October 1962 laid the cornerstone for its first structure, the Dr. Kate Andrews Building. In 1963, the college purchased several adjoining parcels of land to allow expansion of its facilities and to accommodate a projected university.

The advocates of the junior college always intended their project to become a degree granting institution, a plan vigorously opposed by the University of Alberta. At the insistence of the university, the provincial government allowed the college to teach only first-year courses in the early years. Local influence, however, eventually overcame Edmonton's objections and, in 1962, when the college moved to its new campus, it also began to teach second year courses. At the same time, the college board encouraged instructors to work toward their doctorates, improved the library, and laid plans for a $2 million science building. In 1965, the college obtained approval for two-year university status and for a new science building.

The drive to establish a junior college in Lethbridge reflected the planning and consideration that went into the development of the city. Education was big business, a large industry providing jobs to its staff and supporting workers, an activity bringing important economic benefits to the community without any detrimental side effects. It represented a concern with more than economics, a care for the quality of life rather than for more material benefits. Fortunately for Lethbridge, the attention to planning had long and beneficial effects: the city maintained the viability of the downtown, created an efficient network of roads, established pleasant parks and recreational facilities, and founded a superior education system.

The Nikka Yuko Centennial Garden, better known as the Japanese Gardens, in Lethbridge in 1967.

Chapter Eleven

Garden on the Prairie

In many ways the Nikka Yuko Centennial Garden fittingly symbolized Lethbridge's ninth decade. Its subdued simplicity and natural beauty expressed the reconciliation of diverse racial and cultural values into a common purpose. In one way, the garden reflected the harmony and love exuded by the hippie movement of the 1960s. At the same time, however, it represented a refuge in a turbulent decade. The violent demonstrations against authority, materialism, and racism, which marked the late 1960s, did not penetrate the graceful quiet of the garden. Nor did the ravages of the natural prairie environment. In a profound way, the Nikka Yuko Centennial Garden demonstrated the desire of Lethbridgians to make their city a garden on a treeless, windswept prairie.

The idea originated with Chief Abbot Otani of Kyoto, Japan, who visited Lethbridge in 1961 and suggested that the Japanese community should build a Japanese garden. A Buddhist minister at Raymond, Yuteysu Kawamura, discussed the concept with several Japanese leaders who selected a site on the Coutts highway near Lethbridge but failed to secure the necessary funds for the project. In the summer of 1963, however, the director of the local tourist bureau, Kurt M. Steiner, learned of the garden idea and noted it as one way of attracting tourists to the area. By chance, he met Kawamura and discussed the scheme with him. By this time, the project was realistic because the federal government was prepared to sponsor centennial of confederation projects. Within months, the two men contacted many people, organized several meetings, and established the necessary committees.

By the fall of 1963, a brief, prepared for the federal government, recommended the construction of a Japanese garden on a site at Henderson Lake. The proposal delicately skirted the commemorative nature of the garden because bitter memories of the shameful treatment of the Japanese in southern Alberta were still fresh. Consequently, the promoters played down the local connection, seeing the project not as a tribute to the Japanese-Canadians of the region but as a contribution from the Japanese culture to Canada. Despite this cautious approach, the brief did arouse considerable friction within the local Japanese community but the cultural theme carried the day in spite of this opposition. The submission was approved by the Lethbridge Centennial Committee, city council, and provincial and federal authorities. The garden was, in fact, one of the first centennial projects accepted by all levels of government.

The concept of one culture contributing to another became an important factor in the drive for authenticity. The promoters hired Dr. Tadashi Kubo, a Japanese landscape architect, to design the garden, they imported pre-fabricated buildings from Japan, and they surrendered veto powers to knowledgeable Japanese. The gardeners, however, used only Canadian ornamentals because Japanese species were not adaptable to southern Alberta conditions. Specialists from the Brooks Horticultural Station and the Lethbridge Research Station aided in the selection of the plants.

Completed in the summer of 1966, the garden was opened officially on 16 July 1967 by Prince and Princess Takamasu, brother and sister-in-law of the Emperor of Japan. Its name, the Nikka Yuko Centennial Garden, meant Japanese-Canadian friendship.

The enthusiastic reception of the Nikka Yuko project once again revealed Lethbridge's fondness for parks. Nowhere was this more evident than in the development of the river valley. In the 1950s, city council began to move the small houses from the valley, a process virtually completed by 1964. Meanwhile, council developed Indian Battle Park in the area between the CP Rail High Level bridge and the power plant. In February 1969, council approved a parks and recreation commission report, which stated that, "The river valley will be developed as an urban park, catering to the active and passive recreational needs of the city and region. Because of increased emphasis on leisure time activities, the area will become the focal point of the city and will link the east and west areas of Lethbridge." This and subsequent reports reflected the

Nicholas Sheran Park in West Lethbridge.

growing feeling among Lethbridgians that the valley should be preserved and protected for community use.

The 1969 report became the basis of the city's river valley policy. In 1970, at the suggestion of Elizabeth Hall, an ardent naturalist, the city began to purchase small parcels of riverbottom lands. That same year, Neil J. Andrew released the River Valley Corridor Recreational Development Plan. This plan was realized in 1975 in the Lethbridge River Valley Development Scheme which called for the acquisition of the valley of the Oldman River within the city limits, its banks, and sufficient upland prairie to protect its scenic quality. In 1977, however, after the provincial legislature disallowed development scheme by-laws, the city asked Alberta Environment to establish a restricted development area in the river valley to ensure a degree of land use control. The provincial government passed enabling legislation requiring cabinet approval for land use changes in the river valley. The city's plans for park development were secure.

The city's parks policy was but one example of the careful attention to planning so characteristic of Lethbridge's development. In the post-war years, Lethbridge city councils had accepted the need and desirability of town planning. In marked contrast to such cities as Winnipeg or Great Falls, Lethbridge's councillors were sympathetic to the retention of the downtown core rather than to

the enhancement of the suburbs. Generally, they took a midway position between the planners, who wanted tight controls, and developers, who wanted no restrictions on suburban developments.

City planners could not stem the tide of shopping centre construction which became one of the peculiar developments of the last two decades. The trend toward supermarkets and large department stores, coupled with the need for convenient parking spaces, led to the proliferation of sprawling suburban shopping plazas. Containing virtually all the basic shops, the environmentally controlled malls became sterile temples of consumerism. Their managers, attempting to imitate the coziness of downtown shopping, restored to fancy gimmicks, such as boat, car, and fashion shows, miniature midways, and ticket sales.

In 1965, Lethbridge had only one shopping mall — Art Batty's Shopper's World on Mayor Magrath Drive, renamed Holiday Village Mall in 1972, Lethbridge Inn Plaza in 1979, and Sandman Inn Plaza in 1982. But, as the city's population increased, other malls followed. Most of the development occurred on the fringes of the city where land was still relatively inexpensive and promoters could build huge parking lots. In 1967, Canada Safeway and Zellers built Shopper's Plaza, renamed Country Fair Shopping Mall and later Magrath Market Place, on the southern end of Mayor Magrath Drive. Still further south, College Shopping Mall was opened in

Proclamation

Nous, **Marcel Laurin**, maire de la VILLE DE SAINT-LAURENT dans la province de Québec, Canada et

Frank Sherring, maire de la VILLE DE LETHBRIDGE dans la province d'Alberta, Canada,

PROCLAMONS par la présente le jumelage de nos villes, en conformité avec les résolutions dûment adoptées, dans le but de promouvoir les relations d'ordre culturel, touristique, social et économique, entre nos citoyens.

EN FOI DE QUOI nous avons apposé notre signature et le sceau de notre ville, en l'hôtel de ville de Saint-Laurent, ce VINGT-SEPTIÈME jour de JUILLET, MIL NEUF CENT SOIXANTE-SEPT.

Maire de la Ville de Saint-Laurent
Mayor of the City of Saint-Laurent

We, **Frank Sherring**, Mayor of the CITY OF LETHBRIDGE in the Province of Alberta, Canada and

Marcel Laurin, Mayor of the CITY OF SAINT-LAURENT in the Province of Québec, Canada,

HEREBY PROCLAIM the twinning of our cities, in conformity with the resolutions duly approved, in order to promote the exchange of cultural, tourist, social and economic relations in the interest of our citizens.

IN WITNESS WHEREOF we have signed and caused the seals of our cities to be hereunto affixed, in the City Hall of the City of Saint-Laurent, this TWENTY-SEVENTH DAY OF JULY, ONE THOUSAND NINE HUNDRED AND SIXTY-SEVEN.

Mayor of the City of Lethbridge
Maire de la Ville de Lethbridge

The Lethbridge Brewery Garden in 1967, established originally to stabilize the slope adjacent to the brewery by planting trees.

1969 while West Village Mall was finished in 1978. In north Lethbridge the pace was equally frantic. Westminster Shopping Plaza was completed in 1970, Centre Village Shopping Mall in 1971, Chinook Mall in 1978, and Park Meadow Mall in 1979.

Despite the proliferation of suburban malls, Lethbridge's central business district remained the largest and most important shopping area in the city and southern Alberta. The city commissioned several reports on the area, including the Urban Renewal Study in 1966, which examined the deterioration of the central business district and identified the area west of 5th Street as most in need of rehabilitation. That same year, the city improved access to the central core by rebuilding the eastern and western approaches and by upgrading 9th Street South. Finally, in 1972, the Downtown Redevelopment Scheme, which included a provincial government building and a major shopping mall, became the instrument of downtown renewal.

As early as 1966, William Hawrelak, Edmonton's controversial mayor, had proposed a $2 million shopping complex in the rundown

194

area west of 5th Street South. But the scheme, which was the first serious attempt at downtown redevelopment, ended in acrimony. Less than ten years later, Lethbridge Centre Limited adopted Hawrelak's idea and built the city's only downtown mall on 5th Street South. The provincial government added its building in 1976 and the city its new fire hall in 1977. The Lethbridge Lodge Hotel was built in 1978, while Southland Terrace and Chancery Court, two business blocks, were constructed in 1982. The Provincial Courthouse and Haig Tower rounded out the redevelopment of the downtown in 1983.

The increased involvement of the city in economic and physical development caused an inevitable growth in the size of the administration. As early as 1966, overcrowding became a serious problem in city hall. The city moved some of its offices to the former St. Patrick's School, by then called the City Hall Annex, but that did not solve the problem. In 1974, it attempted to secure the old public library in Galt Gardens for the community services department but that plan was cancelled and the Southern Alberta

Fishing at Henderson Lake in the 1960s.

Art Gallery took over the building. Instead, community services moved into rented quarters at 1020-20th Street South. Nevertheless, the problem of overcrowding continued to plague the city administration.

The civic government also suffered some unrest within its own administrative structure. The city's first city manager, J. T. Watson, retired in 1949, and was mainly responsible for the enviable financial position of the city at the end of the war. He had ruled the city with a strong hand, acting first and seeking approval later. Succeeding managers were less successful manipulators of city council and tended to defer to the politicians, becoming administrators rather than managers. In 1967, in 1968, and again in 1973, the city lost two managers and a mayor through sudden resignations. City council tended to blame the problem on the system rather than on the individuals and several times debated alternate forms of civic government. In April 1974, it discussed possible methods of reform with the minister of municipal affairs but could not come to a decision. Consequently, it retained the council-manager form of local government.

City planners could do little about the problem of Lethbridge's airport. By the late 1960s, the civic government could no longer afford to maintain and modernize Kenyon Field. In March 1967, council sold the airport to the federal department of transport, which previously had purchased several parcels of land to extend the runways.

In 1970, Air Canada finally pulled out of the city after years of awkward scheduling and poor service. The national airline was replaced by Walter R. (Stubb) Ross's newly incorporated Time Airways Limited. For some years, Ross's former company, Lethbridge Air Services, had provided a Lethbridge to Calgary service with eight-passenger aircraft. With the support of city council, Ross obtained a five-year license from the federal transport commission. This made financing easier and permitted him to purchase larger airplanes such as two de Havilland Twin Otters in 1971 and a 36-passenger Fairchild in 1974.

The industrialization of Lethbridge in the late 1960s owed much to various federal incentive programs. In 1969, the Department of Regional Economic Expansion, under the Regional Development Act, designated Lethbridge as an area needing economic assistance for the next four years. One of the largest

companies to take advantage of the generous grants program was Swift Canadian, which in 1971 completed a $4.0 million packing plant on 30 acres (12.1 ha) in the industrial park. By 1972, the department of regional expansion had helped several more plants expand or move into the industrial park, including Lethbridge Iron Works, Canadian Dressed Meats, Kirchner Machine, Prebuilt Industries, Custom Engine and Parts, Southern Feeds, Western Canadian Seed Processing, and Western Truck Body.

By the mid-1970s, Lethbridge's industrial park had become large and complex. Accordingly, city council ordered its economic development department to subdivide it and to select names for various portions of the park. The department chose A. C. Anderson, A. W. Shackleford, Palliser and Churchill industrial parks as acceptable names, which were readily approved by council.

In the late 1960s, as the city's residential districts expanded eastward, citizens increasingly complained about odors and other nuisances emanating from the cluster of packing plants, feed mills, stockyards, and feedlots in the area. When city council directed the complaints to the provincial board of health, the local chamber of commerce objected strenuously to the adverse publicity. Arguing that the feedlot-packing plants were vital to the city, the chamber recommended a policy of co-operation and dialogue.

The chamber's pro-business position won out partly through circumstances. Although local packing plants increased their business throughout the 1960s, producers tended to sell directly to the plants rather than at public auction. Consequently, the public stockyards declined in importance and they were scarcely used by the end of the decade. The city purchased the yards in 1981 and three years later demolished them to make way for the Crowsnest Trail project.

While commercial and industrial expansion surged ahead in post-war Lethbridge, centres of research and learning filled an ever-increasing role in the economy of the city. Of particular importance to Lethbridge was agricultural research: the Animal Diseases Research Institute and the Lethbridge Research Station expanded in 1969 and in 1977 respectively, while the Prairie Agricultural Machinery Institute opened on the campus of the Lethbridge Community College in 1975. By 1984, more than 600 people worked on the staffs of various research and educational institutions in the city. In addition, hundreds of doctors, dentists,

Downtown Lethbridge in the mid-1960s when Phase 1 of Downtown Redevelopment was decided upon and the area west of 5th Street was identified as the region most in need of renovation.

lawyers, architects, engineers, and other professionals added to the brains industry, an increasingly important business in Lethbridge.

Vital to the development of the city was the founding of a university. The campaign to bring a university to Lethbridge followed the successful pattern set by the junior college. First came the careful weaving of a community concensus of the need for a university, followed by lobbying of the provincial cabinet, the inevitable feasibility studies, more lobbying, and finally, the reconciliation of diverse interest groups. By 1967, the strategy had succeeded and the University of Lethbridge opened its doors in the Science Building at the Lethbridge Junior College.

Ironically, a bitter controversy erupted after the founding of the university. Students, faculty, and administrators wanted a campus separate from the junior college so that they could establish a distinct identity. They received support from city planners, who for years had advocated the expansion of the city west of the river, and never seriously considered any other location for the university. In December 1967, the board of governors of the university approved moving the university west of the river and the city began to acquire options on farms in the area.

The decision to build the university campus in West Lethbridge aroused a storm of protest. In the first instance, the junior college board, which wanted to extend its control to the university, opposed the move. Its leading spokesperson, Mrs. Kate Andrews, joined with John Landeryou, MLA, to fight it. Equally spirited in their opposition were the North Lethbridge Businessmen's Association, a real estate lobby called the Lethbridge Taxpayers' Association, and several prominent Mormons. Although all the groups had their own selfish motives, they were united in their drive to keep the university east of the river.

Unfortunately, Lethbridge had no representative in the provincial cabinet, hence, Premier Manning's government was not well-informed on the issue. Out of touch with urban issues anyway, the government at first tried to force a plebiscite on the issue and, when that failed, insisted that a connecting bridge to the university not even be discussed for eight years. It reduced the size of the campus to 315 acres (127 ha), and limited the curriculum to undergraduate offerings in art, science, and education. As a result, for several years the site of the campus was about 11 miles (18 km) from the city centre via the No. 3 highway bridge.

Campus in the Coulees

A preliminary master plan for the new University of Lethbridge was unveiled by famed architect Arthur Erickson at a public meeting in Lethbridge on 19 December 1968.

Erickson's plan called for the buildings to be low so that they would fit in with the long, sweeping lines of the prairies. This early concept was reinforced by Erickson's first glimpse of the CP Rail High Level Bridge at Lethbridge. The sweep of the railroad bridge convinced him that it was feasible to design and build a massive structure across several coulees, yet blend it in with the characteristic horizontal lines of the uplands.

The design set the main buildings astraddle two coulees on the edge of the valley on the west side of the Oldman River. Classrooms, offices, laboratories, and residences were to be located in two long, inter-connected buildings with a total length of over 1,000 feet. (Only one has been built to date.) Main buildings were to be connected to prairie level structures such as the physical education building by covered walkways for protection from the wind. Much use was made of earthen berms to conceal upland service buildings as well as features such as parking lots and playing fields.

In 1977, City Council permitted the erection of Fransden Manor Apartments, a highrise that stood out like an exclamation mark on the West Lethbridge skyline and utterly destroyed the effect Arthur Erickson had tried so hard to create.

Despite the obstructionism, university and city authorities persisted and construction began in West Lethbridge during 1970. Designed by famed architect Arthur Erickson, the "Campus in the Coulees" opened in the fall of 1971 and received wide acclaim for its architectural beauty and setting. It also became an important addition to the city's educational services.

After much discussion and debate, Lethbridge finally resolved the public library problem. Although council had approved an expansion to the crowded facilities in 1965 and even stripped back the sods for the excavation, opposition to further encroachment on Galt Gardens scuttled the project. In 1971, council approved

The University of Lethbridge opened in September 1967 with 742 students and 145 faculty and staff members in the Science Building of the Lethbridge Junior College; university offices were located in temporary, rented buildings to the right of the main building.

an $800,000 item in its capital works budget for a new library but further controversy over its location delayed construction. Eventually, the former site of the Central School on 5th Avenue proved acceptable and, in April 1974, Chief Judge L. S. Turcotte opened the new $1.3 million library.

On a more prosaic level, the city also settled the fate of its power plant. The aging plant, with its European machinery, was in need of extensive and costly repairs. At the same time, its generators were incapable of meeting anticipated electrical requirements. In 1960, for example, the city decided to buy power from Calgary Power for the new sewage treatment plant and in 1965 it decided not to install a new generator in the power plant but to negotiate with Calgary Power on the city's future needs. For the next few years the city divided itself between those who fought to renew the plant and those who wanted to switch to Calgary Power. Finally, a 1974 study, commissioned by the city, recommended several alternatives from which council chose the sale of the plant to Calgary Power for about $800,000. The decision sparked an emotional protest, fanned by several political

199

Sod-turning ceremonies for the University of Lethbridge west side campus, 6 September 1969. Premier Harry Strom officiated.

The west side campus of the University of Lethbridge in 1970 in relation to the city and the connecting river valley, by then zoned mostly recreational.

opportunists and the inevitable "Save Our Power Plant Citizens Committee." The public meetings and ensuing hullabaloo failed to inform the citizenry that the collapse of Lethbridge's coal industry had made its power plant obsolete and expensive. The city could obtain its electrical requirements more cheaply from Calgary Power. Eventually, council's will prevailed and it concluded the sale in May 1974.

Care of the aged continued to concern Lethbridgians during the period. In 1966, Devon Nursing Home opened at 13th Street North, absorbing patients from the Galt Nursing Home. That same year, the city transferred patients from the Galt Rehab to the newly-built Lethbridge Auxiliary Hospital, later renamed the Rehabilitation Hospital to stress the restoration of health rather than chronic care. In 1968, four clusters of fourplexes were opened near the Golden Acres Lodge. Another residence, the Blue Sky Lodge, was built on 16th Avenue North in 1973. Recreational, educational and volunteer activities for senior citizens began with the organization of the Golden Mile Senior Centre in Southminster Church in 1969. And, in 1972, Southland Nursing Home opened on 15th Avenue North.

The improvement in quality of life for handicapped persons in Lethbridge owed much to Frank N. Merkl, later a city councillor, and to an organization called Disabled on the Move. Beginning in 1965, Merkl and his associates pressured reluctant city councils to ameliorate the lot of the handicapped. Although the need was great and costs small, the city administration moved slowly and reluctantly to implement such improvements as benches at bus stops and curb ramps at intersections. A service club provided a

---

The Medicine Stone

When the first white settlers came to Lethbridge, they became aware of a granite boulder in the river bottom that had special significance to the Indians. It was called *Mek-kio-towaghs* by the Bloods and the Medicine Stone by the whites.

Mike Mountain Horse, Blood Indian war veteran, was an accomplished writer and recorded a legend of the Medicine Stone. It told how a hunter in what is now West Lethbridge looked across the river to see a figure descending the coulee hill on the other side. The hunter determined that the figure was a medicine pipe man — one who wore a dark red blanket or robe — and noted that he stopped at the foot of the hill and squatted down in the Indian fashion.

The hunter crossed the river near where the CP Rail High Level Bridge now stands. Riding to where he had seen the medicine pipe man he discovered nothing but a solid reddish rock, resembling a man in a squatting position. Failing to find a living person nearby, the hunter offered prayers near the rock in an effort to understand the mystery.

That night, a person appeared to the hunter in his dream and said, "My son, I am the rock you saw. I want you and your children to come and leave me offerings." From that time, the rock was usually laden down with gifts such as bits of clothing, tobacco, or food.

A slightly different version of the legend was obtained from Blood informants by the Rev. John Maclean in 1882. "On the river flat at the mouth of one of the ravines at Lethbridge, not many yards distant from the coal mine, lies a stone, which oftentimes I have seen painted and surrounded by numerous Indian trinkets which had been given it by the Indians. The Blood Indians called it *Mikiotouqse* (The Red Stone). Tradition states that a long time ago a young man lay down beside this stone and fell asleep, and as he lay there he dreamed that the stone spoke to him and said, "Am I the Red Stone?" And the young man said, "Yes, you are the Red Stone." When he awoke he felt that this must be a mysterious stone that could thus converse with him, and he made offerings to it. Until the present day these offerings are made, the Indians believing that by giving it reverence they will be blessed in all things that concern them in this life."

Sometime in the 1930s, with typical contempt for the holy objects of aboriginal cultures, the Medicine Stone was hauled away to be used to reinforce a partial weir, then in use near the waterworks.

In 1984, a party relocated what was believed to be the Medicine Stone on the upper part of the old partial weir and arranged for its removal to Indian Battle Park. Intentions were to locate it near its original site and to dedicate it in Indian fashion.

The replica of Fort Whoop-Up in Indian Battle Park, a Kinsmen Club Confederation of Canada centennial project. The replica was based on NWMP plans now known to be wrong in nearly every particular and, in 1984-1985, was moved and its layout was corrected.

In the 1950s, the area known until the 1920s as "The Point," became an auto wrecker's storage yard and looked like this in 1972.

Callow coach capable of carrying wheel-chair bound passengers on outings in the city. While the handicapped appreciated these minor improvements, the association wanted its members to be able to get to work like anyone else, to go shopping when they wanted, to be able to get around on downtown streets in a wheelchair, and to be able to get into buildings with access to bathrooms, offices, and other facilities on all floors. In 1980, as a result of the International Year of the Disabled, an architectural barriers committee was established to ensure that all city facilities were made fully accessible to the handicapped. In 1983, the city installed an audible traffic signal at the intersection of 6th Street and 4th Avenue South. By 1984, the objectives of the Disabled on the Move had been largely met with the provision of a Handi-Bus service, dished curbs at downtown intersections, ramps and wider doors on public buildings, and simple adjustments, such as lowering paper towel dispensers in public washrooms.

On 11 March 1971, during the second period of a Lethbridge Sugar Kings - Edmonton Maple Leafs hockey game, fire broke out and within 90 minutes destroyed the old ice arena. Fortunately, Constable Eddie Potts, Lethbridge city police, recognized the danger and organized a rapid but orderly evacuation of the building. Home to many fine hockey teams, such as the world championship Maple Leafs of 1951, the Native Sons of the mid- to late 1950s; and the Sugar Kings of the late 1960s and early 1970s, the arena was slated for a major facelift in 1975. Instead, the disaster united the community and it enthusiastically supported the construction of a new building. Within a year, Henderson Lake Ice Arena was completed and in operation.

Lethbridge ended its ninth decade with a spectacular sports display as host of the 1975 Canada Winter Games. The Lethbridge bid for the games was based on a new, regional concept which proposed that the various sporting events be played in various centres throughout southern Alberta with the finals located in Lethbridge. As a result, games organizers had to deal with 15 municipal governments in addition to the provincial and federal administrations. Three years of planning by volunteers of the 1975 Canada Winter Games Society resulted in the smooth running of the games in February 1975. Three thousand volunteers and some paid employees helped to run the 13-day affair and left a lasting legacy.

Among the permanent contributions left by the games was the Canada Games Sportsplex on Scenic Drive, the Stan Siwik swimming pool, the upgrading of numerous sporting facilities in the city and surrounding communities, and the distribution of all sports equipment to clubs and institutions in the region. An olympic-sized oval skating rink caused endless problems for the city, however, and had to be demolished. Intangibly, the games generated regional and national publicity, enhanced community spirit, heightened interest in personal fitness, and advanced amateur sport as an important aspect of community life.

The games were a fitting close to a gentle, tranquil era. A tribute to youth, sportsmanship and health, the 1975 Canada Winter Games fitted the character of Lethbridge. Growing slowly and measuredly, the city had become a pleasant retreat. Isolated from the student disturbances and race riots which raged elsewhere, the city concentrated on the quality of life. Naturally, it experienced some of the social problems of the age, notably the alienation of youth expressed in drug abuse. In 1969, for example, city council received a request to prohibit the sale of glue to children under 16 in order to curb the glue sniffing problem. Meanwhile, the Southern Alberta Teen Organization blamed recent fights at teenage dances in the Civic Sports Centre on drugs and alcohol. Rock-and-roll came into its own and became a vehicle for demonstrations against authority, materialism, and the Vietnam War. Mini-skirts and hippies marked the era and made their way into Lethbridge. But, the human size of the cityscape muted these concerns. Set on the windy, open prairie, Lethbridge was a liveable city, its parks and tree-lined streets providing a tranquil garden in a restless, rapidly changing world.

Downtown Lethbridge, looking toward West Lethbridge, in 1981. Part of the railway relocation area is shown, as is the Downtown Redevelopment or Urban Renewal area.

Chapter Twelve
Modern Lethbridge

In May 1973, Lethbridge removed the fire alarms from the city's telephone poles because practically everyone telephoned emergencies into the fire department, while virtually all calls from the boxes were false. The loss of the alarm boxes demonstrated in a tangible way that Lethbridge had entered the modern, electronic age. Instant communications by telephone, television, and microwave bound the city into a global, electronic network, a factor which represented the greatest transformation in the history of Lethbridge. The small, isolated settlement on an expansive plain had grown into a modern city, fully tied into the metropolitan centres of the world. Television daily beamed events from around the globe into Lethbridge's living rooms. It drew the city instantly into the political, economic, and social problems of the world.

By 1984, Lethbridgians had access to five AM and two FM radio stations. Another small AM station with a very limited range, CKUL, was located on the campus of the University of Lethbridge. The city also enjoyed four television channels, one of which was a repeater from CBC Calgary and the other from the CBC French network in Edmonton. In addition to these services, Lethbridge CableNet distributed signals from four Spokane television channels. Some viewers still were not content with the diversity in programming and soon satellite dishes became a common sight in yards and on rooftops. Capable of bringing in hundreds of channels from the many orbiting satellites, the dishes symbolized how intricately Lethbridge had become enmeshed in the trends of the outside world.

The communication revolution forced a drastic change on one of the oldest news agencies in the city. In 1980, the owner of the *Lethbridge Herald*, FP Publications, was taken over by Thompson Newspapers Limited, which moved in one of its own managing editors in 1982. The new editor concluded that the *Herald* was overstaffed and was operated inefficiently. But, when he fired a staff member, he aroused the anger of many Lethbridgians, some of whom formed the "Committee for Quality Journalism." The

critics charged that the new editor had reduced national and international coverage in favour of local features and more advertising. The bitter dispute between the committee and the newspaper triggered public meetings, demonstrations outside the Herald building, a subscription and advertising boycott, and isolated acts of vandalism. Two new weeklies, the *Lethbridge Weekly* and the *Southerner* arose from the dispute but neither lasted more than a few weeks. Eventually, the furore subsided and Lethbridge accepted the new order of things.

Instant communications caused city officials considerable embarrassment in June 1976. Council, upon being asked to approve a bilingual sign to be placed on the Charles A. Magrath historic marker in city hall, resolved in part that, "the federal government be notified that they can keep their plaque . . . as it is a waste of taxpayers' money." Canadian Press picked up the resolution and soon news items across the country portrayed Lethbridgians as red-necked bigots. The city had to extend apologies, particularly to the citizens of St. Laurent, Quebec, with which Lethbridge had been twinned in 1967.

The electronic information age entered the city administration in the mid-1960s, when a computer firm was hired to process city data. In 1973, when demands on computer services became acute, the city hired a systems analyst and set up a systems and computers department. In 1982, the department persuaded the city to buy its own Sperry Univac computer system instead of contracting out the work as before. Programming a new application system took much longer and was much more expensive than anticipated and it became a heated issue in the 1983 civic elections, coming within 150 votes of defeating long-term Mayor A. C. Anderson. After the election, council decided that, in spite of the costly delays, it would go ahead with its plans to implement the in-house Sperry Univac system.

The city reached a milestone of sorts in 1977 when officials stopped talking of additions and renovations to the old city hall and instead drew plans for a new facility on the old site. Not unexpectedly, the proposal for a new city hall sparked dissent and discussions, forcing planners to reject a number of different designs. Meanwhile, in July 1980, city council authorized its manager to rent two floors of the BLT building to house several city departments and the council chambers. In December 1984, a futuristic plan conceived by Robins Watson Baunton, architects and engineers, was rejected by the electorate.

Another of the significant changes to affect Lethbridge in the 1970s was its expansion west of the Oldman River. This development was a 'planner's dream', an unprecedented opportunity to lay out residential districts, unencumbered by previously built structures. The planners were also able to control spiralling land costs and leapfrog development. They divided the suburb into three 640-acre (260-ha) districts, called Varsity Village, Indian Battle Heights, and Mountain Heights. The first to be constructed was Varsity Village, which was nearest to the university. The plans called for major traffic streets to encircle residential blocks, making it possible to group single family dwellings about cul-de-sac roads.

208

The city invited contractors to bid on serviced lots, the tenders to be accompanied by development plans for about 80 acres (32 ha); it awarded contracts only to acceptable proposals.

Designed to accommodate 30,000 people, the initial demand for West Lethbridge lots was slow. On 11 February 1974, council honoured Mr. and Mrs. J. L. Peart, who had finished their house the previous August, as the first persons to build in West Lethbridge. In May 1976, however, a land rush caught planners by surprise. Applicants camped in line overnight to ensure getting the lot of their choice. West Lethbridge had 10,250 inhabitants by 1983, most of whom lived in Varsity Village. Considerable development had taken place in Indian Battle Heights, immediately to the north, while Mountain Heights, to the south, was still largely untouched.

The influx of people to West Lethbridge contained many young families with school-age children. To accommodate their need for schools, the board constructed Nicholas Sheran Community School on Laval Boulevard in 1981. (Park Meadows School was built on Meadowlark Boulevard in North Lethbridge in 1982.) West Lethbridge still required two more schools but, because existing schools east of the river had 1,400 empty seats, the board bused the extra children to Fleetwood Bawden and Allan Watson schools in the city.

Various congregations established six new churches in West Lethbridge, representing a large proportion of the 16 churches erected in the city in the 20 years after 1965. The Church of Jesus Christ of Latter-day Saints was forced to construct a new edifice on 28th Street and Scenic Drive when an arsonist destroyed its building on 5th Avenue South.

A major political obstacle to the construction of a new bridge across the river to West Lethbridge disappeared in 1971 with the defeat of Harry Strom's Social Credit administration and the election of Peter Lougheed's Conservatives. The city dusted off plans, obtained provincial funds, and, in February 1975, completed the Sixth Avenue Bridge and the 2.1-mile (3.4-km) Whoop-Up Drive, connecting West Lethbridge and the university to the downtown. In 1983-85, the bridge was twinned and the freeway widened to four lanes.

The reluctance of Lethbridge to build the bridge out of its own funds signified another major change in the city's history. With

Lethbridge's city hall was opened in 1948, was inadequate by 1966, and a new city hall was first proposed in 1977. In 1984, the electorate turned down a proposal for an immediate start on a $12.5 million city hall.

the exception of the boom years at the turn of the century, city councillors had established a reputation for parsimony and caution. Perhaps because they were spending their own taxes, they were always reluctant to lavish funds on capital works. After the Second World War all that changed. Both the provincial and federal governments were anxious to expend money on local projects and Lethbridge's civic officials were eager to compete for it. Their persistent and ingenious methods to tap funds from senior governments paid for most of the dramatic changes in the cityscape during the past two decades.

One example of Lethbridge's successful bid for provincial funds was the river valley park scheme. The river and valley, the serpentine entrails of the place, lay at the centre of the city, particularly after the annexation of West Lethbridge. Civic officials had always recognized the recreational potential of the valley and from the early 1950s had launched a program of buying out the owners of land and homes in the valley. But they had been reluctant to spend large sums of money on the park until 1974, when Alberta Culture's Major Cultural and Recreational Facilities Plan assigned $100 per capita on a matching grant basis for major facilities over

Optical and Radio Telescopes

In 1913, a huge telescope was ordered by the Dominion observatory but tests were conducted in the western provinces to discover the point where, throughout the year, there was the greatest dominance of clear sky. Joseph P. Tracey, the city's first industrial commissioner, lobbied vigorously to bring the telescope and observatory to Lethbridge. He submitted locally-prepared briefs, contacted federal ministers and Members of Parliament, and enlisted provincial support. Unfortunately, his efforts came to naught and the telescope and observatory eventually were installed in Ottawa.

In 1984, a joint City Council-University of Lethbridge Committee lobbied federal and provincial governments in an effort to have the headquarters of the Canadian Long Baseline Array (CLBA) based at the University of Lethbridge, which offered a site and buildings as needed.

The CLBA had the potential to be the world's largest radio telescope, an array of at least nine radio dishes scattered across Canada from coast to coast and north to Yellowknife. Canada, with its extreme width, was thought to be an ideal location for such a complex.

The technique, called long baseline interferometry, involved recording data from the nine or more radio dishes to be strung across Canada, creating a radio telescope nearly 5,000 miles (8000 km) in diameter. Data tapes would be taken to a central location for processing and analyses. Each tape would carry a timing signal, superimposed on it by an atomic clock, to allow it to be matched to other tapes with a precision accurate to billionths of a second.

Lethbridge prepared a 50-page booklet entitled "Canada's Window On Space" to explain the concept and to enlist public support. The booklet outlined the many benefits of such an array, not the least of them the possibility of a spinoff of high-tech industry.

One of the proposals submitted by the city was for a nature reserve centre, now the Helen Schuler Coulee Centre, which was built and opened in 1981.

In February 1980, the province unveiled yet another scheme. Called the Urban Parks For The Future Proposal, it outlined a program of assistance to enable some municipalities, including Lethbridge, to provide parks similar to those under development in Calgary and Edmonton. The province agreed to bear 100 percent of initial construction costs, 75 percent of the maintenance costs for the first two years after completion, and 50 percent for the next 23 years.

Lethbridge was quick to take advantage of the scheme. In 1981, council approved a parks proposal or concept plan and submitted it to the provincial government. The city's proposal, called the Community Services Department Urban Parks Program, provided the framework for detailed planning and facility development. It also spelled out the organization required: an urban parks co-ordinator to direct an urban parks project group and to chair a technical advisory committee; and, a five-member urban parks development committee to secure and analyze public input, to recommend projects, and to monitor the entire scheme. Backed by several detailed consultant studies, the parks plan proposed to develop 3,750 acres (1,517 ha) of river valley, the coulees in the Six-Mile Coulee/Lethbridge Community College area, a greenstrip running east from the river valley to Henderson Park, and Henderson Park itself.

Planning, land acquisition, and construction of the Lethbridge river park was estimated to cost $14.8 million but, because the funds were indexed for inflation, when major construction began in 1984 about $22.7 million was available. A major breakthrough occurred in 1983 when provincial authorities accepted a $2.25 million redevelopment of the Sir Alexander Galt Museum and Archives as part of the urban parks program, which from the beginning had stressed only outdoor recreation.

City officials also took full advantage of federal housing improvement funds. As early as 1973, city council discussed the federal government's neighbourhood improvement program and in 1975 placed Westminster, the area bounded by 1st and 7th Avenues and 13th and 23rd Streets north, within the scheme. ORRPC undertook a planning study of the neighbourhood to be used as a basis for future plans. Neighbourhood improvement funds

a ten-year period. The city's community advisory council established five committees to draw up the detailed plans and priorities demanded by Alberta Culture. In April 1976, council approved the Major Facilities Plan and submitted it to the provincial government.

The Quiet Mayor

Andrew Charles Anderson was born in Shabbona, Illinois, in 1910 and came with his parents to Champion, Alberta in 1912. He graduated in pharmacy from the University of Alberta in 1934 and was employed at Kitson Pharmacy in Lethbridge for 14 years. In 1948, he started his own business, now Anderson's Medical Dental Pharmacy (Leth) Ltd.

He became involved in civic politics in 1950 with his election to the school board. Community service included 14 years on the school board, three years on the city recreation commission, 34 years with Rotary, life member of the chamber of commerce, member of the university senate and board of governors, member of St. Michael's hospital board, member of the Alberta Housing council, and on and on.

He became an alderman in 1964 and was chosen by his fellow councillors as mayor upon the resignation of Frank Sherring in March 1968. In September 1984, he became the longest-serving mayor in the history of the city.

Anderson was a central figure in all the important developments in Lethbridge during the past 20 years: park development, establishment of the university, expansion to West Lethbridge, sale of the power plant, downtown redevelopment, railway relocation, and building of a new city hall. Only the last of these was unresolved in 1984.

Anderson was largely instrumental in obtaining many millions of dollars from senior governments for the benefit of the City of Lethbridge. His success lay in a deliberate attempt to be non-controversial, to marshall all the facts, to reach a consensus in council, and then to persuade voters of the correctness of the action. Political opportunists and pressure groups of various stripes surfaced in opposition at all stages of the various developments but, mostly, their very names have been forgotten.

Terry Bland Photo

Andrew Charles Anderson

helped to replace the Lion's swimming pool with a new facility and community centre. In 1975, the federal government initiated the residential rehabilitation assistance program, under which a large number of individual home owners and landlords made applications for renovations on their buildings.

Another area to benefit from federal largesse was the London Road neighbourhood which comprised an L-shaped tract south and east of the downtown core. The whole scheme was administered by the London Road Neighbourhood Association. A general preliminary study in 1975, an economic impact statement in 1978, and the arguments of the Municipal Planning Commission were compiled into an area redevelopment plan approved by city council in November 1980. The objective of all these plans was to ensure

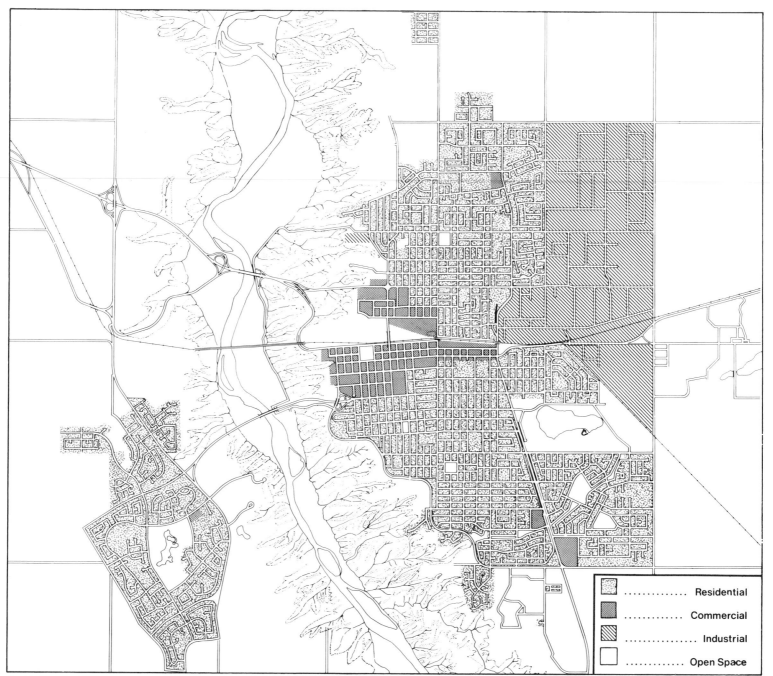

Lethbridge in 1980.

Residential

Commercial

Industrial

Open Space

Nicholas Sheran Leisure Centre in West Lethbridge in 1984.

Nicholas Sheran Community School in West Lethbridge in 1984.

that future developments reflected the needs and concerns of residents in the neighbourhoods and the welfare of the city in general.

In 1979, the federal government agreed to place the Staffordville area and later the Hardieville area in the neighbourhood improvement program. By the end of 1983, the federal government had expended more than $1.25 million in Lethbridge under its various neighbourhood loans and grants programs.

All these programs were overshadowed by the largest beneficiary of senior government funds, the railway yards. Planning for the removal of the yards started in 1970 when Marathon Realty announced that the CPR expected to move the trackage and marshalling yards by the end of the decade and thereby open the property for redevelopment. In May 1974, the federal government passed railway relocation legislation which enabled its transport commission to authorize the relocation of railway yards. Lethbridge became the first small city to apply for such relocation.

As required, the city conducted a series of feasibility studies and prepared plans for the location of the new railway yards and for the use of the released lands. By the mid-1970s, the various studies had determined that relocation would eliminate the division between north and south Lethbridge, would remove an intrusive and unattractive land use from the central area, and would provide attactively planned development opportunities. In 1977, a railway relocation study recommended the removal of the railway yards to Kipp. Also, a transportation report proposed the construction of the Crowsnest Trail to carry east-west traffic through the urban area, to act as an arterial to the downtown, and to provide an opportunity for downtown expansion. The latter report also recommended the extension of Scenic Drive to the north as far as 23rd Avenue, in order to supplement existing north-south roads and to provide a part of a proposed perimeter road around the city.

In 1977, the city prepared several by-laws to accommodate rail relocation. One provided for the development of medium and high density residential and commercial establishments and some light industry, while a second amended the general plan in keeping with the drastically changed transportation and development concepts.

Initially, the federal government was to provide assistance to a maximum of 50 percent of cost but eventually the provincial and municipal governments shared the expense on a 60 to 40 ratio. In 1980, council designated the $80 million Crowsnest Trail as a major continuous corridor in the city, making it eligible for 90 percent provincial funding. The designation also dictated higher standards of design and access control.

By 1980, estimates of the cost of land acquisition and railyard removal totalled $31.2 million, while projected revenues from serviced land sales stood at $43 million. The city mounted a massive public relations campaign to gather support for the scheme. Nevertheless, protestors forced a costly but unsuccessful plebiscite.

In July 1983, council adopted the Railway Relocation Lands Area Redevelopment Plan and a year later the railyards were removed from the city and construction on the Crowsnest Trail was begun. About 95 acres (38 ha) was freed for residential and commercial development but the economic reverses of the early 1980s discouraged real estate promoters. Even as late as 1984, land sales were not encouraging.

Much of the city's success in attracting provincial and federal funds to the city can be attributed to the aggressive work of city councils led by Mayor A. C. Anderson, the quiet, unassuming veteran of city politics. Obsessed with the desire for economic development, he sought out government funding for roads, schools, parks, and industries.

The mayor and his council were backed by a competent planning department at city hall. The formerly cordial relations between Lethbridge and ORRPC deteriorated in the late 1960s. Councillors, annoyed at the slowness of ORRPC, suggested that the city do its own planning. By April 1977, communications between the two bodies were so poor that ORRPC asked for a meeting with the council to confirm newspaper reports that the city was creating a planning department. A month later, when ORRPC was slow to deliver plans on the railway relocation project, the city decided to hire its own planners. In October, despite vocal opposition from a "Concerned Ratepayers' and Renters' Association," the city established the Lethbridge Planning and Development Department. This move served only to increase friction and in 1980 ORRPC reduced city representation from three members to one and the city in turn refused ORRPC membership on its Municipal Planning Commission.

The city had created the Municipal Planning Commission, as well as the Development Appeal Board, in 1968. These bodies were

214

Downtown Redevelopment Area in 1984, showing the Lethbridge Lodge Hotel, business blocks, and the Courthouse.

"Moving the tracks!" *The railway relocation area looking west in 1984.*

"Moving the tracks!" The railway relocation area looking east in 1984.

W. R. "Stubb" Ross C. M.

In the early 1960s, Stubb Ross knew nothing more about running an airline than how to fly the plane. His family ran a 250,000-acre ranch in southeastern Alberta and operated Ranchers' Air Service. Ross had hay fever, which kept him from ranching; his destiny came with a pilot's license.

At the time, Air Canada was anxious to abandon its feeder lines, such as the Lethbridge-Calgary run. Ross saw an opportunity for a small airline and in 1966 set up Lethbridge Air Services, a three-man, seat-of-the-pants flying operation. Ross drove a Volkswagen bus to pick up passengers, a co-pilot warmed up the eight-passenger plane, while passengers picked up tickets from an attendant at a card table. Lethbridge Air Services flew 2,700 passengers in its first year of operation.

The name was soon changed to Time Air and the new airline began to grow with the traffic. Planes were bought, routes were extended, flight frequencies were increased. Reservations and ticketing requirements grew as the airline grew, which enabled Ross personally to finance expansion.

While Ross proved the economic viability of the feeder routes, Pacific Western Airlines (PWA), after 1974 a creature of the Alberta government, tried again and again to take the lucrative Calgary-Lethbridge and later the Lethbridge-Vancouver route from him. Alberta Conservatives were upset at the spectacle of the government-owned airline trying to take over the most profitable routes of a small, privately-owned, regional carrier and, in 1982, pressured the government into selling PWA. Many Albertans credited Ross as being a major cause of PWA's ungainly flight back to the private sector.

In 1984, Ross resigned as chairman of Time Air to become an advisor and honorary chairman of the company.

set up to complement and implement the city's general plan of 1964. The city asked Rockcliffe Partnership of Edmonton to revamp the plan in 1977, a task completed by 1979 and adopted the following year. A new zoning by-law accompanied the new plan, which identified areas suited to new suburban developments and those settled areas requiring redevelopment. The municipal plan, although subject to periodic review and amendment provided the city with the means of directing its future form, growth, and development in a co-ordinated manner.

Lethbridge also sought government incentives to attract industries to the city. In 1974, Palliser Distillers opened a $12 million plant in the industrial park. Three years later, Dresser-Clark occupied the steel fabrication plant abandoned by Horton Steel in 1972. General Foods built a $12 million plant in 1978, to produce beverages and other products for the western market. In 1983, Kawneer Industries opened an equally large plant to manufacture aluminum building products. And later that year, NovaTel Communications announced that it was planning to manufacture cellular mobile telephone systems in a building vacated by AEL Microtel, producer of conventional telephones, which failed to compete with Third World plants. Finally, in 1984, the Premiere group of companies, which included feed formulation and sales, health of animals, and livestock supplies, established itself in the city.

Unfortunately, some of these enterprises failed to survive economic decline in the early 1980s. In triphammer succession, in February 1983, several businesses closed their doors. McGavin's Foods, General Foods, Palliser Distillers, Montagne Meats and AEL Microtel pulled out of Lethbridge, leaving many of their workers to the unemployment lines.

Similarly, Lethbridge's packing plants were overbuilt and in 1984 most of them were in financial difficulties. The older of the plants, plagued by high labor costs and obsolete machinery and design, were only marginally competitive. Moreover, a sharp decline in per capita beef consumption caused a decline in cattle slaughter. The problem was reflected in the checkered history of the plants. Gainers took over the Swift Canadian plant in 1981 but closed it two years later and sold it to Canada Packers in 1984.

Equally disheartening was the short-lived revival of the coal industry. Early in 1981, when everyone expected oil prices to continue rising, Fording Coal, then a subsidiary of CP Enterprises, and Indemitsu Kosan of Japan announced their intention to open an underground thermal coal mine near Shaughnessy. At the same time, Petro Canada sunk a shaft near Coalhurst while Precambian Shield Resources assessed the feasibility of a colliery between Shaughnessy and Picture Butte. The three companies expected to

A TIME AIR "Short" take-off and landing plane over the Oldman River, southern Alberta, about 1978. This type of plane was referred to locally as a "flying boxcar."

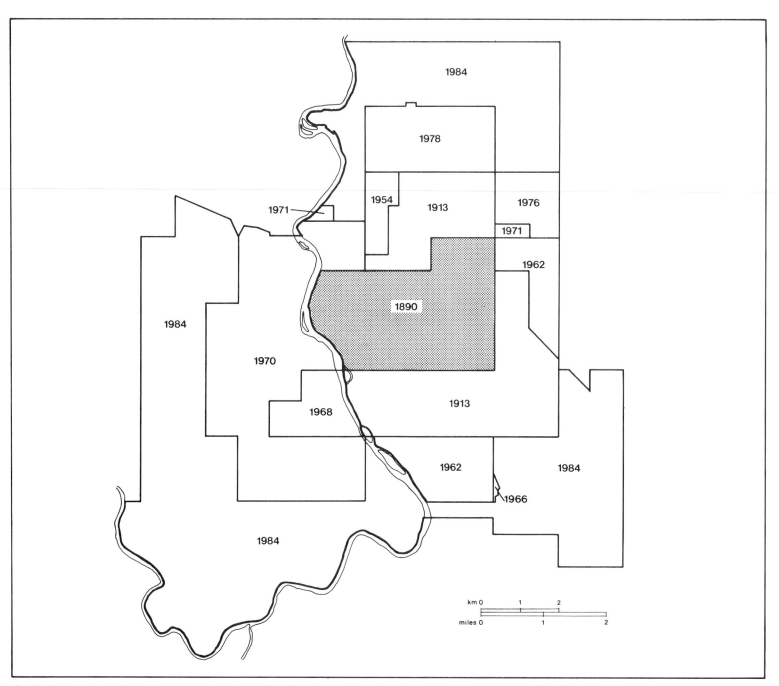

Lethbridge, showing the various annexations from 1913-1984 and the original boundary, which was surveyed by Charles A. Magrath in 1890.

University of Lethbridge campus in 1982.

Anne Campbell C. M.

Anne Campbell was the inspiration and direction behind the Anne Campbell Singers, who in various forms achieved national and international recognition in choral competitions and festivals from the early 1960s onwards.

She started with the Teen Clefs and, by 1967, the choir was good enough to compete internationally at Montreal's Expo '67. Her graduate group was called the Linnets. They were three times to Wales, to Japan, Denmark, Germany, Switzerland, Holland, England, Ireland, and Scotland. Anne Campbell Singers continually receive invitations to sing at prestigious choral competitions and festivals, one of the more recent at Vienna, Austria.

Campbell looked upon choral training as an important part of the educational process. She insisted upon regular and frequent practices, on learning lines, and on working hard and being punctual, all essential to good choral work. Sight reading, enunciation and basic vocal control were other characteristics Campbell demanded of her students. Her students studied under her because they wanted to and all found the experience rewarding.

Campbell was involved with choirs most of her life and directed a senior choir at age 14 in Saskatoon. She gave individual voice and piano lessons for many years. In 1976, in recognition of her services, she was admitted to the Order of Canada and, in 1982, was appointed a lifetime member of the Alberta Choral Federation.

exploit the Galt seam and planned to sell the coal in Japan, South Korean, and other Pacific Rim countries. But falling oil prices in 1982 first stalled the plans and then killed them.

Much more successful was Lethbridge's aviation firm, Time Air. Owned by W. R. (Stubb) Ross, Time Air successfully fought off several attempts by the provincially owned Pacific Western Airlines to fly into Lethbridge from Calgary. The local firm continued to expand and in 1976 bought three of the distinctively shaped Shorts, derisively called 'flying boxcars'. Only four years later, the company purchased two 50-passenger, turbo-prop Dash 7s, adding a third the following year. Meanwhile its passenger load continued to increase and the company extended its routes.

In 1982, Time Air thwarted Pacific Western's fifth attempt to fly the lucrative Lethbridge-Calgary route, as well as a proposed Lethbridge-Kelowna-Vancouver run. Ironically, the company encountered opposition from Lethbridge's city council and its chamber of commerce, both of which wanted Pacific Western's jetliner service. Only the last minute intervention of the federal transportation minister saved Time Air from ruinous competition. It was a hollow victory, however. Faced with an unacceptably high debt: equity ratio Time Air in September 1983 sold 40 percent of its shares to its chief rival. In May 1984, Ross resigned as chairman of the airline he had founded as a one-man, one-plane operation in 1966 and was named advisor and honorary chairman of Time Air.

The increased reliance on funding from senior governments made the city more susceptible to pressure from provincial and federal bureaucracies. From the mid-1970s, for instance, the provincial government pressured municipalities to implement strict environmental controls within their jurisdictions. Assuming that all Albertans were entitled to breathe clean air, drink pure water, and live in unpolluted surroundings, Alberta Environment set ever higher standards, particularly in effluent criteria. Soon Lethbridge's sewage treatment plants failed to meet the regulations. A study showed that No. 1 treatment plant (south of Whoop-Up Drive) was obsolete, while the No. 2 facility (north of Highway 3) was inadequate. The report recommended that the older plant be phased out and the newer one be improved to meet the higher effluent standards. By 1984, plans had reached the design stage and the city was contemplating an immediate $17 million expansion program. Not surprisingly, the city planned to seek provincial or federal funds for the work.

Provincial administrators were even more influential in settling a hospital controversy involving St. Michael's and Municipal hospitals, which raged in Lethbridge at the turn of the decade. A city council resolution in October 1979 noted that hospital services were far from adequate and suggested that the decline was due to the lack of co-operation between the two institutions. The city asked the minister of health and the two boards to consider the consolidation of all hospital services into a single administrative district. The issue was complicated by Mayor A. C. Anderson's membership on the St. Michael's board, which the Municipal board felt prejudiced the city's position on the issue. Many Lethbridgians argued that the two facilities should be renovated but the "Citizen's

In the 1980s, satellite receiving dishes sprouted from many rooftops and in backyards.

Committee for a New Regional Hospital", formed in 1979, rejected that argument and agitated for the construction of one, modern active treatment institution.

Finally, in 1980, while the question was still being argued in the city, the minister of hospitals and medical care informed council that he had decided to make the Municipal Hospital the regional institution and that it would share programming and financing with St. Michael's. But a year later, by the time the city had accepted his position, the minister changed his mind and decided to construct a 330-bed regional referral hospital on the Municipal Hospital grounds, and to renovate St. Michael's to 150-bed capacity. In 1984, the Catholic Hospital Foundation took over ownership of St. Michael's from the Sisters of St. Martha in order to transfer

Dignitaries and members of the Centennial Committee at the 5 January 1985 kick-off to the centennial at a two-hour, sold-out performance in the Sportsplex.

St. Mary's Elementary School Centennial Choir performing at the City of Lethbridge's 100th birthday on 5 January 1985 at a two-hour, sold-out show in the Sportsplex.

control from the sisters' Nova Scotia base to Alberta, where renovation funds were located.

The city also channelled government money into the care of the aged. Seniors increased from 9.1 percent of the population in 1961 to 11.9 percent in 1981. To accommodate their increased numbers, the community built two more lodges for the elderly, the Alberta Rose Lodge at 2251-32nd Street South in 1977 and the Heritage Lodge at 601-6th Street South in 1983. The Devon Nursing Home became Parkland Nursing Home in 1975 and Extendicare (Alberta) began to operate it in 1984. Southland Nursing Home moved to 15th Avenue North in 1975 and was taken over by the Lethbridge Regional Hospital Board in 1984.

By the 1970s, the city needed low-rental, small apartments for those able to look after themselves. Several such complexes were built including Halmrast Manor in 1975, Hardie Manor in 1979, Blue Sky Manor in 1982, and Haig Tower in 1983. The Royal Canadian Legion Housing society constructed Legion Place in 1982 and Legion Arms in 1983. A private developer built Somerset House in 1980. All of these developments removed much of the fear of growing old and becoming incapacitated.

The major facilities plan of 1975 listed as its first priority, "the Civic Centre will be modelled as a multi-use facility with primary emphasis on senior citizens." Completed in 1977, the Senior Centre on 11th Street South became a popular institution in the city. By 1984, about 2,000 seniors used it regularly.

A wide range of facilities were available to senior citizens in Lethbridge in 1984. A list, available from the Senior Centre, included Alert Systems (emergency phone numbers), Ambulance, Blue Cross, Canadian Institute for the Blind, Handyman Services for Seniors, Keep In Touch Program, Lethbridge Handi-Bus, Letter Carriers' Alert, Lethbridge Society for Meals on Wheels, Samaritan, Vial of Life, and many more.

In 1981, the Alberta Securities Commission transferred to the city ownership of Archmount Memorial Gardens, a privately owned cemetery with a long history of financial problems. The same year, city council permitted Martin Bros. Funeral Chapel to operate a crematorium in Mountain View cemetery. By 1984, about 20 percent of the city's dead were cremated, a fact that significantly eased cemetery space requirements.

The Lethbridge of 1985, as it celebrated its centennial, was a vastly different place than the town incorporated in 1891. The

most obvious change was an increase in area from 3,040 acres (1230 ha) to 29,454 acres (11 920 ha), and growth in population from 1,478 to an estimated 60,000. More dramatic was the mushrooming of civic expenditures from a mere $19,963 in 1891 to an enormous $150 million in 1984. Nothing better illustrated the expanding role of government in the everyday affairs of its citizens than the widespread dilation of its budget.

Lethbridgians, like all of western society, participated in the most dramatic social and technological revolution any people had ever experienced. Most of the technology that shaped our lives in 1985 was of extremely recent origin. In 1885, there were no automobiles or household telephones, no radios, no airplanes, no televisions, and no computers. In 1985, it was impossible to imagine a world without these things and the even vaster technologies that they represented. In addition to rapid changes in our technology, we had changed our social organization, our diet, our activity patterns, the substances of daily use and exposure, our patterns of reproductive activity, our methods of tension relief, and human relationships. Automation of the household had drastically reduced the need for physical labor at home; the social implications had been far-reaching. A revolution in telecommunications had brought us from the telegraph, which dominated communications in the 1880s and the best operators could transmit information at 30 words per minute, to the transmission of thousands of bits of information in milliseconds, aided by the telephone and the computer, by microwave relays and orbiting satellites. Yet, while technology produced incredible advances in areas such as medical care, it also created pollution, acid rain, and the threat of nuclear disaster. The destructive nature of the city seemed at times to overshadow the creative forces of the urban community.

Meanwhile Lethbridge, the coal town on the prairies, had managed to become a successful small city while retaining many of its small town values. Its residential areas, with their clipped lawns, neighbors gossiping on patios or around barbeque pits, and its outward-looking literate citizens, demonstrated that civilized life on a human scale was possible in the city. Rooted in agriculture, Lethbridge was sensitive to the seasonality of planting and harvest. Its citizens displayed individual self-reliance and self-confidence, good humor and good manners, concern for neighbors and a readiness to lend a helping hand, and a pride in community and country coupled with a respect for the natural world.

Appendix

Lethbridge Directory, Compiled October 1885

(From: Henderson's North West Towns Directory, 1886-87, pages 329-332).

The list that follows was compiled in October 1885 and purports to list the inhabitants of the new settlement of Lethbridge. The list was hurriedly, even sloppily, done, probably by a reporter who made the rounds of the new town but failed to check his entries. Names were missed, for example, Charles A. Magrath; other names were misspelled. Undoubtedly businesses were missed as well. No women were listed although this was normal for the times. Population was given as 400 in October 1885. It is likely that the population more than doubled from October to December as contemporary observers usually indicated a population of "about a thousand" in December 1885. Some errors are indicated below.

LETHBRIDGE

A mining town at the terminus of the North Western Coal and Navigation Co.'s Railway, distant from Dunmore, a station on the C.P.R., 110 miles; has express and telegraph offices. Pop., Oct. 1885, 400.

Abbot Chas, conductor
Adams J, cow boy
Alexander Lorenzo, milk ranche
Alexander Wm., carpenter
Anderson George, miner
Austin & Davis, saloon
Austin Mark, of Austin & Davis
Bailey Joseph, superintendent RR
Bailey Herbert F.
Barber Alfred, station agent
Barks John, miner
Barnes Fred, miner
Barnes William, miner
Barnes Wm., cook Lethbridge house
Betley [and elsewhere, Bentley] H., of H. Betley & Co.
Betley H & Co., gin [gen] merchants
Bellis Murray
Bickerstaff Alex.

Bisson Oliver, carpenter
Black Drama saloon, Cleveland & Burge, proprietors
Blake John, miner
Botterell Thom., general merchant
Bowen Chas., of Bowen & Morton
Bowen & Morton, restaurant and saloon
Brack John, brakeman
Brady Sam, baker
Brown Lorenzo, carpenter
Budree [Padree] Jeff, proprietor City Bakery
Burgonye J., saloon
Buridge Oliver
Cameron Wm.
Campbell D.A.
Carr Wm, miner
Carny M., miner
City Bakery, Jeff Padree, proprietor
Climie & Robertson, furniture dealers
Climie Robert H., of Climie & Robertson
Clark Bennet, miner
Cleveland S.W.
Cleveland & Burge, proprietors saloon
Cline Jack, saloon lunch counter
Conn James, miner
Coor Arthur, miner
Cord Geo., clerk
Cottrill Chas., carpenter
Cottrill Chas., farmer
Crawford W. M., clerk
Dallas John, miner
Davis Sam, of Austin & Davis
Davis Philip, miner
Day Daniel
Devoe Charles, miner
Dodd Abraham, miner

Dugnay J. A., of Louis H. Dugnay & Bros.
Dugnay Louis H., & Bros., props., Montreal Chop House, Barrowers [Baroness Road] St near Depot
Duff John, clerk
Fixley Christian, of Main & Fixley, horse ranche
Fraser Daniel, carpenter
Fraser N.T., porter private car
Galt E. T., manager North Western Coal & Navigation Co.
Gay W.F., carpenter
Gilbert Joe, conductor
Gillies, Alex.
Gillies Sydney
Glass J. H., teamster, Freighton
Graham S.W., butcher
Greenwood H.F., accountant
Greenwood William, miner
Grist Wm., fitter
Hall Henry
Harrison Albert, engineer
Hartney Harry, train despatcher N.W.C. & N. Cos. Ry.
Hayman John W., miner
Henderson & Hogg, proprietors, Lethbridge house
Henderson Wm., foreman carpenter N.W.C. & N. Co.
Henderson Wm, of Henderson & Hogg
Heney & Whiting [Whitney], prop. Lethbridge stables
Heney Henry, of Heney & Whitney
Higinbotham John D., druggist, stationer and asst postmaster
Hoag Alfred, conductor
Hogg, A.M., of Henderson & Hogg
Hood Paul, miner
Hooper Wm.
Hughes Richard, miner
Irvine John N., of McKuser & Irvine
Jacques Henry
Jessoner Joseph, miner
Jones Thomas, miner
Jones Thos., cook Lethbridge house
Johnston Frank, blacksmith
Johnstone Joseph, miner
Johnstone William, miner
Kean John J., chief sawyer
Kean John, foreman sawmill

Kent Jas., stableman
Kinnear Herbert, carpenter
Kichington William, miner
King Geo., river driver
Kertcher Alf., waiter Lethbridge house
Landgill George, miner
Lennion John, miner
Lethbridge brewery, McKeuser & Irvine, proprietors
Lethbridge House, Henderson & Hogg, proprietors
Lethbridge stables, Heney & Whitney, proprietors
Little E, asst. cook Lethbridge house
Lowther Clarence, miner
Lucas Richard, miner
Lyons Thomas, saloon
McBain Wm., carpenter
McBeath Hugh, clerk
McCaskill Dan
McDonald Dan., stableman
McDonald J. C., miner
McFaul Robert, river driver
McGibbons Chas.
McGregor A., carpenter
McKay Alexander, miner
McKay Daniel G., miner
McKay James, miner
McKay John J., miner
McKay Joseph J., miner
McKuser & Irvine, props., Lethbridge brewery
McKuser Wm., of McKuser & Irvine
McMillan William, miner
NcNab Thos, mechanical supdt.
McNaughton David, engineer
McPherson Thomas, engineer
McWhirter James, miner
Mace W.A., chief sawyer
Main & Fixley, butchers and cattle dealers
Main O.S., of Main & Fixley stock ranch
Manney Issac, painter
Marshall Henry, miner
Mines The Brewer [Brewery], J. H. Noel, proprietor
Morton Albert, of Bowen & Morton
Molloy Hugh, miner

Molloy John, miner
Montreal Chop House, Louis H. Dugnay & Bros., prop.,
  Barrowers [Baroness Road] near Railway depot
Moulton Abraham, miner
Murray D.C., miner
Nightingale & Bailey, bakers
Nightingale Robt.
Niven F.C., clerk
Noel J. H., the Mines Brewery
North Wm., carpenter
Norton Michael, miner
North Western Coal and Navigation Co., E. T. Galt, manager;
  Wm. Lethbridge, president, London, England
O'Brien Patrick, miner
O'Keefe M., road master
Olsen Charles, miner
Olsen William, miner
Perry Jas., miner
Pierce Chas.
Pillion Antoine, engineer
Polley Geo., freight checker
Post office, H. F. Greenwood, postmaster
Ptolemy Thos., clerk
Robertson D.D., of Climie & Robertson
Robertson John, caretaker
Robertson J., brakeman
Robson J.M., bookkeeper for Main & Fixley
Rosenbloom Maurice, miner
Ross Allan
Ross Alexander, miner
Russell James, miner
Sacadore Chas., hewer
Savery Ernest, miner
Scott Thos., carpenter
Seward F., clerk Crown hotel
Sexton Jerry, laborer
Sharp David, mill hand
Simms, J., barber
Smith Robert, miner
Smylie Jas.
Snarth Robert, miner
Stafford John

Stafford William, jun., miner
Stafford William, Superintendent culler [colliery]
Staph Frank, engineer
Stattoford G., carpenter
Stewart Holten, laborer
Sutherland Dan., engineer
Thomson David, miner
Thompson George, miner
Townsend John, miner
Vare James, miner
Vare James, jun., miner
Waghorn W., painter
Watkins, C. W., clerk
Wallworth [Wallwork] Nathan, miner
Warner Jacob, mill hand
Wedlock R., miner
Whitney Wm. D., Heney & Whitney
Whyte Robert miner
Wilson William, miner

Population Growth in Lethbridge, 1876-1981, including Stafford Village, 1891-1911

Year	Population	Numerical Change	Percent Change
1876	2[1]	—	—
1881	4[2]	2	—
1886	1,000[3]	996	—
1891	2,353	1,353	+ 135.3
1896	2,500[3]	147	+ 6.2
1901	2,622	122	+ 4.9
1906	3,228	606	+ 23.1
1911	9,242	6,014	+ 186.3
1916	9,436	194	+ 2.1
1921	11,097	1,661	+ 17.6
1926	10,735	-362	-3.0
1931	13,489	2,754	+ 25.6
1936	13,523	34	+ 0.2
1941	14,612	1,089	+ 8.0
1946	16,522	1,910	+ 13.1
1951	22,947	6,426	+ 38.9
1956	29,348	6,401	+ 27.9
1961	34,911	5,563	+ 18.9
1966	36,837	1,926	+ 5.5
1971	40,856	4,019	+ 10.9
1976	46,818	5,962	+ 14.6
1981	56,624	7,806	+ 16.7

[1]Nicholas and Marcella Sheran, Lethbridge's first citizens.

[2]Nicholas Sheran, his common-law wife and son, and a helper, Fred Whear.

[3]Estimates, based on historical writings (population in October 1885 was 400)

Population Growth by Districts, Lethbridge, 1881-1981

Year	Lethbridge			Total	Change	
	South	North	West		Numerical	Percent
1881	—	—	4[1]	4	—	—
1891	2,153	200[2]	—	2,353	2,439	—
1901	2,072	550	—	2,622	269	+ 11.4
1911	8,050	1,192	—	9,242	6,620	+ 252.5
1921	—	—	—	11,097	1,855	+ 20.1
1931	—	—	—	13,489	2,392	+ 21.5
1941	—	—	—	14,612	1,123	+ 8.3
1951	—	—	—	22,947	8,335	+ 57.0
1961	23,105[3]	11,806	—	34,911	11,964	+ 52.1
1971	26,442	14,346	68[4]	40,856	5,945	+ 17.0
1981	25,843	21,370	7,411	54,624	13,768	+ 33.7

[1]Nicholas Sheran, his common-law wife and son, and a helper, Fred Whear.

[2]Estimates based on about five members per household, the number of households arrived at as follows: 1891, 77 lots were sold and possibly 40 houses were built on the Pierce Addition near Galt No. 3 Mine; 1901, about 25 residences were established along 13th Street North in a community called Little Wigan and about ten more residences elsewhere in the North Ward; and, 1911, 131 names were listed on the Assessment Roll of the Village of Stafford, plus additional residences elsewhere in the area. Also, population of Stafford was shown as 623 in 1906, 753 in 1908, 1,192 in 1911, and "about 1,500" in 1913.

[3]Until 1954, the census was taken by federal authorities and no distinction was made between North and South Lethbridge.

[4]Students in residence at the University of Lethbridge in West Lethbridge.

Mayors of Lethbridge and Period of Service

	Period of Service
Charles Alexander Magrath	1891
Henry (Harry) Bentley	1892-93-96-97-98
Thomas McNabb	1894
William Colpman	1895
Frank Hamilton Mewburn	1899-1900-05
William Oliver	1901-02-03-04
George Rogers	1906
Walter Stuart Galbraith	1907
William Henderson[1]	1908-09
Elias Adams	1910-11
George Merrick Hatch	1912
William Duncan Livingstone Hardie	1913 - July 1928
Robert Barrowman	July 1928-1929-30-31-32-33-34
David Horton Elton	1935-36-37-38-39-40-41-42-43
Alfred William Shackleford	1944-45-46
	October 1952 - October 1955
	October 1957 - October 1961
John Arthur Jardine	1947-48-49
Louis Sherman Turcotte	1950 - October 1952[2]
Thomas Russel Haig	October 1955 - October 1957
Edward Charles Lonsdale	October 1961 - October 1962
Frank Sherring[3]	October 1962 - March 1968
Andrew Charles Anderson[4]	March 1968 -

[1]William Henderson died in office on 13 December 1909 and his term was completed by Acting Mayor C. B. Bowman.

[2]In 1952, date of civic elections was changed from December to October; successful candidates took office immediately, instead of on 1 January of the following year.

[3]Frank Sherring resigned on 11 March 1968.

[4]Andrew C. Anderson was mayor at time of writing.

Members of the Legislative Assembly - Lethbridge Region

Year	North-West Territorial Council or Assembly

1877   Col. James F. Macleod, Stipendary Magistrate and Commissioner, NWMP, an appointed member of the NWT Council

1885   Richard Henry, Viscount Boyle, later the Earl of Shannon (Cons.), the first elected MLA from the Lethbridge region

1887   Frederick William Gordon Haultain (Cons.)

1891   Charles Alexander Magrath (Cons.) Lethbridge District

1898   Dr. Leverett George DeVeber (Lib.)

Province of Alberta Legislative Assembly

1905   Dr. Leverett George DeVeber (Lib.), Lethbridge District

1906   William Charles Simmons (Lib.)

1909   Donald McNabb (Labor)

1909   William Asbury Buchanan (Lib.), Lethbridge City

1911   Dr. John Smith Stewart (Cons.)[1]

1926   Andrew Smeaton (Labor)

1935   Hans Enoch Wight (SC)

1937   Dr. Peter McGregor Campbell (Unity)

1944   John Charles Landeryou (SC)

1971   Richard David Gruenwald (SC), Lethbridge East

        John Victor Anderson (SC), Lethbridge West

1975   Archibald Dick Johnston (PC)[2]

        John Albert Gogo (PC)

[1]Dr. J. S. Stewart was granted military leave from 1915-1919. He was listed as an Independent from 1921-1926.

[2]Cabinet positions were held by F. W. G. Haultain, C. A. Magrath, L. George DeVeber, W. A. Buchanan, and A. Dick Johnston.

Southern Alberta Members of Parliament

Year		District of Alberta	
1887		Donald Watson Davis (Cons.)	
1891		Donald Watson Davis (Cons.)	
1896		Frank Oliver (Lib.)	
1900		Frank Oliver (Lib.)	
1904		John Herron (Cons.)	

Year	Macleod	Lethbridge	Medicine Hat
1908	John Herron (Cons.)	(Medicine Hat-Lethbridge until 1917; Lethbridge-Foothills after 1968)	Charles A. Magrath (Cons.)
1911	Dr. David E. Warnock (Lib.)		William A. Buchanan (Lib.)
1917	Hugh M. Shaw (Unionist)	W. A. Buchanan (Unionist)	Arthur L. Sifton (Unionist)
1921	George G. Coote (Prog.)	L. H. Jeliff (Prog.)	Robert Gardiner (Prog.)
1925	George G. Coote (Prog.)	L. H. Jeliff (Prog.)	Dr. Frederic W. Gershaw (Lib.)
1926	George G. Coote (UFA)	L. H. Jeliff (UFA)	Dr. Frederic W. Gershaw (Lib.)
1930	George G. Coote (UFA)	Dr. John Smith Stewart (Cons.)	Dr. Frederic W. Gershaw (Lib.)
1935	Rev. E. G. Hansell (SC)	John Horne Blackmore (SC)	A. H. Mitchell (SC)
1940	Rev. E. G. Hansell (SC)	John Horne Blackmore (SC)	Dr. Frederic W. Gershaw (Lib.)
1945	Rev. E. G. Hansell (SC)	John Horne Blackmore (SC)	W. D. Wylie (SC)
1949	Rev. E. G. Hansell (SC)	John Horne Blackmore (SC)	W. D. Wylie (SC)
1953	Rev. E. G. Hansell (SC)	John Horne Blackmore (SC)	W. D. Wylie (SC)
1957	Rev. E. G. Hansell (SC)	John Horne Blackmore (SC)	H. A. (Bud) Olson (SC)
1958	Dr. Lawrence Kindt (PC)	Deane R. Gundlock (PC)	Ted Brundsen (PC)
1962	Dr. Lawrence Kindt (PC)	Deane R. Gundlock (PC)	H. A. (Bud) Olson (SC)
1963	Dr. Lawrence Kindt (PC)	Deane R. Gundlock (PC)	H. A. (Bud) Olson (SC)
1965	Dr. Lawrence Kindt (PC)	Deane R. Gundlock (PC)	H. A. (Bud) Olson (SC)
1968	(Riding Abolished)	Deane R. Gundlock (PC)	H. A. (Bud) Olson (Lib.)
1972		Ken E. Hurlburt (PC)	H. T. (Bert) Hargrave (PC)
1975		Ken E. Hurlburt (PC)	H. T. (Bert) Hargrave (PC)
1979		Blaine A. Thacker (PC)	H. T. (Bert) Hargrave (PC)
1980		Blaine A. Thacker (PC)	H. T. (Bert) Hargrave (PC)
1984		Blaine A. Thacker (PC)	Robert H. (Bob) Porter (PC)

Bibliography

Books and Booklets

Anon. 1976. Lethbridge/Southern Alberta 1975 Jeux Canada Games, 11-23 February. Minister of State and Physical Fitness, Ottawa. 197 pp.

Beaty, C. B. 1975. The Landscapes of Southern Alberta: A Regional Geomorphology. University of Lethbridge, Lethbridge. 95 pp.

Bowman, R. F. P. 1973. Railways in Southern Alberta. Occasional Paper No. 4 Whoop-Up Country Chapter HSA, Lethbridge. pp. 40

Bussard, L. H. 1950. Lethbridge Public Schools 1950. Souvenir Booklet, opening of Lethbridge Collegiate Institute. 22 November 1950. 20 pp.

Byrne, W. J. 1973. The Archaeology and Prehistory of Southern Alberta as Reflected by Ceramics. Mercury Series, Paper No. 14, National Museum of Man, Ottawa. Vol. 3 of three.

Carpenter, J. H. 1975. The Badge and the Blotter. D. W. Friesen & Sons, Altona, Manitoba. 157 pp. (A history of the Lethbridge City Police Force.)

Carter, David J. 1980. Behind Canadian Barbed Wire. Tumbleweed Press Limited, Calgary. 334 pp.

den Otter, A. A. 1972. Irrigation in Southern Alberta 1882-1901. Great Plains Journal II, No. 2: 125-137.

den Otter, A. A. 1982. Civilizing the West: The Galts and the Development of Western Canada. University of Alberta Press, Edmonton. 395 pp.

Fooks, Georgia G. 1975. A History of the Lethbridge Herald 1905-1975. MA thesis, Brigham Young University, Provo, Utah. Sir Alexander Galt Archives, Lethbridge. 237 pp.

Fooks, Georgia G. 1978. The History of the Lethbridge Community College. Board of Governors, LCC, Lethbridge. 325 pp.

Higinbotham, J. D. 1933. When The West Was Young. Ryerson Press, Toronto. 328 pp.

Holmes, O. G. 1972. Come Hell or High Water. University of Lethbridge, Lethbridge. 141 pp. (An account of the founding years of the University of Lethbridge.)

Johnston, A. 1966. The Battle at Belly River. Robins Printing, Lethbridge. 40 pp.

Johnston, A. 1966. Boats and Barges on the Belly. Herald Printing, Lethbridge. 48 pp.

Johnston, A. 1977. To Serve Agriculture: A History of the Lethbridge Research Station 1906-1976. Can. Dep. Agric., Ottawa. Hist. Series No. 9. 59 pp.

Johnston, A. 1984. CP Rail High Level Bridge at Lethbridge. Occasional Paper No. 12, Lethbridge Historical Society, Lethbridge. 40 pp.

Magrath, C.A. 1935. The Galts: Father and Son *and* How Alberta Grew Up. Lethbridge Herald. Pp. 64, illus.

Marshalsay, Barbara, and Margaret Wheeler. 1981. Lethbridge News and Macleod Gazette 1882-1900: A Subject and Biographical Index. Ronalds Western Printing Limited, Lethbridge. 264 pp.

Mewburn, F. H. 1928. The 25th Battery, Canadian Field Artillery (Canadian Militia) 1908-1914. 24 pp.

Poelman, Leah. 1981. White Caps and Red Roses. Ronalds Western Printing Limited, Lethbridge. 355 pp. (The history of the Galt School of Nursing 1910-1979.)

Steele, C. Frank. 1961. Prairie Editor: The Life and Times of Buchanan of Lethbridge. Ryerson Press, Toronto. pp. 196.

Van Luven, Lynne. 1980. Nikka Yuko Centennial Garden: A History. Ronalds Western Printing Limited, Lethbridge. 36 pp.

Articles

Anon. 1939. Some Local Breweries That Make It Go! The Brewer's Digest, Vol. XIV, No. 10: 24-37.

Anon. 1962. This Is Lethbridge, Alberta: Canada's Award Winning City. Prairie Towns and Cities Magazine for 1962: 1-12.

Anon. 1970. Lethbridge Expands Rapidly. Financial Post, 16 May 1970. Fourth Section, page L1.

Anon. 1981. Coal in Canada. Coal Association of Canada, Calgary. 2nd Edition, p. 48.

Buchanan, Ruth. 1983. What Is The Herald Controversy All About: Lethbridge Magazine, Spring 1983. Pp. 28-29.

Geiger K. W. 1965. Bedrock topography of Southwestern Alberta. Report No. 65-1, Research Council of Alberta, Edmonton. 14 pp.

Horberg, Leland. 1952. Pleistocene drift sheets in the Lethbridge region, Alberta, Canada. Journal of Geology 60 (4): 303-330.

Johnston, A. 1984. Nicholas and Marcella Sheran: Lethbridge's First Citizens. Alta. Hist. 31 (4): 1-10.

Reeves, B. O. K. 1978. Head-Smashed-In: 5500 Years of Bison Jumping in the Alberta Plains. Plains Anthropologist Vol. 23 (82): 151-174.

Reeves, B. O. K. 1981. The Rocky Mountain Eastern Slopes: Problems and Considerations. Pp. 31-38 in Moore, T. A. (ed.) Alberta Archaeology: Prospect and Retrospect. Archaeological Society of Alberta, Lethbridge. 108 pp.

Tyre, Robert. 1972. Lethbridge: A Western Showcase of Economic Progress. Trade and Commerce Magazine. July 1972 issue.

Winchester, N. Brian. 1979. Citizen participation and influence in Lethbridge, Alberta. Annual Meeting, Canadian Political Science Association, Saskatoon. 23 pp.

Reports

1927. Bull, E. W. Report on City of Lethbridge Power Conditions. Typed manuscript in City Clerk's office, City Hall, Lethbridge. 21 pp.

1929. Watson, J. T. General report covering existing and future estimated conditions in connection with the City of Lethbridge Electric Plant. Herald Printers, Lethbridge. 18 pp.

1951. Carrothers, G. A. P. Survey for planning in 1951: A study of factors affecting the growth of Lethbridge. University of Manitoba, Winnipeg. 153 pp.

1958. City of Lethbridge Interim Development By-law No. 2416. Prepared under The Town and Rural Planning Act (1955).

1960. Analysis of the survey for the General Plan of the City of Lethbridge. Oldman River Regional Planning Commission, Lethbridge.

1964. Bowie, G. W. City of Lethbridge: Recreation Survey. Parks and Recreation Commission, Lethbridge.

1964. By-law No. 2528. A By-law of the City of Lethbridge pursuant to provisions of The Planning Act (1963), to adopt a General Plan.

1965. A Study to Examine and Report upon the Feasibility of Developing University Facilities in Lethbridge. Hu Harries and Associates, Edmonton. 59 pp.

1968. Future City of Lethbridge expansion and University location. Prepared by ORRPC, Lethbridge.

1969. Hobart, Charles W. Recreation in the City of Lethbridge: A survey of interests, activities, and opportunities. Dep. Youth. Research Division. Three volumes, Chapters I-XIV. 440 pp.

1969. City of Lethbridge: Urbanization of West Lethbridge. Prepared for ORRPC, Lethbridge. 50 pp.

1975. Hall, E. B., B. Lacey, and R. M. Bartlett. Major Facilities Plan 1975-1985. Community Services Directorate, Lethbridge.

1976. Lethbridge Railway Relocation Study: Examination of alternate development options. Damas & Smith Limited. 20 pp.

1976. Study of land uses in the Downtown Phase II Area, City of Lethbridge. ORRPC, Lethbridge. 73 pp.

1976. City of Lethbridge: Lethbridge Transportation Study. De Leuw Cather Canada Limited, Edmonton. 125 pp.

1977. Ho, S., G. McNab, and G. Kuhl. Westminster Neighbourhood Study: Guidelines for evaluating multi-family development applications. City of Lethbridge Planning and Development Department, Lethbridge. 26 pp.

1978. City of Lethbridge: Report on computer services. Finance Committee, City Council, Lethbridge. 43 pp.

1978. Report on the route location of the Northwest Parkway. Reid Crowther and Partners Limited, Calgary. 43 pp.

1979. Urban Parks Proposal. Alberta Recreation and Parks, Edmonton. 20 pp.

1979. Downtown Phase II Area Redevelopment Plan. City of Lethbridge Planning and Development Department, Lethbridge. 42 pp.

1980. City of Lethbridge General Municipal Plan. Adopted by By-law No. 3573. Rockcliffe Partnership Architects Planners. 96 pp.

1980. City of Lethbridge Land Use By-law No. 3574. 187 pp.

1980. Uplands and Valleyview Policy Statement and Area Structure Plan. Stanley Associates Engineering Limited. 76 pp.

1981. Sir Alexander Galt Museum Design Development. Robins Watson Baunton, Lethbridge. 14 pp.

1981. Route Location and functional planning study of Crowsnest Trail. Reid Crowther and Partners Limited. 77 pp.

1981. Parks Proposal Lethbridge: Community Services Department Urban Parks Proposal. City of Lethbridge. 18 pp.

1982. Lethbridge Regional Hospital: Project description. Submitted in support of Development Permit Application. Cohos Evamy and Partners, Calgary, 14 pp.

1982. Kalman, H. D. Sir Alexander Galt Museum: A study of the potential for continued use of the Galt building. Historic Sites Service, Edmonton. 55 pp.

1983. Preliminary Design Report on the Expansion of Wastewater Treatment Works. Underwood McLellan Limited, with Gore and Storrie Limited, Lethbridge.

1983. Urban Parks Master Plan: Urban Parks Project, City of Lethbridge. Lombard North Group, Calgary. 90 pp.

1983. Kennedy, Margaret, and Brian Reeves. Historical synthesis and assessment Lethbridge Urban Parks project: Indian Battle Park and Nature Reserve. 159 pp.

1984. Historical Interpretive Master Plan: City of Lethbridge. Marshall Macklin Monaghan Western Limited, Edmonton. 151 pp.

1984. City of Lethbridge: Lethbridge Transportation Study. Executive Summary. DelCan of Leuw Cather Western Limited. 45 pp.

Miscellaneous

Council Minutes, City of Lethbridge, 1891-1983, inclusive. In office of the City Clerk, BLT Building, Lethbridge.

City of Lethbridge Police Reports, 1914-1916 and 1928-1982. In Buchanan Collection, Lethbridge Public Library.

Various issues of Lethbridge newspapers: Lethbridge News, Lethbridge Semi-Weekly News, Lethbridge Morning News, Telegram, Lethbridge Daily Herald, Lethbridge Herald, from 1885-1984. Mostly on microfilm, Lethbridge Public Library, Lethbridge.

Chiste, Arrigo. (nd) A history of the Village of Stafford 1900-1913. Typed manuscript in Sir Alexander Galt Archives, Lethbridge. 19 pp, maps.

History of the 2nd Canadian Anti-Tank Regiment, Royal Canadian Artillery 1939-1945. (It included the 20th Battery from Lethbridge.) Typed manuscript, Sir Alexander Galt Archives, Lethbridge. 26 pp.

History of the 33rd Field Squadron RCE (Militia), Lethbridge. Typed manuscript, Sir Alexander Galt Archives, Lethbridge. 4 pp.

History of the 6th Canadian Light Anti-Aircraft Regiment, RCA. (112th Battery, Lethbridge, was a part.) Typed manuscript, Sir Alexander Galt Archives, Lethbridge. 35 pp.

Holyoak, F. G. History of the 39th Battery, Canadian Field Artillery, 1914-1918. Typed manuscript in Sir Alexander Galt Archives, Lethbridge. 23 pp.

Johnston, A. 1982. Lethbridge — A Business History: The story of the Chamber of Commerce. Typed manuscript in Sir Alexander Galt Archives, Lethbridge. 188 pp.

National Defense RCAF RG 24 E-7 RCAF Record Books and Diaries. No. 8 Bombing and Gunnery School, Lethbridge. Folder 52.4, Public Archives of Canada, Ottawa. On microfilm.

National Defense RCAF RG 24 E-7 RCAF Record Books and Diaries. No. 5 Elementary Flying Training School, Lethbridge and High River. Folder 53.1, Public Archives of Canada, Ottawa. On microfilm.

National Defense RG 24 C-4 Prisoner-of-War files. Mostly restricted but some available on microfilm. Public Archives of Canada, Ottawa.

Index